Adiel Lejbovitz

D1570439

מסורה

ArtScroll Series®

Rabbi Nosson Scherman / Rabbi Meir Zlotowitz

General Editors

SUC

Published by

Mesorah Publications, ltd

CESS!

Bringing out the best
in yourself — and others

by

Rabbi Moshe Gans

FIRST EDITION
First Impression . . . August 1996

Published and Distributed by
MESORAH PUBLICATIONS, Ltd.
4401 Second Avenue
Brooklyn, New York 11232

Distributed in Europe by
J. LEHMANN HEBREW BOOKSELLERS
20 Cambridge Terrace
Gateshead, Tyne and Wear
England NE8 1RP

Distributed in Israel by
SIFRIATI / A. GITLER—BOOKS
4 Bilu Street
P.O.B. 14075
Tel Aviv 61140

Distributed in Australia & New Zealand by
GOLDS BOOK & GIFT CO.
36 William Street
Balaclava 3183, Vic., Australia

Distributed in South Africa by
KOLLEL BOOKSHOP
22 Muller Street
Yeoville 2198, Johannesburg, South Africa

THE ARTSCROLL SERIES®
SUCCESS!
© Copyright 1996, by MESORAH PUBLICATIONS, Ltd. and Rabbi Moshe Gans
4401 Second Avenue / Brooklyn, N.Y. 11232 / (718) 921-9000

ISBN
0-89906-521-X (hard cover)
0-89906-522-8 (paperback)

Typography by Compuscribe at ArtScroll Studios, Ltd.

Printed in the United States of America by Noble Book Press
Bound by Sefercraft, Quality Bookbinders, Ltd. Brooklyn, N.Y.

Acknowledgments

There are many people who must be recognized for helping make this book possible. To these people I owe a debt of gratitude.

To Rabbi Chaim Pinchos Scheinberg, Rabbi Moshe Aharon Stern, Rabbi Abraham Twerski and Rabbi Zelig Pliskin, for reviewing the manuscript and writing letters of recommendation. Also, to Rabbi Matisyahu Solomon for reviewing the manuscript and approving its contents.

To Rabbi Avrohom Turin, Rabbi Shmuel Blech and Aryeh Markovitch, for analyzing the manuscript and sharing their valuable thoughts.

To my mother, Mrs. Miriam Gans, for her support and appreciation of this project. To my father, יעקב יצחק בן מנחם מענדל ז״ל, for his support of this project. He was a seeker of truth, and the epitome of honesty and sincerity. May the good that comes from these pages be a merit to his memory.

To my parents-in-law, Mr. and Mrs. Meyer Rosenberg, for their encouragement of this project.

To my brother-in-law and sister-in-law, Nechemiah and Esti Rosenberg, for making the contacts and technical arrangements in Israel.

To Rabbi Meir Zlotowitz, Rabbi Nosson Scherman and Rabbi Sheah Brander, who accepted the manuscript for publication. Once again, I am proud to be part of their special contribution to contemporary Jewry.

To Avrohom Biderman of the ArtScroll staff, who supervised every stage of this project and helped assure a high standard of quality; to Fayge Silverman, whose expert editing greatly enhanced the book; to Mrs. Mindy Stern for her meticulous proofreading; to Mrs. Chaya Gitti Loevy for pagination and Mrs. Esther Feierstein for typesetting.

To my wife, whose constant encouragement brought about this publication. As I was beginning the project and telling people that I was writing a book, she not only took me seriously, but also pushed me to continue during the trying times. May Hashem answer all her prayers and grant her *success*! in all her endeavors.

Rabbi Moshe Gans

Adar, 5754 / February, 1996

Table of Contents

Introduction

We all want success and happiness. All too often, though, it eludes us. At times, it seems as if we are going through life in the slow lane while everyone else is passing us by. So we ask:

How can I be more successful?
How can I be a happier person?
How can I motivate myself?

Sometimes we don't know whom to turn to for the answers. Other times, we have the solutions but don't know how to implement them. So we do what we think will bring us fulfillment. This would be reasonable, assuming we do the right things. However, we often do the wrong things, thinking that they will move us forward when instead they take us backward.

Without guidance, relying on only intuition and guesswork, it is unlikely that anyone will find the right answers — especially in a culture that promotes misleading notions about success and fulfillment.

Our society constantly bombards us with invalid, self-defeating ideas, telling us that we cannot control our thoughts; that we are stuck with our negative attitudes; that happiness is a result of having the things we want; that success means achieving a goal, and no matter how hard one tries, anything short of its completion is failure. With these ideas continually creeping into our hearts and minds, it is no wonder that we often take misguided paths toward improving our lives.

The purpose of this book is to offer solutions. Rooted in the Torah and the world view of our Sages, the ideas in this book suggest a practical approach to attaining more success and happiness in life.

What do you long for? A comfortable life-style? Success at your job? A desirable salary? Good relationships? Well-behaved children? A higher level of spirituality? This book can help you come closer to those goals.

Many self-improvement books make the claim: "Follow the suggestions outlined here and you are guaranteed success." This book does not make such bold assurances. As the old Yiddish saying goes: *"A mentch tracht undt G-dt lacht,"* meaning, "A person makes plans but G-d does what He wants."

However, the book offers another assurance: "Follow these suggestions and your chances of success will be increased." While we do not have control over future outcomes, we do have influence over our own lives. By doing the right things, we can *increase our chances* of success.

> A person's actions never directly bring about the outcome, because a person just does the action with his hands and the outcome is determined by Hashem . . . Since a person does not directly bring about the outcome — rather, through his actions he is assisted from Above — the more effort he puts into achieving success, the more Hashem will assist him (Rabbi Chaim Shmulevitz, *Sichos Mussar*, 5732:13).

Our effort makes a difference, because effort begets success. As King Shlomo, the wisest of all men, repeatedly remarked in *Mishlei*, success can be expected from a diligent person and failure from a lazy person.

Attitude: the root of our influence. Attitude is important because if we are unmotivated, undisciplined, irresponsible, unfriendly or cynical, we will not do the things that increase our chances of success. And if we lack self-confidence and expect too little of ourselves, we may actually sabotage a desirable outcome.

We are not stuck with our attitudes. We can change. We can improve the way we see the world and the way we see ourselves. Even if we were born into families that bred our low self-confidence and negative, self-defeating attitudes, we can develop a new, positive attitude. And even if our inner drive is dulled as a result of problems on the job, the loss of a loved one, or failure to reach important goals, we can learn to look at those situations in a more positive light. With a new attitude and a revitalized inner drive, we will begin to do the things that increase the chances for success.

"But," you may ask, "is it really possible to change a personality? If I have a negative attitude or low self-confidence, if I am unhappy or constantly do things that sabotage success, can I really change?" The answer is yes. You can break old habits and character traits and develop new ones. *Chazal* told us that with enough practice, practical attitudes and behaviors become second nature. They become part of your very fiber.

Breaking faulty character traits is not only possible, but is an obligation incumbent on every human being.

> The purpose of life is to break the character traits that have not yet been broken. Therefore, one must constantly strengthen himself, because if he does not strengthen himself, what is the purpose of his life? (Vilna Gaon, *Mishlei* 4:13).

You may recognize some of the ideas in these pages as the mumbo-jumbo of popular psychology and ivory-tower academicians. You may say, "This is too abstract for me. I need practical, hands-on methods that I can use now."

This book strives to break down those abstract ideas into practical suggestions that can be used immediately. It may require a second or third reading, and it certainly requires practice, but in time these ideas will no longer seem foreign. So don't put the book down or flip to another chapter whenever you come across a novel idea. Keep on reading. Experiment with the suggestion.

Even if you are not able to implement some of the suggestions, there is still value in knowing that they exist. When you are aware of these concepts, you can try to make them part of your life. Even if they bring about a twenty-percent improvement, your situation will be twenty-percent better than it was before. Relatively speaking, this is significant progress. But if you are not aware of the possibilities, it is unlikely that you will even come close to this sort of improvement.

Help children improve their attitudes. The second purpose of this book is to help you bring out the best in children. Whether you are a parent or teacher, the greatest service you can provide children is to help them become happier, more successful individuals. Once you have put these concepts into practice yourself, you will be in a position to guide and influence children to practice these principles, too.

Wisdom of *Chazal*. There is a third purpose to this book — to introduce readers to the wisdom of *Chazal*. Our Sages were not antiquated, armchair theoreticians whose heads were high in the clouds. They were sensitive, practical people, fully in touch with human nature. Their insights were true in their times, and they are true now.

This is more than a quick "how-to" book. It is designed to help the reader understand *why* each suggestion works. This is important because each principle has its basis in human psychology, and when we understand the connection, it becomes part of our modus operandi. We come to understand the concept and are enthusiastic about implementing it. We have more control of it and act in ways that produce the best results.

Many of the ideas presented in these pages are repeated throughout the book. This is intentional. Some ideas are so vital that they deserve repetition and emphasis. Other ideas are novel and abstract, and need repetition to enhance their understanding.

Many of the ideas presented here may seem elementary. They are still worth mentioning because, as the venerable Rabbi Moshe Chaim Luzzato wrote in *Mesilas Yesharim*, matters that are most obvious tend to be overlooked and forgotten. Furthermore, what is simple to one reader may be unfamiliar to another reader.

After writing my first book, *Make Me, Don't Break Me*, which dealt with motivating children, people asked, "It's nice to have a book about motivating my kids. But what about me? I need motivation, too. Why not write a book about personal motivation?" This book addresses these requests. But even after reading it, there is no easy road. Motivating oneself requires work. Old, ineffective mind-sets will have to be replaced with productive ones, and old, self-defeating habits will have to be replaced with new, self-enriching practices.

You can do it. You were born with the seeds of greatness. Your potential is greater than you think. You have the power to manage life's challenges and come out a winner. It is my hope that this book will provide some of the essential knowledge and skills which you can use to become everything you *can* be, and also to help your children along the way.

Chapter One

Live Positively

The brothers Reb Shmelke and Reb Pinchas approached the Maggid of Mezeritch with a provocative question: "The Talmud tells us that we must bless Hashem for misfortune with the same happiness that we bless Him for good fortune.[1] How is it possible to do this?" The Maggid told them to pose their question to Reb Zushe of Hanipol. Reb Zushe was an extremely poor man who often lacked the basic necessities of life, yet he was always happy. He was the ideal person to answer their question.

Following the Maggid's suggestion, the two brothers went to the study hall in search of Reb Zushe. When they found him, they told him that the Maggid had said he would be able to help.

Reb Zushe was puzzled. He said, "I am surprised that the Maggid sent you to me. You should really speak with someone who has experienced suffering in his life. As for me, I have only experienced good things. Nothing bad has ever happened to me."[2]

Reb Zushe was destitute. He lacked basic necessities. He, of all people, should have been able to explain how it is possible to bless

---

1. Talmud *Berachos* 54a.
2. *Midor Dor*, p. 216, cited by Rabbi Z. Pliskin in *Gateway to Happiness*, pp. 65-66.

Hashem for misfortune. But he felt he had never experienced suffering or misfortune; therefore, he considered himself incapable of providing an explanation. He was in a set of circumstances that most people would consider pitiful, yet he was happy.

How could Reb Zushe feel this way? How could he have dissociated himself from the obvious truth that things were not going well for him? Had he entered a fantasy world, where he was in total ignorance of the reality in which he was living?

Indeed, Reb Zushe was aware of the reality. He knew he was far from being affluent, but this did not interfere with his general outlook on life. He controlled his mind to look at life positively. He had a positive attitude — one so strong that he believed he was the recipient of only good fortune. He perceived his predicament differently from the way most other people in his situation would see it. He perceived his life so differently that he actually believed he was not lacking a thing.

There is no doubt about it — Reb Zushe was a special individual. However, he did not accomplish the impossible. And this is the lesson for us. Like Reb Zushe, we all have the capacity to live positively, happily and productively under conditions that most people would consider distressful. We all have the ability to manage ourselves inwardly and control our minds to respond positively to life's challenges. This chapter will describe some techniques that can be used to develop a positive personality and a positive outlook on life. And as we will soon see, this attitude is an important element of success. First, we will discuss the Torah requirement to live positively.

We Are Required To Be Positive

There was once a poverty-stricken man by the name of Nachum. He was blind, his legs were amputated, and he lived in a house fit to be condemned. Nonetheless, Nachum responded to every distressful event with the words "*Gam zu letovah* (This is also for the good)." He saw — even better, he *found* — a benefit in every event, even if the event seemed negative. People called Nachum "*Ish gam zu* (the man who always says '*gam zu*')" and held him in high esteem.[1]

Chazal suggested that every person adopt the same positive attitude toward all of life's challenges. In other words, we should look

---

1. Talmud *Taanis* 21a.

positively at every event, whether it is distressful or not, as Nachum did. This is what positive living means.

Here are some comments made by *Chazal* concerning positive living:

> A person should always be accustomed to say, "All that Hashem does is for the good" (Talmud *Berachos* 60b).
>
> A person must bless Hashem for bad occurrences as he would for good occurrences (Mishnah *Berachos* 9:1).[1]
>
> The *Shechinah* (presence of Hashem) does not rest on a person through gloom, laziness, laughter, irreverence, talk, or idle chatter, but through joy in connection with a *mitzvah* (Talmud *Shabbos* 30b).[2]

Let's examine the wording of these statements: "*The Shechinah does not rest on a person through gloom . . . but through joy*"; "*A person must bless Hashem for bad occurrences*"; "*A person should always be accustomed . . .*"

We are led to one conclusion: There is a requirement to be positive toward everything — all the time. We must develop a positive attitude toward life's events and feel that every event is beneficial, even if it appears to be a misfortune. In the Torah scheme of things, there is simply no place for negativity! Radak made the point succinctly:

> "The word of Hashem is upright, and all His deeds are with faith" (*Tehillim* 33:4) . . . They [people] praise the bad with joy and delight, as well as the good, because they perceive the bad as good (Radak, ad loc.).

Look for the good in everything. When it rains, it is not enough to stand by idly and watch; find the benefit in each and every drop.[3] Similarly, when walking down the street, do not go untouched by the fresh air, the sight of a clear blue sky, the sounds of children laughing and birds chirping; rather, fill your lungs and enjoy the fresh air, and open your eyes and ears to the scintillating sights and sounds that surround you.

---

1. Talmud *Berachos* 60b explains that the blessing here refers to accepting the occurrence with joy.
2. See Rashi there: "It is a *mitzvah* to bring the *Shechinah* upon oneself."
3. Rabbi Yeruchom Levovitz, *Daas Chochmah U'Mussar*, Vol. 3, p. 26.

The requirement to be positive applies to our outlook on people as well. The classic example is the prohibition of *lashon hara* — that is, speaking negatively about others, even if it is the truth.[1] Here is a question: *Emes*, truth, is at the top of the list of moral obligations. If so, what can possibly be wrong with sharing it with others? If the information is true, why shouldn't everybody know it? The answer is simple: Knowing the negative, albeit the truth, serves no positive purpose. It causes hate, quarrels and arguments.[2] All one can do with the information is look down on the person about whom the comments were made.[3]

Rabbi Shlomo Freifeld went one step further. He said that *lashon hara* is more than speaking negatively about others; it is speaking negatively — period. We are expected to confine our speech — and thus, our attitudes — to the positive.[4]

The Torah requires many other positive behaviors. We must love other people and help them whenever possible.[5] We are obligated to perfect our *middos* by avoiding hate, anger, revenge, jealousy, cruelty and bearing a grudge. We must even attain the most positive state of mind — happiness:

And you shall be happy with all the good that Hashem, your G-d, gave to you and to your household (Devarim 26:11).[6]

> A person should not be a jokester, nor should he be depressed or mournful, but he should be happy (Rambam, *De'os* 2:7).
>
> It is a big *mitzvah* to be in a perpetual state of happiness. One must strengthen himself with all his power to avoid depression and bitterness, and to be only happy all the time (Rabbi Nachman of Breslov, *Likutei Etzos, Simcha* 30).

---

1. *Vayikra* 19:16. Although this verse refers directly to talebearing, *lashon hara* is included. See *Sefer Chofetz Chaim, Pesicha Lavim* 1, and *Sefer HaChinuch* 236.

2. *Sefer HaChinuch* 236.

3. See *Sefer Chofetz Chaim*, Section 1, Rule 4:10-11: When asked to describe a man or woman for the purpose of a potential marriage, or when warning a child to stay away from certain people who have bad *middos*, one is required to say the truth even if it is negative. Unlike other negative actions, these are constructive; therefore, they are really positive.

4. Heard from Rabbi Freifeld in a speech delivered at Yeshivah Sh'or Yoshuv.

5. *Vayikra* 19:18.

6. Also see *Devarim* 28:47.

Begin to live positively. After concluding that positive living is a Torah requirement, let us ask a practical question: How can a person begin to live positively after years, or even a lifetime, of negative or indifferent thinking?

We could enter into a lengthy discourse — a "*mussar shmuess*," as it is called in yeshivos — on *bitachon*, the belief that all occurrences are predetermined by Hashem for our benefit. We would elaborate on how people with *bitachon* put their faith in Hashem and, as a result, enjoy a positive outlook and peace of mind.[1] We would also stress that having *bitachon* virtually guarantees positive living, even after years of being negative.

The *bitachon* approach is valid; with *bitachon*, a person can certainly become more positive. However, some people have a problem with it. Take, for example, the person who has negative tendencies or a negative personality, always putting a pessimistic twist on life's events. Because his perception of life's events is so downbeat, he may have a problem relating to the *bitachon* approach, which puts life's events into a positive light. Another example is the person whose belief and/or faith in Hashem is weak in the first place. With shaky convictions, he has a problem connecting effectively with concepts of *bitachon* altogether.

Furthermore, to master *bitachon*, one must invest a great deal of time, effort, study and thought. Even after making these investments, growth is a gradual process which takes months or years. If people who are weak in *bitachon* had to depend solely on discussions about *bitachon* to maximize their potential for positive living, they might not reach that goal for a long time. Even worse, they might never become the positive individuals they could otherwise be. So how can these people become more positive? They can supplement the *bitachon* approach with another approach. This does not mean they should abandon the pursuit of *bitachon*; on the contrary, they need to work on *bitachon*, study it, and make it part of their personalities. But they should augment it with another approach in order to accomplish even more. As they become more positive, their *bitachon* may grow as well.

Indeed, many of us are "*k'tanei emunah* (small in faith)."[2] We

---

1. *Chovos HaLevavos*, beginning of *Shaar HaBitachon*.
2. This term is found in Rashi, *Bereishis* 7:7.

have *some* imperfections in our faith and we have *some* negative tendencies in life. With this limitation, a *mussar shmuess* alone may not be enough to motivate us to reach the high levels of positiveness we are capable of reaching.

To give us a boost, we can do two things: develop a positive attitude and practice the Habits of Positive Living. First, we will discuss the important topic of attitude.

Attitude Shapes One's Perception of Reality

There is a story of a little girl who was looking for something to do. She asked her father for an idea. He found a large picture of the world and tore it into small pieces. Then he told his daughter, "Show me how smart you are and put the picture back together." He expected her to work at the project for at least one hour, but after a very short time the little girl taped all the pieces together. Her father was amazed and asked how she did it so quickly. She showed her father the other side of the picture and replied, "You see, there is a picture of a man on the other side. I put him together and then the world became put together." The father replied, "That's right. When a person is put together, his world is also put together."

Exactly what does "put together" mean? How can we define a person who is "put together"?

A person who is "put together" knows what is important and is reasonably confident of his ability to reach his goals. He has a clear, orderly outlook on the world, and finds merit in life's so-called "negative" events. With this attitude, he is "put together." And so is his world, meaning that his perception of the people and events around him is also clear and orderly.

Think of a time when you felt sad or upset. Maybe the feeling was the result of losing a job or not being able to find a job. If it was, did you get the idea that the world is unexciting and lacks opportunity?

Maybe the sadness was the result of an illness. In your melancholy state, did the world seem depressing and cheerless?

Maybe you were upset because of a failing relationship. Since you were feeling rejected, insulted or betrayed, all other people may have seemed untrustworthy or unappealing.

Whatever the problem was, you were in a negative or confused state of mind, and you perceived the world with the same attitude.

Why? Because you were not "put together," and neither was your world.

Now recall a time when you felt happy and productive. Perhaps you received a compliment or an increase in salary. How did the world seem then? You probably saw the world as a bright place and full of opportunity. You probably viewed people in general as friendly and welcoming. You felt "put together" — and you saw the world the same way. Your attitude — that is, the way you see other people and things — shaped your perception of reality.

Observe the hustle-bustle of people walking on a busy street corner. Just for a moment, suppose one of those strangers suddenly dies. Now that this person is no longer alive, would the world continue to move forward? As you continue observing the busy corner, you would conclude that the world is progressing quite well without him.

How would a close friend or relative react? They would find it very difficult to live without their loved one. The loss would bring about a change in their outlook; yesterday they saw the world as bright and exciting, but today it is dark and meaningless. To them, the world is upside-down and it will take time to correct itself.

While the death of this individual affects friends and relatives, it has no effect on others. Why? Because they never had a relationship with him and feel no loss. Each group judges life's events differently, and the way they judge the event is determined by their attitude.

Sometimes, we even project our attitude onto others. When I ask schoolteachers to assess the morale of the teaching staff, those with low morale usually judge the general morale as low, while the ones with high morale generally judge it as high. Each group perceives the attitudes of the others to be similar to their own. Why? Because their own attitude determines their perception of the world around them.

During the forty years that the Jewish people were in the Sinai Desert, they ate *mon*. All in all, the *mon* had very desirable qualities, yet many people did not appreciate it and even considered it a burden. Why? Because they wanted ordinary food, not the *mon* with its supernatural qualities. They had a general attitude of discontent, and their negative attitude toward the *mon* was a reflection of it. Their attitude determined their perception of reality.[1]

----

1. Rashi, *Behaalosecha* 11:7.

At another time during that forty-year period, the Jewish people accused Hashem of hating them.[1] How did they come to this preposterous conclusion? It was a result of their own hatred toward Hashem. Because they hated Hashem, they assumed that Hashem hated them. This is human nature. We assume that other people's feelings for us are similar to our feelings for them.[2] In other words, a person's attitude determines the way he judges reality.

At yet another time during the forty-year period in the desert, the Jewish people came to a spring of bitter water. In recounting this incident, the Torah writes, "They were bitter." Simply speaking, "they" refers to the water. However, the Kotzker Rebbe suggested that "they" refers to the people. *Because* they — the people — were bitter, everything they tasted was bitter.[3] Their attitude shaped their perception of reality.

A plastic surgeon once noted that after he straightened his patients' crooked noses, some saw no difference. Although their features had truly improved, these patients did not perceive it that way. In their eyes, they were still ugly. The plastic surgeon discovered that these people had bad self-images. He theorized that their negative attitude played a role in determining their perception of reality.[4]

Your attitude toward other people is so powerful that it determines the way you interpret everything they say, even if their remarks are inoffensive.

> "Hatred arouses quarrels. Love covers up all transgressions" (*Mishlei* 10:12) . . . If one person hates another, and the other person says something trivial to the first, it provokes the first to begin quarreling. The cause of the quarrel is not the remark; rather, it is the hatred the first has for the other person. Due to his hatred, he is aroused at the remark of the other person, even though it is not something that should cause a quarrel. But if the first person truly loves the other, his love covers up all transgressions (Vilna Gaon, ad loc.).

---

1. *Devarim* 1:27.
2. Rashi and *Sifsei Chachamim* there.
3. *HaRebbe M'Kotzk*, Beton HaSefer Pub., 1952, p. 94.
4. Dr. Maxwell Maltz, *Psycho-Cybernetics*, Pocket Books, 1960, pp. 6-7.

This point reflects a principle every employee knows: If the boss likes you, he will look kindly on you and favor your work. But if he does not like you, he will find problems that are not even there.

It all starts with attitude. When attitude is positive, perceptions are positive. When attitude is negative, perceptions are negative. People interpret the world around them in ways that are consistent with their attitudes, whether the conclusions are valid or not.

With a positive attitude, the most life-threatening event can be interpreted in a positive way. This is how Rabbi Eliyahu Lopian interpreted an episode in the life of Rabbi Moshe Schwab.

Rabbi Schwab lived in London during the Second World War. One time, he was in an area of London being bombed by the *Luftwaffe* (German air force), and he had to take refuge in a shelter. Long after the war, he related this incident to Rabbi Eliyahu Lopian, describing the fear he and his family had experienced during the air raid. Rabbi Lopian responded, "How fortunate you are to have experienced the fear of death." Rabbi Lopian's attitude was positive, and he saw something positive in the most life-threatening occurrence.[1]

Why do the righteous suffer in this world? This familiar question is based on a misconception that suffering means ill health, lack of financial stability, and the like. A truly righteous person, however, does not perceive these conditions negatively. A righteous person, by definition, sees the benefit in all occurrences. He does not think he is suffering, even if his health is poor or he lacks financial stability. A righteous person has a positive attitude and perceives everything around him in a positive way.[2]

Sarah, our matriarch, illustrated this ideal. The Torah tells us that all her years were equally good.[3] Although she experienced much distress in her life, she understood that every inconvenience was for her benefit, and because her attitude was positive, she never felt distraught over her challenges. In *her* eyes, all her years were equally good.[4]

---

1. *Maarchei Leiv*, Vol. 1, p. 25, cited in *Gateway to Happiness*, p. 59. Rabbi Lopian probably made reference here to *Avos* 2:15: "Repent one day before you die."
2. *Darkei Mussar*, p. 57, cited in *Gateway to Happiness*, p. 55.
3. Rashi, *Bereishis* 23:1.
4. *Rabbi Zushe of Anapoli*, cited by Rabbi Z. Pliskin in *Growth Through Torah*, p. 52.

All this points toward our central theme: A person's perception of a particular event, person or thing is a function of his own attitude. A person acts and feels according to the image his mind holds, not necessarily according to the way things really are. A person carries certain mental images of himself, events and people around him, and he tends to behave as though these images are the truth, whether they are or not. For this reason, the way a person sees the world creates the world that he sees.

If a person's attitude is positive, he tends to see himself, the world and other people positively. If a person's attitude is negative, he tends to see himself, the world and other people negatively. Why is this important to know? Because we are obligated to view life positively, and if our attitude has such a strong influence on the way we see everything else, it stands to reason that we must first correct our attitude before correcting the way we see the world.

Many events are neutral, but judgments are not. Suppose an ordinary person had to put shoes on another person's feet. He would probably feel degraded. But a shoe salesman looks forward to it. Why do these two people judge the same action so differently?

Because each tells himself something different about the action. The shoe salesman tells himself that putting shoes on other people is an opportunity to make more money, so he perceives the action as positive. But the ordinary person has no desire to sell shoes. He tells himself that putting shoes on other people is debasing, so he perceives the action as negative.[1]

Putting shoes on another person's feet is really neutral; it is neither good nor bad. However, each person judges the event in his own way, based on his own perception.

Suppose an acquaintance passes you on the street and does not greet you. You may begin to wonder: Why does he act this way? You really don't know. And without asking him, all you can do is make an assumption. You can assume that he really wants to greet you but is too shy to do so; then you do not become upset. You can tell yourself that he does not even see you, in which case you also do not become upset. Or you can conclude that he no longer likes

---

1. Rabbi Eliyahu Dessler, *Michtav M'Eliyahu*, Vol. 1, p. 265.

you (disregarding the Torah guideline of giving the benefit of the doubt). Then you become upset.

What is the truth? The event itself is neutral — an acquaintance did not greet you, which in itself does not indicate a thing. Only after you tell yourself that it is good or bad does it become that way — and it becomes that way to you alone, because the judgment is based on personal perception.

Suppose you asked another person to call you a fool, and he did so. Would you be insulted? Of course not. But suppose your boss said it, and he was serious. How would you feel then? You would probably be hurt. When the other person makes the derogatory statement, you know that he does not mean it. Thus, there is no reason to be insulted. But when the boss says it, you assume that he means it, and you feel insulted.

The event itself is neutral — someone made a remark. Depending on what you tell yourself about that remark, your judgment will either be positive, negative or neutral. Your judgment depends more on how you process the remark than on the words themselves.

Until now we have been discussing how attitude affects the way we perceive ourselves, the world, and all its events. But there is more. Our attitude also affects the way others perceive us. This, in turn, brings about success or failure in our endeavors. Read on.

The World Mirrors Our Attitude

There was once a boy who constantly failed to reach his goals. When he told his mother that he was ready to give up, she took him to the edge of a canyon and told him to yell, "I hate you." He did this, and an echo came back: "I hate you, I hate you, I hate you, I hate you." Then she told him to yell, "I love you." He did this, and an echo came back: "I love you, I love you, I love you, I love you." She then said, "You see? What you put into the world is what it gives back to you, only multiplied. If you work at your goals, the world will treat you as a winner; if you give up, the world will treat you as a loser."

That is attitude. The world sees it and mirrors it right back. If you walk on the street with a feeling of love and value for others, people will return the same feeling. If you act grumpy or walk around with a scowl on your face, others will treat you the same way.

A person who lacks self-confidence and constantly anticipates failure typically behaves with a feeling of inadequacy. As other people detect his attitude, they in turn do not put much trust in him either, so they never offer him any real opportunities to succeed. He ends up a failure — exactly what he thought would happen.

On the other hand, if he is self-confident, others detect his attitude and trust him. They then provide opportunities for him to succeed. The more he succeeds, the more opportunities for success come his way. Anticipating success, he increases the chances of becoming the successful person he always thought he would be.[1]

Why does it work this way? Because one's attitude is reflected in his behavior, which in turn sends subtle signals to the world about how he feels. Others detect these signals and respond in kind. A person determines, to a large degree, how the world responds to him.

This is what happened when Moshe Rabbeinu sent the twelve spies to survey *Eretz Yisrael*. When they returned from their mission, they reported, "We were in our eyes as grasshoppers, and so we were in their eyes."[2] First, they saw *themselves* as inferior. Afterwards, the inhabitants saw them as inferior. The inhabitants mirrored the same opinion that the spies had of themselves.[3]

Dr. Martin Seligman, a noted researcher, conducted a study concerning the way people interpret and explain the world around them. He said that people have either a positive or a negative explanatory style. One of Dr. Seligman's findings was that insurance salesmen with a positive explanatory style sold more insurance than their colleagues who had a negative explanatory style. Dr. Seligman suggested that the customers mirrored the style of their salespeople. This in turn increased or decreased the likelihood of the salesman's success.

We hear about people who triumph over adversity. They are solution-oriented, determined to make adversity work for them. They have a positive, can-do attitude. They believe that there is no such thing as a hopeless situation; rather, there are only situations in which people can lose hope. They see themselves as winners, and

---

1. See Rabbeinu Yonah, *Mishlei* 3:6: One can increase the possibility of success if he works with the belief that Hashem will help.

2. *Bamidbar* 13:33.

3. Heard from Rabbi Avrohom Turin in the name of Rabbi Eliyahu Meir Bloch.

the world treats them as winners. This increases their chances of success at whatever they do.

On the other hand, we hear about people who surrender to adversity. They have a negative, defeatist attitude. They are problem-oriented and lack determination. They see their situations as hopeless and give up the struggle, believing they are victims of awful circumstances. They see themselves as losers, and the world treats them as losers. This increases their chances of failure at whatever they do.

Now consider this: If attitude controls both the way we perceive the world and the way the world perceives us, doesn't it stand to reason that if we improve our attitude we will be able to improve our own perceptions, as well as the perceptions that others have of us? Can we consciously improve our attitude? Read on.

Controlling Attitudes

Some people think they do not have control over their minds, emotions or attitudes. To these people, a mind is like a trash can; they allow any thought, feeling or attitude to enter, whether it is appropriate or not. This is a mistake.[1]

> A person has the ability to train his thoughts in any direction he wants . . . Even if his thoughts occasionally wander and begin to be concerned with irrelevant matters, he has the ability to redirect his thoughts to the proper course so that they will be appropriate once again. It is like a horse that turns off its path and begins to go on another. The rider can seize the horse by its reins and redirect it onto the proper path. It is exactly the same with thoughts; as soon as a person sees his thoughts deviating from the proper path, he must seize them and redirect them to the proper way (Rabbi Nachman of Breslov, *Likutei Etzos, Machshovos Vehirhurim* 16).

We *choose* what goes into our minds. Some people choose a positive attitude and receive the benefits that come with it. Some choose a negative attitude and are pulled down with it. The choice is ours; we are in control.

---

1. Rabbi Simcha Zissel Ziv, cited in *Tenuas HaMussar*, Vol. 2, pp. 149-150.

Suppose you are screaming at a family member when suddenly you hear a knock at the door. You open the door and behold, a good friend is standing there. How would you greet him? Would you scream at him, too? Or would you gather your composure and greet him calmly? Of course, you would become calm and friendly. You would probably not even allow him to know that you just lost your temper.

This sort of occurrence happens all the time in one form or another. It proves that people do select their emotions and attitudes. Otherwise, how would they be able to make such instant emotional shifts?

We are expected to thank Hashem for misfortune in the same way that we thank Him for good fortune. If we do not have control over our attitudes, how can we force ourselves to see good in what appears bad?

We are expected to correct bad *middos*.[1] If we cannot control our attitudes, how would we be able to avoid hatred, jealousy, arrogance, temptation and honor-seeking?

Even more, how could Hashem punish us for not being happy?[2] If we had no control over attitudes, we would not deserve to be punished.

From all this, it is obvious that we do have control. We have the power to change our attitudes. Through practice and self-discipline, one small step at a time, we can develop the skill of controlling our minds.[3] Rabbi Simcha Zissel Ziv said it succinctly:

> When a person is about to exercise a bad *middah*, such as hatred or jealousy, he should motivate himself not to allow the hate and jealousy to find root. He should seek ways of resisting the implantation of these *middos* (Rabbi Simcha Zissel Ziv, *Chochmah U'Mussar*, Vol. 2, p. 224).

Reaction and proaction. When faced with a challenge, we can deal with it in a positive way or a negative way. This is called *reaction*; it is the way we respond to a particular set of circumstances.

---

1. Vilna Gaon, *Mishlei* 4:13.

2. *Devarim* 28:47.

3. Rabbi Simcha Zissel Ziv, cited in *Tenuas HaMussar*, Vol. 2, pp. 149-150. Also see *Cheshbon HaNefesh* 16 and 108, and Chazon Ish, *Emunah U'Bitachon* 1:15.

To be reactive, something has to be happening. Whether it is a person, event or thing, there is something going on to influence our lives in some way.

Proaction is something else. There are no events, people or things calling for a response; rather, we look at our set of circumstances and take the initiative to make something good or bad happen. Proaction can work in action or in thought, in either the positive or negative direction. Obviously, our discussion addresses the positive direction.

Our forefather Avraham illustrated proactivity. He was not satisfied to wait until someone in need came to his doorstep for help; he went out of his way to find people whom he could assist.[1] Avraham learned to be proactive from Hashem:

> Emulate Hashem; just as He is gracious and merciful, you should be gracious and merciful (Talmud *Shabbos* 133b).
>
> The Torah writes, "You shall go after Hashem, your G-d."[2] How can a person be like Hashem? Hashem is a consuming fire![3] Rather, it means that you should go after the *middos* of Hashem: Just as He provides clothing for the unclothed . . . you should also provide clothing for the unclothed; Hashem visits the sick . . . you should also visit the sick; Hashem consoles mourners . . . you should also console mourners; Hashem buries the dead . . . you should also bury the dead (Talmud *Sotah* 14a).

Hashem is proactive. He looks for opportunities to satisfy the needs of His creatures. People are expected to do the same.

Reactivity and proactivity are two ways of expressing our general attitude. We will first discuss how to react positively in times of challenge. We will then discuss the important topic of proactive living.

Living Positively in Times of Challenge

Challenging situations arise frequently. Although the conditions are undesirable, we can nevertheless react positively to them. There are three ways to react positively, each requiring a deliberate effort:

1. Rashi, *Bereishis* 18:1.
2. *Devarim* 13:5.
3. *Devarim* 4:24.

1. Find benefits and opportunities in the event or its outcome.
2. Find a solution and pursue it, instead of dwelling on the problem.
3. Ignore the unpleasantness of the event.

We will now explain these approaches.

Find benefits and opportunities in the event or its outcome. There are benefits and opportunities in every set of circumstances. There are even benefits in one's greatest failure; by learning something from the experience, he knows how to perform better next time. By doing this, one can transform tragedy into a major victory.

Yosef, the son of our forefather Yaakov, realized this. His brothers threw him into a pit and left him to die, then sold him as a slave to some passing merchants. The merchants took him to Egypt where they sold him as a slave. In Egypt, Yosef was convicted of a crime he never committed and was thrown into jail. Even after he was freed, he continued living in this foreign country, estranged from his family. Indeed, Yosef lived through adversity.

Yet Yosef saw the benefit in these seemingly ugly events — his opportunity to save an entire nation by stockpiling food for a potentially deadly famine. And when he and his brothers reunited, he assured them that he had no thought of revenge. Although the brothers had brought about all his problems, he still said, "You were thinking bad about me but Hashem was thinking good, so that I should help a large nation survive."[1]

Yosef was not bitter toward life's events or toward his brothers. Instead of focusing on his brothers' offensive actions, he focused on the benefits of the outcome — the survival of the entire Egyptian nation. Instead of lamenting over the fact that he was a victim of circumstance, he saw himself as the conduit of a Heavenly plan.

Have you ever been fired from a job? Do you know someone else who has? As unpleasant as it may be, many people in this situation report that they actually benefited from the event or its result. Some made use of their free time to achieve personal and professional goals which they had ignored beforehand. Others reflected on their mistakes — the reasons they were fired in the first place —

---

1. *Bereishis* 50:20.

and made corrections. They learned about their weaknesses and used the lessons for professional growth. They proceeded to the next job with added skill and confidence. They transformed an unpleasant experience — what many people call "failure" — into a personal victory, and came one step closer to real success in their lives.

Rabbi Yechezkel Levenstein wrote that the events which caused him suffering also brought about good fortune; every event that was challenging in the beginning proved to be beneficial in the end.[1] This is what *Chazal* meant when they said, "All that Hashem does is for the good."[2]

Even if the benefit is not obvious, the event may simply be an opportunity to reap a Heavenly reward for dealing with it properly. For this reason, Hashem gave our forefather Avraham ten tests, or ten types of adversity — so that he could overcome the obstacles and earn a Heavenly reward. His difficulties were really blessings in disguise, all intended for his ultimate benefit.[3]

You are never a failure or a victim of circumstance — unless you *choose* to be. Even if the failure was your fault, you have the power to move forward and make something of yourself. Yes, you may be a mistake-maker, but you are also a mistake-breaker. A mistake is not bad unless you do nothing constructive with it. By learning from the mistake and improving yourself, you become a better person.

Find solutions. There was once a man who was hospitalized with cancer. He was convinced that his illness was caused by a bad diet, heavy smoking and a general lack of attention to his health. He became depressed and constantly talked about how he was to blame. Friends and relatives were unable to boost his morale, until one man came to visit. The visitor told his sick friend, "The problem is in the past. The consequence is in the present. The cure is in the future. Until you stop focusing on the past and the present, you will not move into the future, where the cure is."

This made a strong impact on the ill man. He realized that by harping on the problem, he was constantly living with it and becoming part of it. He began to realize that he had a limited amount of energy which he was using for unproductive ends. So he began

---

1. *Ohr Yechezkel, Michtavim,* p. 326.
2. Talmud *Berachos* 60b.
3. Ramban, *Bereishis* 22:1.

to focus on the prospect of a healthy future and what he could do to create it. He became solution-oriented, and his ambition to become healthy improved.

Many people deal with problems the same way. Instead of directing their energy toward the right thing — the solution — they direct their energy toward the wrong thing — the problem. They worry, mourn, replay the event, talk about what they "could'a, should'a, would'a done." They concentrate on the problem and remain depressed and aggravated. But this serves no purpose because, as the sick man learned, the cure is in the future.

When a person is bitten by a poisonous snake, he can run after the snake or tend to the bite. If he focuses on the snake — the problem — the poison will spread throughout his body and kill him. If he focuses on the bite, though, he can stop the poison from spreading. Yes, the snake will get away, but by addressing the problem, he will be saved. He can be problem-oriented or solution-oriented. Obviously, the consequence of one is desirable; the consequence of the other is undesirable.

Chazal have told us that the challenge of mastering the entire Torah is insurmountable. Although it is impossible to master the entire Torah, we are still required to do the best we can.[1] In other words, we should not be *troubled* by a challenge; rather, we should use our energy to do what we can to *overcome* it, to the best of our ability.

When Rabbi Eliyahu Meir Bloch came to America, he received news that his family might have perished in the Holocaust of Europe. Nevertheless, he pursued his goal of opening a yeshivah. On the Purim following the confirmation that his family had indeed perished, he was in a happy state. He did not allow his loss to interfere with his goal of rejoicing. He could have become depressed and troubled over his problems; instead, he created a mission and set new goals.[2]

You can do the same, whether the event is big or small. The next time you miss a train or a flight, don't beat yourself up for having arrived late. Whether it is your fault or not, by dwelling on the problem your mind becomes so tied up with it that you are not able to think of a solution. Instead say, "That's all. It's over." You arrived

---

1. *Avos* 2:15-16.
2. Heard from Rabbi Avrohom Turin.

late, the train or plane departed, and nothing can change it now. You can use your energy instead to devise an alternate plan.

Similarly, the next time you miss a deadline at work, don't waste any time or energy worrying about the negative consequences. It's over. You cannot change it now. Instead of giving the problem center stage, use your energy to devise another strategy.

The next time you are expecting guests and the house is not in order, don't become anxious and cry, "What am I going to do? What am I going to do?" Instead, decide what has to be done and do it. Be solution-oriented, not problem-oriented. Don't give the problem undue attention. Be part of the solution, not the problem.

Ignore the unpleasantness of the event. Some problems may not have a benefit or a solution. What can you do in these cases? Ignore the unpleasantness.

For example, you are driving to work in the morning and a car from another lane suddenly cuts you off. You become irritated and say to yourself, "What a bad driver! He almost caused an accident! Why do they allow such people to drive anyway?" While your blood boils and you become more and more tense, the one who committed the dastardly offense continues driving merrily along, oblivious to his terrible crime.

In an attempt to ease the tension, you look for a benefit in the event. But you cannot find one. So you think about a solution to the problem. Once again, there is none; the misdemeanor was already committed and nothing can be done about it now. Since you see no benefit or solution, the best reaction at this time is to ignore the unpleasantness. Accept the fact that there are less-than-perfect drivers in the world and forget about the incident. By ignoring the unpleasant event, you spare yourself unnecessary anxiety.

When one person speaks offensively to another, the recipient may say, "He makes me so angry!" as if the offender is forcing him, against his will, to become angry. The truth is that nobody can force another person to become angry. The recipient here *chooses* to become angry in reaction to the other person's behavior. But if he wants, he can totally ignore the unpleasantness of the incident.

This was the way Hillel reacted to a person who tried to anger him. It was Friday, and Hillel was busy preparing for Shabbos when a man came to his doorstep to pester him with an assortment of foolish questions. Each time this person approached Hillel, Hillel ignored the unpleasantness of the event and patiently answered the man's question.[1]

Help children deal positively with challenges. Children also have their share of obstacles. To a child, it is no simple matter to be turned down for the school play or athletic team. And when a child is rejected by others or becomes the victim of a classmate's insensitive remarks, it can be devastating. Whatever the circumstance, adults can help children find a benefit in the event or its outcome. Here is an illustration:

> Yitzy wanted to be in the school play. He rehearsed for the audition and was confident that he would be accepted. The judges, however, rejected him. He became depressed because he had spent a great deal of time rehearsing and felt that he deserved a chance.
>
> When Yitzy's mood improved, his father suggested that he practice playing his electric keyboard. Music was very important to Yitzy, but while he was preparing for the audition he had not been able to spend much time practicing.
>
> Now that Yitzy had time to practice music, he once again derived fulfillment from it, and he even made plans to join the school band. His father told Yitzy, "You see, if you had been part of the school play, you would not have had time to develop your musical talent." Yitzy then realized that his "failure" to be part of the school play enabled his success in music.

Yitzy's father did a masterful job of helping him see a benefit in the outcome of his problem. However, children sometimes focus on a problem with such intensity that they actually refuse to see a benefit. What can parents do then? If they were to give a lecture about *bitachon* and suggest that the child relax and search for benefits, the child may resent it and may even dig his feet deeper into the ground.[2] At times like this, parents may just have to wait to discuss the issue until the child becomes more receptive.

---

1. Talmud *Shabbos* 31a. *Chazal* there recommended that all people practice this trait.
2. *Avos* 4:19. See Maharal, *Derech Chaim*, there.

Adults can also help children learn to find solutions to their problems. Here is an illustration:

> Shira came home upset over an argument she had with a friend. After she calmed down, her mother asked her what happened.
>
> As they discussed the incident, Shira realized that she had caused the problem by provoking her friend; she had made some "cute" remarks, which actually insulted her friend. She now decided never to make those remarks again.
>
> Shira's mother then encouraged her to apologize to her friend and make a fresh start. Shira did so, and not only did her relationship with this friend improve, her relationships with all people improved.

Some parents might let their daughter sit and bemoan her predicament without their intervening. They would justify their approach by saying, "She is a big girl. She can find solutions to her own problems. This is the only way for her to learn independence. If she wants to sit and dwell on the problem, there is nothing I can do about it."

What would this accomplish? It would help the child become a problem-oriented individual. But Shira's mother taught her daughter that finding solutions to problems is more beneficial than letting the problem remain unsolved. With this attitude, Shira will increase her chances of success at anything she does.

Ignoring unpleasant events, as we have discussed, is the third way of dealing with challenge. Let us illustrate how adults can help children learn this skill.

> Moshe was playing with a ball while a neighbor watched from his backyard. Every time Moshe dropped the ball, the neighbor laughed. Moshe was insulted and came inside to tell his mother.
>
> Moshe's wise mother listened, and then asked him to find a solution. He said that the neighbor enjoyed making fun of others and there was no way to stop him. Seeing that there was no solution, his mother said, "Try to understand that he has a problem, not you. And since you do not have a solution, try to ignore him."

Moshe went back to the yard and continued playing ball. The neighbor continued laughing at Moshe's errors, but when he saw that he was being ignored, he stopped.

Not only did Moshe make peace with the problem by ignoring it, his behavior eliminated the problem altogether.

Many children in this predicament become angry and yell or hit. Sometimes they even have to be physically restrained. However, when children are able to ignore an offender, as Moshe did, they can proceed with their lives peacefully and productively.

Finally, the most powerful way for adults to help children be positive is to be positive themselves. When adults are challenged by a difficulty and react positively, children see them as role models and emulate their behavior.

Positive living is not always easy. It is not easy to be positive when you do not feel that way, especially when you have already begun building up the momentum of a negative reaction. Even if you have not yet begun to react negatively, you may have a natural urge to do so, in which case you need a great deal of self-discipline to shift the impulse from negative to positive. Discovering benefits, finding solutions and ignoring unpleasantness — especially when your tendency is to ruminate over the problem — may create a stressful internal conflict, especially if the problem involves an offender with hurtful intent.

What can you do to help make the shift from negative to positive? Practice the Habits of Positive Living. These habits will help you build a positive personality. But it doesn't stop there. You can also increase the chances of success at whatever you do. This is the topic of the next section.

The Eleven Habits of Positive Living

Earlier, we discussed the difference between reaction and proaction. We *react* to events that are already occurring and that trigger some sort of a response. We *proact* to events that do not present any particular challenge or trigger any particular reaction. From the *Chazal* presented earlier, it is clear that we are expected both to react and to proact positively. *Chazal* demand that we live positively at all times, with a positive attitude toward all events, people and things, whether or not they present a challenge. In other words, we are required to have a positive personality.

A person with a positive personality does not wait to be positive until he is challenged by some sort of difficulty. Instead, he creates and maintains a positive attitude, with or without a challenge. He acts, thinks and speaks positively. His attitudes and behaviors are expressions of a personality whose very fabric is positive. He is a happier, more peaceful person, because his outlook on life — his world — is peaceful and "put together." Other people sense his attitude and reflect it back to him. As a result, he experiences fewer unpleasant occurrences. And when unpleasant occurrences do arise, his positive reaction is natural and without extraordinary effort. Thus, his life is happy and peaceful.

How can you develop a positive personality? By practicing the Habits of Positive Living. These habits foster the positive attitude they represent, creating a calmer, happier YOU, better equipped to proact and react successfully to all of life's events. We will now present the eleven Habits of Positive Living.

1. Act Positively

There is a widespread belief that a person's actions follow his attitudes, but that his attitudes do not follow his actions. This means that if a person thinks negatively, he will act negatively, and if he thinks positively, he will act positively. The premise is that no matter how he acts, his thinking will remain the same until he makes a change within his mind and heart, with logic and emotion, through self-study and/or psychotherapy.

According to this presumption, a person with a bleak outlook on life can improve his attitude only after he enters his own mind and makes a change through some sort of psychological process. Even if he *acts* with high spirits, as though he were upbeat, he will not begin thinking that way until he makes the change from within. Why? Because according to this belief, a person's attitude must be changed from within; it is not influenced by his actions.

Similarly, a person who lacks self-confidence will begin to think more highly of himself only after he convinces himself, through logical and emotional processes, that he is worthy and competent. Even if he performs with an artificial display of confidence, his real attitude will persist until he makes the change from within his mind. Why? Because according to this belief, a person's actions do not influence his attitude.

The presumption that a person can improve his performance by improving his attitude is correct. However, the presumption that a person can only improve his attitude through psychological processes and not by acting in a particular direction is incorrect. *Chazal* have told us that a person can change his attitude by going through the motions. In other words, attitude follows action in the same way that action follows attitude. The *Mesilas Yesharim* made this point succinctly:

> Just as the trait of zeal is the result of an inner drive, an artificial act of zeal can create an inner drive. One who does *mitzvos* with speedy body movements conditions himself to have a similar inner movement, where a yearning and desire for *mitzvos* continually grow within him. But if his body movements are sluggish, the movement of his spirit will also be suppressed . . . If a person's desire to serve Hashem is not strong enough, he should willfully act with zeal so that his desire will become a natural instinct, because outer movements stir inner ones. If he uses what is readily available to him, he will also attain what is not readily available; he will become happy and enthusiastic as a result of his willful outer movements (*Mesilas Yesharim*, Ch. 7).

The *Sefer HaChinuch* also elaborated on this concept:

> A person is influenced and impressed by his actions. His heart and all his thoughts always follow his actions, whether they are good or bad. If an evildoer who only thinks of evil suddenly becomes inspired and occupies himself diligently with Torah and *mitzvos*, even if it is not for Heaven's sake, he will begin to be good and his evil inclination will become subdued by his actions, because his heart follows his actions. And if a righteous person who is totally committed to Torah and *mitzvos* occupies himself with frivolous matters — if, for example, the king

appoints him to an unethical job — and he is occupied all day with that work, he will lose his righteousness and become an evildoer, because of the principle that every person is affected by his actions. For this reason, Hashem assigned many *mitzvos*,[1] so that they will capture all our thoughts and we will be totally occupied with them, and our share in the next world will be enhanced — because, as a result of our good actions, we are influenced to be good people, fitting to receive a favorable share in the next world . . . You should look carefully at your job and other activities because you are drawn to them; you will not draw them to you. Do not be so confident as to say, "I am a sincere person with a strong belief in Hashem. I have nothing to lose by occasionally sitting with others who joke and poke fun at matters that do not bring about sin. I will not be drawn after them." Be careful not to do this because you will become like them (*Sefer HaChinuch* 16).

The *Mesilas Yesharim* and *Sefer HaChinuch* both share the secret of creating a positive attitude: Act positively. *Act* enthusiastically, and become enthusiastic. *Act* happy, and become happy. *Act* confidently, and become self-confident. Attain any desired attitude by *acting* the attitude. Just go through the motions.

This is the "outside-in" approach. It states that positive behavior begets a positive attitude, and that negative behavior begets a negative attitude. Attitude follows action.[2] Over time, the "outside-in" approach does have its effect. Some experts suggest that it doesn't even take so long; after twenty-one consecutive days of practice, you will begin to feel the results. And once you reach the three-week mark, you are on your way to internalizing the attitude permanently.[3]

Act confidently. If you have low self-confidence, you can become more confident by acting confidently. This does not mean that you

---

1. *Makkos* 3:15: "Hashem wanted to give merit to the Jewish people; therefore, he increased for them the Torah and *mitzvos*."

2. See Rabbi Yeruchom Levovitz, *Daas Chochmah U'Mussar*, Vol. 1, p. 114: Our psyche understands the language of action, not the language of logic. Also see Vilna Gaon, *Mishlei* 4:26: Habits are developed through consistent action. They then become part of a person's nature.

3. Dr. Maxwell Maltz, *Psycho-Cybernetics*, Pocket Books, 1960.

should act haughtily or arrogantly; rather, act the way that people with healthy self-confidence act. For example, when introduced to a stranger, give a firm handshake and a friendly smile; stand upright with your head and shoulders high; speak with poise and clarity; express your opinions as if they count; and give value to the feelings and opinions of the new acquaintance.

While putting on the act, you may feel silly, dishonest or unworthy of friendship. You may secretly want to shrivel up and disappear. The way to improve self-confidence, though, is to go against those tendencies by acting confidently. Although you may feel guilty of being intellectually dishonest to yourself now, you will become a truly self-confident individual later. Your life will be enriched, along with your chances of success.

Act happy. Many people think happiness is the by-product of good fortune and peace of mind. They say that happiness cannot be controlled; rather, when one is in a setting conducive to happiness, it will come automatically. According to this presumption, a person who wants to become happier must seek those conditions and/or focus on the cause of his unhappiness and make the correction.

This is a mistake. As we mentioned earlier, happiness is a trait that can, and must, be refined. In other words, we can control our happiness the same way we can control any other trait. Along these lines, Abraham Lincoln, who was known to experience bouts of severe depression, once said, "Most people are about as happy as they make up their minds to be." Happiness does not happen to us; we make it happen. It is our decision to be happy or unhappy.

How can you become happy? Act the role of a happy person, even if it feels insincere. Walk with a bounce and an upright posture, and assume a gait that radiates joy and cheer. Talk with enthusiasm and greet others with a cheerful "Hello." Smile, even if there is nobody around. Many people find that the simple act of turning up the corners of their mouths to form a smile changes their mood. Try it; you may become a believer.

A wise man once said, "A smile is a crooked line that sets a lot of things straight." When you smile and act happy among other people, it tells them that you like them.[1] The result is that people feel

---

1. See *Torah Temimah, Bereishis* 49:12.

appreciated, and they respond in kind. This brings about more fulfilling relationships, and life in general becomes enriched.[1] Smiling and acting happy, then, have two benefits: They cause you to feel happy and they bring about a desirable response from others.

Once a person becomes happy, his chances of general success are increased, because the degree of success one achieves in life is often dependent on his level of happiness:

> A strong desire within a person generates power, enhances thought processes, helps overcome laziness and propels him in the path of wisdom. For this reason, the Torah warned against not being happy,[2] because lack of happiness is lack of strong desire; they are one and the same. And anything that enhances desire enhances success (Rabbi Simcha Zissel Ziv, *Chochmah U'Mussar*, Vol. 2, p. 172).

Does this mean that unhappy people perform their tasks poorly? Absolutely not. Unhappy people frequently outperform their peers; however, they perform inadequately in relation to their *own* potential. They do not succeed in any area of life to the degree that they otherwise could. As Rabbi Simcha Zissel said, unhappy people do not muster up enough concern, desire and enthusiasm to be peak performers.

Is it dishonest to act out an attitude? Is the "outside-in" approach fraudulent? Isn't it more honest to act true to your attitude than to be one person on the outside and another on the inside?

Furthermore, isn't the "outside-in" approach a form of brainwashing? Shouldn't intelligent people be expected to use logic, not mind games, to convince themselves of a new way of doing things?

The answer to these questions may be found in the answer to another question: Even if the "outside-in" approach is a form of brainwashing, how is it any different from the negative brainwashing that a person has performed on himself in the past? Let us explain.

Suppose a car salesman is asked to perform brain surgery. What would be a healthy response — "I can do it" or "I cannot do it"? This

---

1. See *Tiferes Yisrael* and Rabbeinu Yonah, *Avos* 1:15.
2. *Devarim* 28:47.

person is not trained in surgery. He cannot possibly succeed, and it is unreasonable for him to think that he will.

Now suppose a qualified neurosurgeon is asked to perform the same surgery. He is trained and certified, and has the right to feel confident of success. But instead, he feels incapable. His nagging feeling of inadequacy gets in the way and chokes off his creativity every time the prospect of surgery comes up. When this man says, "I cannot do it," he is being unreasonable.

Many people are like this. Although they are qualified to perform the task at hand, they nevertheless feel inadequate. In many cases, the underlying reason is that they take all the negative things that others have said about them, from infancy until the present, and synthesize them with their own negative ideas about themselves, all of which lead them to the conclusion that they cannot succeed. To make matters worse, they are convinced that they are right because they are their own most reliable assessors. "Who," they reason, "knows me better than myself?" This conclusion is a mistake. Let us explain.

A person is the product of all the input he receives about himself over a lifetime. He stores up everything that other people have ever said about him, along with everything he has been saying about himself. Some input is positive and some negative; some is true and some false. Typically, he does not differentiate; rather, he accepts it all and becomes a product of it. As a result, his unique "conditioning" is formed.

When a person is about to formulate an opinion about himself, he first consults with his conditioning. If his conditioning is positive, he will generate a positive opinion of his abilities, and if his conditioning is negative, he will generate a negative opinion. Since he is relying on his conditioning, his view of his abilities may be distorted, yet he always thinks it is true.

In other words, a person's perception of himself is not objective; rather, it is the product of his conditioning, which is either real or distorted, depending on the influences that have impacted on his life. While he thinks his perception is true, he really has been "brainwashed," or hypnotized, by all the input that conditioned him in the first place.

It stands to reason, then, that a capable person who expects to fail has really been brainwashed to think of himself as inadequate. He is being as dishonest and unreasonable, so to speak, as the unqualified person who expects to succeed. What they believe is their greatest advantage — being close to themselves — turns out to be their greatest disadvantage.

Let us return to the original question: Is the "outside-in" approach a form of brainwashing? In a way, it is. But this brainwashing process is no worse than the brainwashing process that formed one's negative conditioning in the first place! The only difference is that he is now working in a positive direction.

Is the "outside-in" approach dishonest? No, not at all. If one knows that he is qualified, the only reason he would ever expect to fail is because his negative conditioning tells him that he is inadequate. But if he would realize that these preexisting ideas are distorted, he would have no reason to think of himself as incompetent. It stands to reason, then, that acting on his existing negative attitude — real though it may seem to him — is the unreasonable thing to do, because it is distorted.

If he were to act, however, on the assumption that he is capable of succeeding — as insincere as he may *feel* — he is not being unreasonable or dishonest at all, because he really is qualified. Going through the motions of confidence when a person knows he has the qualifications is an honest and objective way of dealing with his situation. For the person who is qualified, acting confidently — as dishonest as it may seem at the time — is less fraudulent than acting *without* confidence!

A person who lacks self-confidence and only goes through the motions is not being one person on the outside and another on the inside. When he realizes that the inside person is handicapped with a distorted view and dismisses that view in favor of his true qualifications, he is being both honest and objective. And when he uses actions to create new attitudes, he is not brainwashing himself; he is aligning his inside with his true abilities. This, in turn, enhances his chances for success and happiness.

The person with low confidence has a choice. He can continue thinking negatively about himself and allow it to interfere with his success in life. Or he can begin to think positively and increase his chances of success. What he thinks about himself has the power to enrich his life, so why shouldn't he give himself the advantage? The "outside-in" approach is a proven way of giving oneself that advantage.

Improving *middos*. The "outside-in" approach can be used to correct any *middah* or attitude. A mean person can become kind, a cruel person can become merciful, and a faultfinder can become a "good-finder."[1] Is this dishonest? It is certainly no more dishonest than being mean, cruel or hypercritical.

Unhappiness is another *middah* that can be corrected with the "outside-in" approach. Some people become unhappy when they work hard to reach a goal and fail. They think that the situation calls for unhappiness, and they allow themselves to feel that way. "After all," they say, "I invested so much time and effort for nothing. I have a right to be unhappy."

Even if they feel this way, they should still act happy. Is this dishonest? No. The Torah requires people to be happy. Happiness, then, is the morally legitimate state of mind to strive for, no matter how one actually feels. If one comes to this truth through an outward action, insincere as it may seem, it is not dishonest.

The truth is that no situation warrants unhappiness, unless one decides to be that way. Happiness or lack of it is a decision which a person makes after judging a situation and superimposing his personal values and conditioning on it. The problem is that one's judgment may be misguided and his values may be wrong. But because he thinks he has the advantage of knowing himself best, he trusts his own opinion.

His conditioning, however — the force that formed his opinion in the first place — may be distorted. It may be his single greatest handicap. Therefore, when he acts happy, even insincerely so, he should realize that his negative feeling is based on a deficient judgment, while his current action is based on an objective judgment.

Help children act out new attitudes. Adults can help children become happier and more self-confident by teaching them the motions of happy, confident people. As they act that way in the real world, they will begin to feel it inside too.

At first, however, children should only be expected to "put on an

---

1. See Rabbi Simcha Zissel Ziv, *Chochmah U'Mussar*, Vol. 1, p. 100: A person can correct a bad trait by acting as if he has the corresponding good trait.

act" in one or two encounters per day. As they become more comfortable, they will be able to do it more frequently.

Some children behave in socially unacceptable ways, not out of spite or arrogance, but because they are unfamiliar with appropriate behavior. Whether the children speak in an offensive tone of voice, use inappropriate words, or are insensitive to the feelings of others, adults can help them improve by demonstrating socially acceptable behaviors and role-playing with them.

What if the children do not cooperate? There is no benefit in forcing children to act positively when they have no interest in doing so. As the saying goes, "You can lead a horse to water, but you can't make it drink." Therefore, it is usually better to encourage children to *want* to behave appropriately, and leave the rest up to them. Sometimes, rewards or persuasion can motivate them to make the change. At other times, throwing down the challenge and encouraging them to experiment just once or twice is effective.

2. Talk Positively

Just as actions have an impact on a person's attitude, speech has an impact, too. Both reinforce the attitude in the same direction they are expressed. How an individual talks about the events and people in his life affects the way he ultimately feels about everything in his life.

> Speech is powerful. If a person becomes accustomed to speaking in matters of Torah and holiness, it will influence his thought processes and his heart (Rabbi Eliyahu Dessler, *Michtav M'Eliyahu*, Vol. 4, p. 257).

There is an old saying: "If you have nothing good to say, don't say anything at all." While this is a nice saying to follow, it is not enough to satisfy the habit of talking positively. Instead, this habit would prescribe, "If you have nothing good to say, find something good and say it." This is proactive and has the effect of creating a strong positive personality. Rabbeinu Yonah discussed this point:

> King Shlomo said, "Sinners look for guilt";[1] that is, the sinful evildoer talks about the negative points that he sees

---

1. *Mishlei* 14:9.

in people. He is like the fool who passes a carcass and says, "This carcass has such a bad odor." But "among the upright is good will";[1] that is, the upright person only talks about the good points of others. He is like the wise person who passes a carcass and says, "Its teeth are so white"[2] (Rabbeinu Yonah, *Avos* 5:20).

Why is the person who calls attention to the carcass's bad odor considered foolish and the person who calls attention to its white teeth considered wise? Aren't they both correct? Yes, they are; however, in regard to the proper way to talk, the wise one focuses on the positive and the fool focuses on the negative.

Here is another question: Couldn't the wise person simply pass the carcass and say nothing? Why did he look for the good and talk about it? Because he was proactive, on the lookout for something positive in order to call attention to it. He practiced the habit of talking positively.[3]

To become accustomed to this habit, it is a good idea to replace commonly used negative phrases, pertaining to people, events, things, and even oneself, with positive phrases, even if you feel insincere about it. Here are some examples.

A. Your neighbor is a gossip and also blasts her stereo into the late hours of the night. When someone begins to talk about her, you can say what you think (ignoring the prohibition of *lashon hara*) or say something positive.

- Replace "She is not a very nice person" with "She is a wonderful cook."

In this example, the negative point is entirely avoided. Although the positive point may not have the same degree of importance as the negative point, say it anyway.

---

1. Ibid.

2. See also Rabbeinu Yonah, *Shaarei Teshuvah* 3:217: "The *tzaddikim* praise and honor people for every attribute they have, and the *reshaim* look for people's faults and mistakes so that they can put them down."

3. See Rabbeinu Yonah, *Shaarei Teshuvah* 3:217: Two people passed the carcass at the same time. After the first made his negative comment, the wise one made his positive comment. In this scenario, it is possible that the wise one spoke positively only to show the first person that one should not be negative, and not because he was proactive. Had the first not said anything at all, the wise one may also not have said anything.

B. Your landlord wants to evict you, or your boss is pressuring you heavily. These are major problems. You can dwell on the problem or think of a solution.

- Replace "Oh no, I have such a problem" with "Here's the solution . . ."

Problems are negative, and dwelling on them accomplishes nothing. Solutions are positive, and dwelling on them is productive.

C. It is a vacation day. After waking up, you look out the window and see thick clouds hanging in the sky. Is the day ruined?

- Replace "The weather is terrible" with "It is going to be a productive day. We will finally be able to complete that home improvement project."

The weather may be terrible, but it does not have to ruin your day. Anybody can turn a dreary day into a productive one by looking for opportunities to pursue.

D. You are asked to deliver a speech at your school's annual banquet. You have never spoken in public and are having second thoughts about doing it.

- Replace "I can't do this" with "I have not yet done this . . ."

Calling attention to what cannot be done is problem-oriented and negative. However, when you say that you have not yet done the task, it indicates an expectation to do it and to succeed.

E. Your boss asks you to write a report. You are not in the mood to do it. How committed should you be?

- Replace "I will try to do it" with "I will do it."

Trying is not positive enough. It hints at the possibility of not doing the task altogether. "I will," though, is a clear commitment to action.

F. Your spouse is ill and asks you to take over a particular chore. A husband may be asked to do the laundry; a wife may be asked to drive the children to school. What should your attitude be?

- Replace "I have to . . ." with "I want to . . ." or "I will."

"I have to" suggests a degree of unwillingness, as though there is some coercion. "I want to" indicates a definite desire to do the task.[1]

G. You are working for a delivery service and an established customer calls for an emergency delivery.

- Replace: "If I can, I will" or "I hope I will" with "I will."

What do "If I can" and "I hope" mean? They are conditional and do not indicate any sort of definite commitment. "I will," on the other hand, is a clear commitment.

H. You just competed in a sports match and lost. How should you view the event?

- Replace: "I failed" with "Next time I will do it better."

Focusing on failure is negative. Instead, look for the lessons that emerge from the failure.[2]

In these examples, you exercise your "positive muscles" while allowing your "negative muscles" to atrophy. Your feelings and attitudes will eventually follow in the same direction.

So the next time somebody asks how you are doing, don't say, "Not too bad" or "Could be better." Say instead, "Great!" — even if you don't mean it. An enthusiastic, positive evaluation of your set of circumstances makes the situation seem a little easier. It makes you feel better and helps you appreciate what you have. And if you are concerned about telling a lie, there really is truth in this statement; the quality of any situation is decreed from Above to be the best for you.[3]

Some go one step further, suggesting that we replace other commonly used terms having a subtly negative tone with terms that have a positive tone. For example, the clock that wakes people up in the

---

1. See Rambam, *Shemoneh P'rakim: Mitzvah* performance requires the "I-have-to" attitude.

2. An exception is the *mitzvah* of *viduy*. When repenting for sins, one is required to focus on the failure by saying, "I sinned."

3. An exception is an ill person who wants another person to pray for his health. He may tell the second person about his problem.

morning is commonly called an "alarm clock." Alarms are frightening; they are sounded when a building is on fire or is being burglarized. The suggestion, therefore, is to call it an "opportunity clock," because when the clock rings you have the opportunity to wake up and make an impact on the world.[1]

Along these lines, we should call the two outermost sides of a loaf of bread "the beginnings" instead of "the ends."

All this may seem silly, but by avoiding negative-sounding words we are making a conscious effort to develop a positive personality. With enough repetition, our thoughts and attitudes will also begin to go in that direction.

It is interesting to note that *Chazal* referred to night as "light" in an effort to avoid negative terms.[2] Also, the Torah once avoided the word "impure" to describe certain animals and instead referred to them in a lengthier way, as animals "which are not pure," to teach the same lesson.[3] Maybe the intent here is to create a positive personality.

Help children speak positively. You can help children adopt this pattern by showing them ways of modifying daily speech habits. But what if a child does not want to talk positively? Can you do anything, short of coercion, to help him or her talk more positively?

Here is an idea: After the child makes a negative comment, say, "I now understand how you feel. Now I would like to hear you say something positive." Show understanding, albeit without condoning, while prompting the child to focus on the positive and to talk about it.

While this idea is effective, there is something that will have an even more powerful impact. Be a role model. Never call another person a derogatory name, even if it is apropos. Don't let a child catch you dwelling on problems, even if those problems are real. Don't sit down at the dinner table and say, "Everything I eat turns to fat," even if you have a serious weight problem. When a child is about to leave for school, don't say, "Now, don't you get run over in traffic" when a simple reminder to be careful would do.

---

1. An exception is the person who is not motivated to wake up by thinking about the opportunities of the day.
2. Talmud *Pesachim* 3a.
3. Talmud *Pesachim* 3a, referring to *Bereishis* 7:8.

If it is appropriate, let children know when you are making an effort to talk positively. Tell them that you were about to say something negative but instead replaced it with something positive. This imbues children with the notion that speaking positively is a choice which is in one's own hands.

So far, we have discussed the habits of acting positively and talking positively. Another closely related habit is thinking positively. We will discuss this next.

3. Think Positively

We mentioned earlier that we are not hostages to the thoughts that enter our minds; rather, we can entertain or reject any thought we want. This is where the habit of positive thinking comes in. When we practice positive thinking, we take control of our minds by allowing only positive thoughts to enter. How can we master the habit of positive thinking?

Replace negative thoughts with positive thoughts. In regard to the *yetzer hara* (evil inclination), *Chazal* said, "If you meet up with this ugly thing, drag him to the house of Torah study."[1] Similarly, when you begin to entertain negative ideas, replace them with positive ideas.[2]

Controlling thoughts may not be easy, and here are some tips to help make it possible:

A. Don't force thoughts from your mind. There is no way to force a thought out of the mind; on the contrary, trying to drive a thought away forcibly can actually reinforce its hold on you. Instead, relax and gently look for other thoughts to replace the unwanted one.[3]

B. Improve your concentration. The stronger your power of concentration, the greater your ability to take control of your thoughts. What can you do if your power of concentration is weak? Improve it through practice.

Practice concentrating on a single thought for a short period of time one day, and slowly increase the concentration time every day.

---

1. Talmud *Kiddushin* 30b.

2. *Cheshbon HaNefesh* 108.

3. Rabbi Yisrael Salanter, cited in *Tenuas HaMussar*, Vol. 1, p. 284. Also, *Cheshbon HaNefesh* 16 and 108.

In this way, you will develop the skill of concentrating, enabling you to think about anything you want for extended periods of time.[1]

C. Fill your mind with positive thoughts. Occupy yourself with activities that stir positive thinking. Read books that present appropriate, positive ideas. Listen to audio-cassettes while driving a car, riding the bus or walking on the street. Avoid reading or listening to stories about hate, selfishness, deceit, corruption, vulgarity or depravity. And avoid the mother of all negativity — television.

Some people make a list of their goals and rewards for reaching them. Then they make a plan of action to reach those goals. Every day, they review the goals and think of ways to reach them. Their minds become filled with positive thoughts of success and reward.

D. Look for the good in all people, events and things. We are all familiar with faultfinders. Their antennae are always focused on people's faults. The habit of thinking positively, though, suggests that you become a "good-finder," with your antennae focused on the good points of other people, events and things.

When you look out the window, stand in a crowd of people, or walk down the street, find pleasant sights to admire and sounds to enjoy. Like the wise man who passed the carcass and looked at its white teeth, look for something positive to think about. Once you become accustomed to finding the good in other people and things, the result will be a more positive YOU.

If you are a habitual faultfinder, you may feel awkward looking for the good in everything. Don't let this feeling stop you. Changing habits always feels awkward. Try, for example, removing your wristwatch and placing it on the opposite hand. It will no doubt have an awkward feel. Nevertheless, after a short time you will become used to it. It is the same with any habit.

But what if another person does something that appears inappropriate? How can you be a "good-finder" in this situation? You can give him the benefit of the doubt. As long as you can think of a valid reason for inappropriate behavior, assume that this is why the other person did it.[2]

The habit of "good-finding" changed the life of one office secre-

---

1. *Cheshbon HaNefesh* 16.
2. *Avos* 1:6.

tary. She felt that nothing was going right at her job and that the people in her office were not nice, and she sought the advice of a professional counselor. The wise counselor told her to stay with the job, because wherever she would go she would have the same problem. He also advised her to make a list every day of any positive occurrence.

At first, she was only able to think of things such as receiving a salary, and having a chair to sit in and a desk to write on. But as the days and weeks went by, she became more attuned to positive occurrences and was able to add more "good-findings" to her list.

Some time later, she visited the counselor and mentioned that things were beginning to improve at the office. She reported that the other workers were even becoming nicer.

What she did not realize was that the workers were really the same; it was her attitude that had changed. Because she had become a "good-finder," her perception of everything around her took on a totally different twist. And she was now enjoying the benefits of it.

E. Don't allow another person to hurt your feelings. When someone hurts your feelings, how might you react? Assuming that you forgo the option of *tochachah* (rebuke), you can either internalize the insult and become hurt, or accept the fact that the world is full of insensitive people and dismiss the offense.

This is in your control, because nobody can hurt your feelings without your consent. You can only be hurt if you give the other person permission to hurt you.

Ignoring offensive people is not easy. One strategy that will help is to objectify the offender. Willfully perceive the offender as some sort of object. Say to yourself, "Take a look at that specimen. Isn't it interesting how this thing has the intelligence to come up with such ideas?" By depersonalizing the offender and viewing him or her as an object, you become no more insulted than if you had an encounter with just such an object. Your emotions become dissociated from the offense, and you do not become hurt.

F. Negative thoughts are damaging. A radio talk show host was once encouraging listeners to call in and express their ideas about a certain controversial topic. He said, "All I am asking you to do is to express your ideas. Ideas are harmless. There is no damage in thinking about them or expressing them." This person was making a big mistake.

> Do not say that only actions have a value or penalty, and thoughts alone have none. Do not say this, because in reality the heart influences the body; a person's pleasure or pain is mainly dependent on the thoughts of his heart (Rabbeinu Yonah, *Mishlei* 15:13).

A person is where his thoughts are.[1] Think positively, and become that person; think negatively, and become that person. If your thoughts are bitter, critical, sarcastic or vindictive — with no positive purpose — so are you. If your thoughts are kind, gentle, forgiving, sympathetic and full of love, so are you.[2] While negative thinking may be unappealing or offensive to others, its greatest harm is to you.

Contrary to the opinion of the talk show host, inappropriate ideas are indeed harmful.

G. Adopt a positive inner voice. When you make a mistake — whether it concerns your job, a friend, a family member or a task — do you put yourself down? Some people do. They think to themselves, "You are so stupid. What is the matter with you? Why are you so incompetent? You made this mistake because you are a born loser. You have always failed, and you will always be a failure." Even before attempting a difficult task, they say to themselves, "There is no way on earth you are going to do this. You are a loser."

Then there are people who are kind to themselves. When something goes wrong, they tell themselves, "You did your best! Don't worry. You'll do better next time." Even before attempting a difficult task, they are supportive of themselves, saying, "Go on. Try it. You can do it."

These self-directed monologues are a person's "inner voice." The inner voice provides feedback on his or her actions and thoughts. Everybody has one; some voices are positive and some are negative.

What kind of inner voice do you have? Is it kind, supportive and sympathetic, or is it critical, vindictive and unforgiving? Does it

---

1. Rabbi Yeruchom Levovitz, *Daas Chochmah U'Mussar*, Vol. 2, pp. 6-7.
2. See Me'iri, *Mishlei* 27:21.

assume different tones at different times, or is it constantly the same? Knowing what kind of inner voice you have is important because, as we shall soon see, you will then be in a position to change it. But first, let us talk about the origination of the inner voice.

Your inner voice is the product of your conditioning. From infancy, your mind has been receiving input about yourself from many sources: parents, relatives, siblings, friends, teachers, etc. Whatever you did or said, their support or lack of it impacted upon your psyche. You synthesized these inputs with your own notions of yourself, resulting in your personal conditioning. This conditioning is the source of your self-image; it is the reason you think of yourself as you do. And your inner voice is the voice of that self-image; it is nothing more than a reflection of what you think about yourself.

As a child, you did not choose which information to accept and which to discard. You trusted your parents and valued what others said about you. You heard a wide variety of subjective opinions and believed what you heard, although much of it may have been negative, distorted and clearly false. Without analysis or evaluation, you absorbed it all and formed a self-image. Your inner voice then became the spokesman of that self-image.

Suppose a person grew up in a critical home where parents criticized every mistake or misgiving. Children typically do not dispute the messages they hear from their parents; they accept their parents' word as valid. So this child, too, believed his parents and soon began to believe that he was truly inadequate.

Although his parents may also have been aware of his attributes, the fact that they only talked about his deficiencies led him to believe that he was deficient. How was he to know otherwise? All he had heard were negative comments about himself. So as time went on, this child formed a negative image of himself, and his inner voice became the spokesman of that image.

Even as this child enters adulthood, his inner voice continues to express negative ideas about himself. It is as critical as his family had always been, condemning him for mistakes and discouraging him from taking on new challenges. And unless he does something to subdue his inner voice, he will probably enter old age hearing the same condemnations.

On the other hand, a person growing up in a nurturing home synthesizes all the positive input he receives and starts believing that he is worthy and competent. His inner voice, the voice of his positive self-image, expresses encouraging ideas about himself. It says such things as, "I can do it. I am a capable person. If I make a mistake, that's okay. I'll do better next time." This child will probably go into old age with a supportive inner voice.

Since your self-image is the product of your conditioning and not necessarily the product of truth, it stands to reason that your inner voice is not necessarily the voice of truth. It may be selling you short by underestimating your true capabilities. Therefore, the critical remarks you make about yourself cannot be trusted; they are too subjective, tainted by the slanted opinions of others. When you say to yourself, "You are so stupid" or "You cannot do it," it is probably the result of some negative, false conditioning.

You can change your inner voice. One way to make the change is to talk back to it. When you hear the voice criticizing you, respond that it is irrational and unreliable. Say, "You are a remnant of my childhood, and I am not going to rely on you. So I made a mistake; now I know how to do it better. I am a capable person, and with this new skill, I will succeed."

When you are about to begin a task and your inner voice says, "You can't do it," talk back to it. Say, "I have the qualifications to succeed. I am not going to listen to you. You are only a reflection of some negative ideas instilled many years ago by some unreliable people."

Suppose a drunkard called you a derogatory name. Would it bother you? Of course not. He is drunk, incapable of making a rational judgment. Treat your inner voice the same way; it is the product of mixed inputs and is incapable of making a rational judgment. Don't give it so much respect by heeding every nasty comment it makes. Treat it as though it were a drunkard.

Another way to subdue your inner voice is to discover its origin. Recall who in your life said those things to you. For example, suppose you had a sister who criticized you every time you dropped something by saying, "What in the world is wrong with you!?" Now, as an adult, you find yourself saying the same thing every time you make a mistake. Once you realize that the opinion you are expressing is really not yours but your sister's, and that you are allowing her to control you even in adulthood, it may be easier to stop criticizing yourself.

So far, we have described three Habits of Positive Living — acting, talking, and thinking positively. There are eight more habits that can help you become a positive person.

4. Practice Self-Suggestion Techniques

If you are trying to refine a bad *middah,* improve a relationship with a friend or family member, or get a raise or a desirable job, you can increase the chances of success by putting thoughts of success into your mind. Practice on the inside what you need on the outside, and when it comes time to perform, you will do better. This concept is called self-suggestion. We will now discuss two self-suggestion techniques: visualization and self-talk.

Although these two techniques are thoroughly discussed in Chapter Two, we will briefly present them here as Habits of Positive Living.

Visualization. Visualization is a mental rehearsal of an upcoming event. Before performing a task, imagine performing well and feeling good about it. Be specific; visualize what you will say and do, and even how you will say and do it. In your mind's eye, perform the task successfully.

Suppose you will be going for a job interview. Before the event, imagine entering the employer's office, smiling, and greeting the interviewer with a firm handshake. Think of some questions you may be asked and visualize answering them with poise, clarity and confidence. Then imagine feeling good about the interview.

Suppose you want to improve a relationship. Create an inner image of being warm, outgoing, talkative, caring and friendly with that person. Visualize the person responding favorably.

The more you visualize future success, the greater the chance of succeeding. By the time you actually perform, you have already been there, in your mind, many times.[1]

Self-talk. In this technique, you repeat inspirational statements to yourself about your ability to achieve certain goals, whether they concern a physical performance, improving a *middah,* changing an

---

1. Rabbi Eliyahu Dessler, *Michtav M'Eliyahu,* Vol. 4, pp. 252-254.

attitude or learning a new skill. The following are some examples of inspirational slogans: "I see the positive qualities in everything"; "I am not a failure because I learn from all experiences"; "I am a positive person." Constantly repeating these ideas causes you to internalize them. They become part of your attitude and affect the quality of your performance.[1]

One person used self-talk to stay on a diet. He made a tape-recording of slogans such as, "You have the power to avoid any food you want to avoid. You are a thin person. Your waistline gets smaller every day." Every morning while getting dressed, he listened to the tape recording. During the day, when the tape was not available, he would repeat the same ideas to himself. He reported that the self-talk was the reason he lost so much weight.

As we mentioned earlier, your inner voice constantly repeats messages. Some are negative, such as, "I am so stupid," "Nothing ever goes right," "I am a failure and will always be one," and "Everything I eat turns to fat." Some are positive, such as, "I am capable," "Many things go right, and when they don't there is a lesson for me," and "I am usually successful in my efforts." If your inner voice is negative, don't let it control your mind. Create another inner voice by willfully repeating positive, inspirational messages about yourself.

If you feel awkward or foolish repeating slogans that you do not believe, don't stop. In time, all the positive messages will make an impact upon your attitude.

5. Associate with Positive People

The Rambam explained how the behavior of other people influences us:

> Man's nature is to be drawn after his friends, in both attitude and action, and to behave like his fellow countrymen. Therefore, a person must associate with righteous people and always sit near wise people so that he may learn from their ways. He must avoid evildoers so that he will not learn from their actions (Rambam, *De'os* 6:1).

---

1. Rabbi Yisrael Salanter, cited in *Tenuas HaMussar*, Vol. 1, p. 253; Rabbi Yeruchom Levovitz, *Daas Chochmah U'Mussar*, Vol. 1, p. 114; *Cheshbon HaNefesh*, Ch. 1.

The people with whom we associate have a powerful influence on us, so powerful that the Rambam recommended living as a hermit rather than living among people who behave improperly.[1]

Avoid negative people. Walk away when they spew their words of hate, gossip and dissatisfaction. Instead, seek out people who exemplify the positive goals you are trying to achieve. Associate with them and let their positive attitudes influence you.

Associating with positive people is especially important when you are going through some sort of adversity. They can be supportive and help make the challenge easier to conquer, whereas negative people may make the problem look even bigger.

6. Understand Success and Failure

When measuring success, don't compare your performance to the performance of others; rather, compare it to the one you *could* have, assuming that you utilized all your talents and capabilities. If you have used all your resources, consider yourself a success — even if someone else does it better.

And when you make a mistake or fail, focus on the lesson learned from the experience. Look for the growth factor in every failure and anticipate doing better the next time. Take the attitude that failure is nothing more than a stepping stone, an opportunity to improve on the next try. These ideas will be discussed thoroughly in Chapters Three and Four.

7. Look for Your Inner Strengths

There was once a man of modest income who owned a farm. He worked diligently until he heard that diamond mines were being discovered all around the country. He wanted to become rich quickly, so he sold his farm and went prospecting for diamonds.

One day, the man who bought his farm crossed a stream on the property and found a large stone in the water. Not knowing what type of stone it was, he took it home and placed it above his fireplace. Some time later, a guest noticed the stone and inspected it. He informed the owner that the stone was a raw diamond, so the

---

1. *De'os* 6:1.

owner ran out to the stream in search of more stones. He soon began to mine his property, and it became one of the most heavily producing diamond fields in the area.

In the meantime, the first owner, who had gone prospecting, never found his riches. Even worse, he had made a mistake for which he never forgave himself: Instead of looking right under his own two feet, he had gone elsewhere to look for riches. He had possessed his own field of diamonds but never developed it.

There is a moral to this story: Don't go elsewhere to discover success. Explore yourself to find your riches in life. How? First, take a look inside yourself for your own inner strengths. You have many talents and abilities, sometimes buried very deep, waiting to be tapped. Find them and become all you can become.

Even when you are faced with a challenge, turn inward and discover the resources you were born with. Don't give up on yourself; instead, mine your own field of diamonds. You may have just what is needed to overcome the obstacle.

8. Be Adaptable

Chazal said, "The wealthy person is the one who is happy with his share in life."[1] This person does not get upset when things do not go his way; instead, he rolls with the punches and adapts to challenges. Yes, he tries to overcome challenges and rectify inconveniences, but if he cannot make the adjustment, he accepts the situation as it is and finds other opportunities on which to focus.

This attitude is captured in the following prayer used by Alcoholics Anonymous:

> G-d, grant me the serenity
> to accept the things I cannot change,
> the courage to change the things I can,
> and the wisdom
> to know the difference.

9. Avoid Worrying

People spend a great deal of time worrying about events that will never occur or those over which they have no control. For

---

1. *Avos* 4:1.

example, an air traveler worries that his plane will arrive late, causing him to miss an important appointment; a businessman worries that his successful business will collapse; a housewife worries that one of her neighbors dislikes her; a mother worries that her healthy child will contract a disease.

None of these people have any valid basis for their concerns. The odds are that the worst will never happen. And even if it does happen, there is nothing that can be done about it now other than to take reasonable measures to avoid the calamity. Then all one can do is pray for the best.

Worrying that calamity will strike is negative and detracts from a positive outlook. To achieve the goal of living positively, it must be avoided at all costs.

"Okay," you may say, "I understand that it detracts from a positive life-style. But what can I do to stop myself from this habit?"

Here are seven ideas to help you deflect worry. They are not listed in order of importance; each person may find a different idea helpful.

A. Consider the fact that worrying will not improve the situation or reduce the chances of the crisis occurring. It is an emotion which has no bearing on reality.

B. Consider the fact that when you worry, you are expending mental energy. This energy could be better used for more productive activities such as creating safeguards or getting involved in a totally different project. Once you are involved in a productive project, your worries will begin to dissipate.

√ C. Use the *bitachon* approach. Strengthen your belief that everything that happens in life is predetermined by Hashem for your benefit. If you are convinced of this, you will not suffer discomfort over a hypothetical disaster.

D. Consider the fact that worrying is making you a negative person, the opposite of what you want to be and what the Torah expects of you.

E. Make an objective analysis of the situation and ask how you can change it. As simple as this sounds, many people become paralyzed by the thought of impending hardship.

They forget to use their greatest asset — their ability to think their way out of the problem.

F. Ask what the worst possible scenario would be if things do not work out the way you would like. Very often, the worst possible scenario is not unbearable at all.

G. Live in day-tight compartments. Focus on today's goals and responsibilities. Put tomorrow's concerns into an imaginary box and put the "box" up on a high shelf in a closet. You can go to the box any time you want, but not today. Today you are only concerned with today's issues.[1]

10. Be Solution-Oriented

When a problem arises, a solution-oriented person uses his energy to correct the situation instead of dwelling on the problem. A problem-oriented person, though, uses his energy to hash and rehash the problem. While he may have an interest in resolving his difficulty, his major focus is on the problem.

You can become a solution-oriented person by learning problem-solving strategies. As you internalize these methods, you will become a more positive person. Here are some strategies:

Don't become anxious over problems. When I was engaged to be married, an older friend approached me and asked if I was nervous. With some embarrassment, I admitted that I was. My wise friend replied enthusiastically, "Good. I'm glad. You are normal!"

My wise friend's message was, "It is common for someone in your position to be nervous. Don't become anxious over it. Don't become overly concerned about your feelings. Instead, direct your attention to other productive affairs."

The Steipler Gaon was known to tell people, *"Yedder einer hut zein peckel."* This means that everyone has his own set of problems, whether it is nervousness over getting married, illness, financial issues or relationship difficulties. Problems are a normal part of everyday life, and everyone has them. The only people who do not have problems are in the cemetery.

When you are challenged with a problem, take the advice of my wise friend and don't become overly concerned. Recognize that it is

---

1. Rashi, *Bereishis* 6:6.

only natural to have problems; just as you have a set of teeth, ears, hands and feet, you have a set of problems. It is all part of normal living. Knowing this should help you relax and focus on solutions and other productive thoughts.

Rename the problem. The word "problem" conjures up negative ideas. It is an unappealing word with a negative ring. If, in some way, you could make this word sound less menacing, you might be able to deal with problems more comfortably. For example, call them "challenges" and say that you are "triumphing over challenges." Or call them "opportunities" and say that you are "growing and learning from opportunities." Call them "minor inconveniences" and say that you "deal with minor inconveniences." There is more appeal in "challenges" and "opportunities," even in "minor inconveniences," than there is in "problems." The simple act of renaming a problem may make the burden of dealing with it lighter.

Follow a problem-solving process. There are some logical steps one can take to solve a problem. These steps apply to all types of problems, ranging from the simple to the severe. While these steps may sound elementary, they are not used often enough.

A. *Recognize the problem.* Recognize that things are not going the way they should.

B. *Analyze the problem.* Know exactly what you want and what you are not getting. Try to discover the cause of the difficulty. Ask, "What can I do about it?" Ask, "Who is involved and who should be involved?" Formulate options which may alleviate the problem.

Gather all the information necessary to create a solution by discussing the issue with people who have had similar experiences. Don't rely solely on the information you currently have; rather, learn from the experiences of others. This will enable you to repeat successes, not mistakes.

C. *Select the best solution.* Review the alternatives you formulated during the analysis. Make a list, preferably in writing, and weigh the advantages and disadvantages of each alternative. Prioritize the options and make a plan of action.

D. *Implement the solution.* Accept the plan of action whole-heartedly and with no regrets. Make a commitment to the solution and live up to it.

E. *Evaluate the solution.* After you have begun to implement the solution, ask, "Does the solution work? Does it need revision or modification?" The original decision is not carved in stone; it can be changed. If it needs improvement, adjust it.

Take risks. Whenever you embark on a new plan of action, you enter unknown territory. The solution has not been tested yet, and it may not work. Yes, there is a risk of failure, but if you abandon the plan because of the risk, you will be left in the same position as when you started. Instead, focus on the rewards of success and look at the risk as an integral part of the solution process.

When you commit yourself to a new plan of action, you create a new set of circumstances for yourself. You create a new opportunity that can lead to successes which may otherwise never occur. This is the payoff in taking the risk. Some people, though, choose the path of least resistance by avoiding risks. They choose the status quo and allow opportunity to pass them by. These people will get only what the status quo makes available and will be only as successful as the situation allows.

Successful people will tell you that they have achieved goals — whether it is in the financial, personal, social or familial arena of life — *because* they took risks. They know that every new plan has a chance of failure, but they are not afraid of failure; they see it merely as the cost one pays for growth. They know that the more risks they take, the greater their chances for success. They are always on the lookout for new opportunities which will put them on top, and they throw themselves into their experiences with a "can-do" attitude.

Help children become solution-oriented. We can help children achieve this orientation by offering guidance at the appropriate times. When a child has a problem, encourage him or her to look at it in a relaxed manner. Help the child realize that problems are part of everyday life and cannot be avoided.

Help a child rename problems. For example, if a child does not enjoy doing math problems, rename the task by calling them "math challenges." The child may then look at her work more positively, because a "challenge" has more appeal than a "problem."

You can give a child an invaluable tool for life by teaching her a problem-solving process. Guide the child through the steps and encourage her to take risks. Here is a story that illustrates this process:

> Sarah never participated in classroom discussions. The teacher took her to the side and asked why she did not participate. Sarah responded, "I know the answers, but I want to make absolutely sure they are correct before I say anything. By that time, someone else answers."
>
> The teacher decided to help Sarah become a risk-taker. First, she helped Sarah appreciate her academic strengths by pointing out that she was qualified to respond correctly. She then showed Sarah that the odds of making a mistake were small; Sarah herself acknowledged that her answers were usually correct. Then she outlined for Sarah how the benefits of participation outweigh the penalty of failure.
>
> Sarah began participating in class. As a result, she progressed more than anyone had anticipated. She became a risk-taker and succeeded because of it.

When to seek professional help? A problem should never be so formidable that it interferes with one's daily activities, consuming that person with fear or worry. Still, some people are reluctant to seek the advice of others. King Shlomo, however, tells us that seeking the advice of others is the trait of a wise person.[1]

11. Stretch Your Mind; Think

Using your mind to think is the eleventh Habit of Positive Living. This may seem elementary; after all, doesn't everyone think? Not really. Psychologists say that people use only a fraction of their thinking ability. They may concern themselves with simple household and business routines, but this is not real thinking. They may be able to talk with friends for hours, but this is also not thinking;

---

1. *Mishlei* 12:15.

it is the gift of gab. Thinking is creative. It stretches the mind to solve problems that have no easy solutions. Thinking creates new plans of action that satisfy previously unaddressed needs. Thinking sends a person in new directions rather than repeating old habits. It helps him to break away from the routine and venture toward something higher.

When faced with a challenge, don't lose hope or make guesses about how to deal with it. Instead, stop everything, sit down in a quiet place, take a pad and pencil, and stretch your mind to think of logical ways of dealing with the issue. People who have done this are amazed to discover powers they were never aware of.

Help children learn to think. When a child is faced with a challenge and immediately gives up hope, don't let him get away with it. Sit down with him and discuss options. Encourage him to think creatively by asking questions that force him to stretch his mind.

Adopting the Habits of Positive Living

Two definitions of "habit" are offered by *Webster's Ninth New Collegiate Dictionary*: 1) An acquired mode of behavior that has become nearly or completely involuntary. 2) A costume, characteristic of a calling, rank or function. One definition sees a habit as a behavior and the other sees it as a garment. It would seem that there is no connection between these two definitions. But there is.

The habitual behaviors that we develop are not accidental. We adopt them because they are consistent with our personalities. Like a well-fitting garment, habits are worn by our personalities. And because they fit our personalities so well, we keep them.

And just as we can change a garment, we can change a behavioral habit. This is important, because many people think that they are stuck with their styles and habits. If they are negative, critical, unhappy or problem-oriented, they think that they are not able to change. This is a mistake. No one is stuck with his style or habits. Everyone is capable of change.

There are two ways of making the change. One is to change the personality, and then find new habits to fit it. As discussed earlier, this is the "inside-out" approach, which requires an initial change within the mind and heart. This change can be achieved with logic and emotion, through self-study and/or psychotherapy.

The second way of changing habits is to consciously and deliberately develop new and better habits. The personality then outgrows the old habits and begins to fit into the new ones. This is the "outside-in" approach, which we discussed earlier.

We are not locked into our habits simply because we have learned their patterns and have grown comfortable with them. If we learned to be unhappy, critical, problem-oriented and negative, we can replace these habits with new ones and become comfortable with them.

One Step at a Time

Changing old attitudes and forming new ones entails breaking habits that are deeply entrenched in our personalities. We cannot totally and completely undo years of conditioning in a few days, months, or even years. Reconditioning takes a great deal of time and effort, and progress comes in small steps. One of the greatest threats to improvement is the attitude "I must see a change tomorrow." We mentioned earlier that it takes time before one can even begin to see a small change.

Appreciate the Power of Choice

Everything we have been discussing hinges on choice: choosing to react positively to challenge; choosing to act, talk and think positively; choosing to associate with positive people; choosing to be solution-oriented. We do not have to stand by and watch life act upon us. We can make things happen by choosing appropriate attitudes and behaviors.

We have the choice to think and act the way we want. This is important, because what we choose will affect our lives. The way we think and act — whether it is positive or negative — determines what we will get out of life. Much of what we will get is what we choose to get, through our behaviors. It is up to us. It is our choice.

The Blessing of Positive Living

> The person with a good heart is always feasting (*Mishlei* 15:15).

How can we recognize a person with a good heart? He is cheerful. He is thankful for everything he has. He is not jealous of others or sad over what he lacks. In his eyes, he is wealthy and has everything he needs. In other words, he has a positive attitude.[1]

King Shlomo said that such a person receives the blessing of perpetual joy. And after reading this chapter, we can go one step further. We can say that by being positive, a person *creates* the blessing that he receives. The choice of living positively results in a better life; thus, we can create the blessing of perpetual joy by making that choice.

In the beginning of this chapter, we were introduced to Reb Zushe, the impoverished man who said that he never saw a day of suffering in his life. We asked how Reb Zushe could feel this way. How could he have dissociated himself from the obvious truth that things were not going well for him?

Maybe we have the answer now. Maybe Reb Zushe's secret was his attitude. Certainly, Reb Zushe had true *bitachon* and believed that all the events in his life were decreed by Hashem for his benefit. But he also had the emotional strength to view those events with happiness.[2] He may have developed this capacity by controlling his attitude and practicing the Habits of Positive Living. Maybe, by managing himself in this way, Reb Zushe created his own blessing of perpetual joy.

---

1. See Rabbeinu Yonah and Vilna Gaon on *Avos* 4:1.

2. If *bitachon* goes hand in hand with happiness, Reb Shmelke and Reb Pinchas would not have asked their question. The answer would be elementary; the person with true *bitachon* is, by definition, happy. But since they had the question, we might deduce that *bitachon* and happiness do not necessarily go hand in hand.

Chapter Two

Expect the
Best from Yourself

*D*id you ever have a goal you thought you could not reach? Perhaps you wanted to learn a new skill, make a new friend, correct a bad *middah,* achieve an academic goal, or get a desirable job. You thought you might not be able to do it, but instead of dropping the idea, you vigorously pursued it. In the end you succeeded.

What brought about this success? Up until now, you never expected it to happen, so why *did* it happen? Many factors contributed: skill, motivation, determination and doing the right things at the right times. One factor in particular played an important role — the high expectation you set for yourself. You expected the best from yourself, and all your subsequent actions became aligned with that expectation. This is called a self-fulfilling prophecy, also known as the Pygmalion effect.

A prophecy is self-fulfilling when the expectation of an event induces behavior that increases the likelihood of the event. This is not an abstract idea or concept; it is a reality, a fact of life. A person tends to act in accordance with his set of expectations, thus bringing about the expected outcome.

A self-fulfilling prophecy can work vis-a-vis a person's expectation of himself and his subsequent behavior, or his expectation of someone else and that person's subsequent behavior. We will be discussing the first — how a person's *self-expectancy,* as we will call it, induces behavior that increases the likelihood of that outcome.

The Self-Fulfilling Prophecy

Rabbi Moshe Feinstein discussed self-expectancy and the self-fulfilling prophecy. He explained why we should always expect the best from ourselves:

> Many people do not reach their potential and also become sinners because they degrade themselves or the matter at hand. For example, a person thinks he cannot do great things such as learn Talmud with all its commentaries. He therefore does not learn because, according to his opinion, it will not help to know anything anyway. The result is that he is unable to learn and he becomes an ignoramus (*Darash Moshe,* p. 111).

This person has low self-expectancy. He feels he is incapable of learning, and his expectation of failure induces the very behavior that increases the likelihood of that outcome.

There are many stories that illustrate the effect of self-expectancy. For example, a case history is documented about a man who was suffering from an advanced case of cancer. He was admitted into a hospital where doctors administered Krebiozen, a new "wonder drug." Although he was close to death when he was admitted, his condition improved dramatically after taking Krebiozen. After several months, he was discharged from the hospital. Afterward, however, he was informed that Krebiozen was no longer considered effective against cancer. The man relapsed and was re-admitted to the hospital.

In the hospital, he was told that researchers had reviewed the Krebiozen case and once again held that it was effective. He was given injections of what he thought was Krebiozen but in reality was only a saline solution. His condition improved, and he was once again discharged.

After some time, the American Medical Association announced conclusively that Krebiozen was ineffective against cancer. The man lost all hope, suffered a relapse, was readmitted to the hospital, and died within several days.[1]

This man experienced the "placebo effect," a well-documented type of self-fulfilling prophecy. He expected his treatment to result in a particular outcome, and through the power of mind-over-matter, he induced that outcome.

Whenever medical researchers test a new drug, they consider the placebo effect. They divide their volunteers into two groups, an experimental and a control group. The experimental group receives the actual drug, while the control group receives a harmless sugar pill or saline solution. Volunteers do not know which group they are in; they are all told that they are receiving the real drug.

Researchers have found that when people *think* they are receiving the real drug, they often improve, even if they are actually receiving a fake, or placebo. Conversely, when people *think* they are receiving a sugar pill or saline solution, their symptoms often remain the same, even if they receive the actual drug. To test the true potency of the new drug, therefore, researchers make all participants *think* they are receiving it. Both groups have equal expectations, and the skewed effect of the self-fulfilling prophecy is factored out from the findings.

The placebo effect illustrates the self-fulfilling prophecy. It shows that the response people expect to have increases the likelihood of that very outcome.[2]

We see the effects of the self-fulfilling prophecy in all areas of life. Consider, for example, the young woman who believes she is unattractive and unworthy of marriage. Her attitude is, "I am ugly. Nobody will want to marry me." So she acts the part by dressing unfashionably and taking poor care of herself. She carries herself with a lowered head and stooped shoulders, and she may even talk unclearly. Eligible men become alienated as a result of her unappealing behavior.

---

1. Robert Rosenthal and Lenore Jacobson, *Pygmalion in the Classroom*, Holt, Rinehart and Winston Inc., 1968, p. 14.
2. Ibid., p. 15.

This woman's negative self-expectancy induces the very behavior that increases the likelihood that her expectation will come true.

Suppose, on the other hand, that she thinks, "I am a worthy person. I have many attractive points. And I deserve a fine husband." She would portray a totally different personality by dressing fashionably and carrying herself with greater confidence. In turn, she would attract eligible men.

I am acquainted with a person who, after going through a major setback, went on a job interview. Although he was highly talented, he went in with low self-confidence, feeling incapable of succeeding at the job.

During the interview, he played the role of an incapable person, exhibiting low enthusiasm, a meek tone of voice, timid body movements and an unconvincing choice of words. His behavior was an expression of his attitude.

His negative self-expectancy led him to play the role of a loser, which caused the interviewer to perceive him negatively. Because of his negative expectation and subsequent behavior, my talented friend was rejected in favor of a man who was less capable, but who projected strong self-confidence.

I am acquainted with a child who failed a mathematics course because of her negative self-expectancy. She did not understand the subject and failed every test. When the teacher tried to tutor her, she did not even make an effort to understand. She had a defeatist attitude and often said, "I'm bad in math. I'll never understand it."

The teacher decided to discuss the problem with the child's mother. As they talked, she discovered that the mother also had a negative attitude about herself, only stronger. She said, "I was never good in math. My sisters and brothers weren't. None of my other children were. My family is just not good in math." Her mind was made up, and her attitude was so negative that she did not even agree to a plan of action.

The mother expected failure and indirectly taught her daughter to expect failure, too. She conveyed the message in many subtle and not-so-subtle ways. The daughter "knew" she would do poorly — it was in her genes. So she gave up without even trying.

In this story, the mother helped her daughter believe that she was not good in math. She was a co-conspirator in her daughter's negative self-fulfilling prophecy. If she had been supportive of the girl's ability, the self-fulfilling prophecy may have gone in the other direction, increasing her chances of success.

The same is true of employees and students who perform well when managers and teachers expect it. They begin to believe what the manager and teacher say, and in turn expect the best of themselves. Then they commit themselves to the task and make the necessary effort to succeed. Their behavior is consistent with their expectation, increasing the likelihood of a positive outcome.[1]

Olympic athletes are also acquainted with the power of positive self-expectancy. By the time these athletes reach the Olympics, most are on a similar level of mastery. So what factor singles out the leader from all the others? Researchers say that it is his mental ability. The champion has the strongest self-confidence, the most disciplined power of concentration, and the most intense belief that he can win. Although his skills may be no better than those of the other contestants, the champion wins because he expects the best from himself and makes every effort to meet that expectation.

The lesson for us is that if we expect the best from ourselves, in any area of endeavor, we increase our chances of success. We perform better with high self-expectations. The Me'iri said it succinctly:

> An intelligent person must try to discover what he needs and not give up hope of achieving it by thinking that his goals are unreasonably high. If he works with a thoughtful, logical and determined effort, he will succeed in most cases (Me'iri, *Mishlei* 21:22).

The Me'iri suggested making a thorough study of every opportunity. After reviewing the available courses of action, choose the one that holds the greatest promise. Adopt a positive attitude about your talents, and expect to succeed. Take risks and do not allow fear or self-doubt to interfere. With proper research and a positive attitude, you will succeed in most cases.

This was the attitude of the artisans who constructed the *Mishkan* after the Exodus from Egypt. They were not trained in architecture, masonry, embroidery, weaving, diamond-cutting, gold

---

1. Rabbi Klonimus Kalmish Shapira, *Chovas HaTalmidim*, Ch. 1, citing Sh'lah; Rabbi S. R. Hirsch, *Yesodos HaChinuch*, Netzach Publishers, p. 63.

and silversmithing, or any of the other necessary arts. But they did have untapped talents. They recognized their talents and came forth to volunteer their services.[1] They had a drive to undertake the project, and they accomplished because of that drive.[2] In other words, they expected to succeed — and they did.

> The artisans who constructed the *Mishkan* were not experts, nor did they ever formally learn their skills; rather, they had a feeling that they were fitting for the work, and they were secure in their abilities . . . A student who gives up on himself will not meet his potential in learning, and the student who feels secure with his strengths and believes that he will excel in Torah . . . will become strong and able; he will progress and become successful (Rabbi Chaim Shmulevitz, *Sichos Mussar*, 5732:26).

In our daily living, we constantly set expectations for ourselves, often without even realizing it. For example, before we begin to read a book, we typically flip through the pages and consider its length and difficulty. Only if we think we have the time and ability to complete it — that is, an expectation to succeed — do we begin reading. It is the same when we accept a communal responsibility. First, we consider the challenges involved and the skills needed. Only after deciding that we have what it takes to succeed do we get involved.

Even before performing the simple task of throwing a ball, we first consider our ability. We may say to ourselves, "I'm a klutz. I will look funny throwing this ball," or we can choose to think, "It is only a ball. I can do it. And if I can't, who cares?" We only throw the ball if we think that we will succeed.

Our performance in any activity becomes a reflection of our expectation. The lower the expectation, the smaller the chance of performing well; the higher the expectation, the greater the chance of performing well.[3]

Wouldn't it be nice if we could control the expectations we have of ourselves? Then we would increase our chances of success in

---

1. Ramban, *Shemos* 35:21.

2. Rabbi Yeruchom Levovitz, *Daas Torah, Shemos*, p. 348.

3. While there is a special assistance from Above in matters related to *mitzvah* performance, expectations still play a role in non-*mitzvah* matters, too.

whatever activity we do. Is it possible to control self-expectancy? Or must we simply make peace with what we *think* we can do and work with the potential we *think* we already have?

Indeed, we *can* control our expectations. But before discussing this important point, we will review some important ideas about reality, perceptions and human conditioning. These concepts will help us appreciate our innate control.

Reality, Perceptions and Conditioning

In Chapter One we described the way in which our attitude determines our perception of reality. This explains why an unproductive person has a bleak outlook on the world, while a productive person has a brighter outlook. It explains why a shoe salesman enjoys putting shoes on another person's feet while an ordinary person feels degraded.

How a person perceives the world is the way the world *is* to him or her. This perception becomes his or her reality. Since each person has a different set of attitudes, each has a different perception of reality. Thus, every person has his or her own world. Indeed, each and every person is an "*olam katan*," a small world unto him or herself.[1]

The perception we have of ourselves may be different from the perception others have of us. Not only do we perceive the world differently from others, we also perceive ourselves differently from the way others see us. For example, there are people who think they have good *middos*, yet others think they have poor *middos*. There are people who consider themselves inept, yet others consider them clever and skilled. And we all have had at least one instance when others thought we acted in an unfriendly manner, yet we thought we acted in a friendly manner.

To illustrate this idea, try this experiment. Tape record yourself talking with another person. Afterwards, play it back. Listen to your expressions, choice of words and tone of voice. People who have done this say they cannot believe they are listening to themselves. What they hear is much different from what they thought they were communicating. Sometimes, they even think the tape recorder is broken.

---

1. This term is used by the masters of Jewish ethics and philosophy.

Well, the tape recorder is not broken. The real problem is that up until now, these people only knew how they sounded to themselves. Now, for the first time, they hear how they sound to others. And they find it hard to believe.

The wise old adage goes, "If two people say you are drunk, lie down." Even if you didn't drink anything, there is a reason people are saying you are intoxicated. Their perception of you is different from your perception of yourself.

Perceptions are expressions of our conditioning. From infancy, we have been receiving messages about ourselves and the world around us from parents, siblings, friends, relatives, teachers and total strangers. As explained in Chapter One, we synthesized all this information with our own ideas and became conditioned by it. This conditioning formed our self-images and many of our attitudes and personality traits. These factors in turn determine the perceptions we have of ourselves and everything around us.

To illustrate how your perceptions reflect your conditioning, let us say that as a child you were constantly criticized for being irresponsible. Even if it was not true, you probably believed it anyway. This opinion remained with you and helped to condition you. Now, as an adult, you continue to think you are irresponsible, although it may not be true, and you therefore avoid tasks that require any sort of responsibility.

Perceptions are fixed. The perception we have of ourselves and the world around us is an integral part of our personalities. Like any other personality trait, it is fixed and cannot be easily changed. The following exercise illustrates this point.

Look at the drawing on the page 79. Do you see an old woman or a young woman? Whenever groups of people are given this exercise, some participants say the woman is old and some say she is young.

Now look at the two pictures on page 80. One is of an old woman, the other is of a young woman. Which is the one you saw in the drawing on page 79? If you saw an old woman, try to look for the young woman. And if you saw the young woman, look for the old one. At first, you may have some difficulty seeing the image in a new way, but if you relax your eyes and allow yourself to see the other woman, you will.

It is fascinating to see how people hold on tenaciously to their original perceptions. But once they make the effort to see the other face, they realize there is another way to perceive the drawing.

Which is right? There is no right or wrong perception here, only different ones. It is the same with any perception. You cannot debate the validity of your perception over another's, because the other believes his perception is just as real as you think yours is.

Now concentrate on another thought or object for a minute. Afterwards, look at the first picture again. Do you see the old woman, the young woman, or both? Most people immediately see the same woman they saw the first time. Even though they have been shown the other image, their original perception remains dominant.

In much the same way, all our perceptions, whether they concern ourselves or others, are fixed aspects of our personalities and cannot be easily changed. Even if we understand another perception, our own remains dominant.

A fixed perception is the reason that the Jewish people, in their flight from Egypt, were afraid to fight the Egyptians who were pursuing them. Although there were 600,000 Jewish men against a much smaller Egyptian army, they still feared the enemy. This was because they had been conditioned their entire lives to fear the Egyptians. Their perception was fixed and could not be easily changed.[1]

It has been suggested that for this reason Yosef's brothers did not recognize him even after he hinted at his true identity. Their perception had always been of an unbearded Yosef, and now that he had a full beard they could not perceive him anew. Their perception was so ingrained that even when Yosef disclosed himself they did not believe him until he revealed his *bris milah*.

To summarize: Perception is a product of conditioning; it is a fixed part of one's personality; the perception one has of himself is different from the perception others have of him; and one's perception creates his reality. With this foundation, we can proceed to the main focus of this chapter — the way in which our self-perception either holds us back from success or propels us to reach our potential in any area of life, whether it pertains to character refinement,

---

1. Ibn Ezra, *Shemos* 14:13.

financial growth, or family and social relationships. We will discuss this next.

Self-Imposed Limitations

Sometimes people perceive themselves as having limited capabilities. It may be true, but it may be nothing more than a distorted perception. Even worse, their negative self-perception may hold them back from fulfilling their full potential. We call this a self-imposed limitation.

Self-perceptions and self-imposed limitations. Imagine a steel beam two feet wide and ten feet long on the ground next to you. Some friends offer you twenty dollars to walk across the beam. Easy enough. So you walk across and collect the prize. Then they raise the beam four feet and offer you fifty dollars to walk across. You think, "What is the worst that can happen? Even if I fall, it is only four feet. Besides, I know I can do it, because I just walked across the same beam when it was on the ground." You walk across and collect the fifty dollars.

Then they raise the beam one hundred feet in the air and offer you one thousand dollars. You think about it and decide to go. "After all," you reason, "when the beam was four feet off the ground, I walked across it so easily. It's the same beam, so why shouldn't I be able to walk across now?" But just as you start, you look down and begin to lose your balance. After wobbling for a few moments, you turn back.

This beam is two feet wide, so why are you not able to keep your balance? "Because," you say, "it is one hundred feet in the air." But you walked across the same beam when it was four feet in the air, so why can't you keep your balance now?

Because you have imposed a limitation on yourself. You think, "It is difficult to keep my balance so high up in the air. There is a good chance that I will fall. The prize is just not worth the chance of falling." So even though you did not lose your balance on the last two attempts, you quickly lose balance now. You have imposed a limitation on yourself, and as a result you do not fulfill your true potential.

What keeps you back, then, is not *who* you are but what you think you are *not*. Indeed, you are the same person who walked across the beam when it was four feet off the ground; however, your thinking is now different. Because you tell yourself that you cannot manage, you quickly lose your balance and do not attempt the walk. You behave consistently with your self-perception, even if it means forfeiting a thousand-dollar prize.

The perception you have of yourself plays a pivotal role in all areas of your life. It dictates to you what you are capable of achieving. Whether you are about to read a book, throw a ball, undertake an academic pursuit, or walk the beam, you first consider the ability you think you have. You act on your self-perception because you trust it, whether it is true or not.

What you *think* you can do is what you can do. Who you *feel* you are is who you are. In life, you only go as far as you *think* you can go.

Consider, for example, a person who grows up in a family of cantors and singers. He thinks his voice is bad, so he avoids activities that involve singing. And if he thinks his voice is so bad that it cannot improve with training, he will not even seek the training. The result of his negative attitude is that he will never enjoy this activity and will not join others in a singing event.

This person's self-perception acts as a screen. Just as a wire screen separates the large particles from the fine particles, his perception of his capabilities is the screen that separates the activities he will pursue from those that he will avoid. In this case, he screens out all options related to singing. His self-imposed limitation keeps him from an entire sphere of enjoyable opportunities in life. He is kept back not because of *who* he is, but because of what he thinks he is *not.*

Isn't this what the man in Rabbi Feinstein's example did? He thought he would never know anything, so he screened out all options related to learning. With his self-imposed limitation, he maintained his ignorance. He was kept back not because of *who* he was, but because of what he thought he was *not.*

We are all exposed to opportunities that we screen out because we think we cannot achieve them. One example is the novice schoolteacher who, after the first few days of classes, discovers that he has an unusually large number of weak students in his class. He thinks, "I am new at this, and the position calls for someone with a lot more experience. There is no way I can overcome this challenge. I cannot possibly succeed. Maybe I should look for another job." He thinks he cannot succeed, so he screens out the possibility of performing well and considers leaving the job.

Another example is the sensitive newlywed who discovers that her new husband has a temper. She confides to a close friend, "While we were going out, I thought he had such fine *middos*. Now I find out he has a terrible temper. I am not capable of dealing with it. I am a sensitive person and have no skills in dealing with temperamental people. How can my marriage possibly work?" She thinks she will never deal successfully with her husband, so she screens out the possibility.

Consider the office worker who has a difficult boss. She tells a colleague, "My boss is so difficult. If I say 'yes,' he says 'no.' If I say 'hot,' he says 'cold.' He is so critical, it seems that whatever I do is never good enough for him. I always avoided people like this. I can't come to work every day and put up with this!"

All these people have the same assumption — "I don't know how to overcome the challenge; therefore, I should give up." They perceive themselves as incapable and have screened out the possibility of learning to deal with the problem and overcoming it. By limiting themselves to the status quo, they will go as far as the status quo allows, and that is not very far at all.

On the other hand, they could say, "I have a problem. But I am not going to let it beat me. I am going to think of a solution. And if I have to, I will seek advice from experts." This positive attitude empowers them to find solutions and, as the Me'iri and Rabbi Feinstein point out, can change the situation entirely.

You get what you expect. The saying goes, "Treat yourself as you *think* you are, and you will remain as you are. Treat yourself as if you were what you *could* be and *should* be, and you will become what you could be and should be." This does not mean that you can completely control the level of success you have. There are many other factors, internal and external, working for and against that success. Rather, the saying expresses the idea that you play a primary role and have a strong influence on your own life. Through your expectations, you influence — not control — your behavior, both positive and negative.

For this reason, it is important to see yourself in a positive light. When you expect great things from yourself, you are driven to go further than you otherwise would go. Once you believe you can achieve, your behavior becomes consistent with the anticipation and you find the resources to make it come true. In other words, your *attitude* determines your *altitude.*

The expectation/motivation connection. Suppose a person does not expect to succeed at a particular task. Will the promise of a reward motivate him to succeed? It is hard to know. But the odds are that if he expects to fail, he will not take the incentive seriously. "After all," he reasons, "I will never see the reward anyway." Besides, he probably has no inner drive to do his best because he "knows" that he will not succeed anyway. Although he would like to reach the goal, he loses his motivation and gives up.

The desire to succeed is obviously not enough to drive a person to work for success; there has to be an expectation attached to it. Once he has both the expectation and the desire, he has more of an inner drive and becomes more susceptible to the motivational influence of a reward.

Take, as an example, a real estate agent who is paid on a commission basis. The more houses he sells, the more commission he earns, and the closer he comes to his dream of a company-sponsored all-expenses-paid vacation. Although he wants a higher income and the vacation, he feels that he is capable of selling only five houses per year, hardly enough to receive those benefits. How much effort will he put into selling homes? It is hard to know, but the odds are that he will not put in the same effort as if he expected to sell twelve houses per year.

This agent has a desire to succeed, but it is not enough to push him to reach his potential. Without *expecting* to perform better, he will not perform better.

A person gets what he expects. When he expects a certain outcome and is motivated to get it, he works harder than if he did not have that expectation.

Be a thermostat, not a thermometer. Why do people impose limitations on themselves? Because they have absorbed so many negative ideas about themselves that they feel incapable of success.

They are like the person who stubs his toe, and when other people say, "Look what you have done. You cannot possibly succeed in your condition," he listens, even if he really could succeed. He is a victim of his own conditioning, giving credence to anybody who has ever said something negative about him.

People who impose limitations on themselves reflect the negative opinions of their environment in the same way that a thermometer reflects the temperature of its environment. They say things like, "People have always said that I am incompetent. I agree. I will never do it. I can't." As a thermometer, they pay attention to what others say and respond to it.

But if they acted as a thermostat, things would be different. As a thermostat *controls* the temperature of its environment, they could put some *control* into their lives. Instead of having constricting self-perceptions based on past failures and the negative input of others, they could take some control and say, "Let me see what I can learn from all this. Let me see how I can do it right. I can become a winner." By perceiving past failure as an opportunity to do things right the next time, by taking the criticism of others as a gentle nudge to become even more competent, they can take control over their attitudes and boost their self-expectancy.

Chazal said that a person proves how strong he is by his ability to control his *yetzer hara,* not by winning a boxing match; that a person proves how wealthy he is by being happy with his circumstances, not by amassing material wealth; and that a person proves how wise he is by wanting to learn from everybody and everything, not by showing others how much wisdom he has acquired.[1]

Chazal told us that strength, wisdom and wealth are all products of the way one utilizes his mind. Success in these areas comes from within; it is an inside job, where each individual can choose the attitude that will define his degree of strength, wisdom and wealth. Like a thermostat, every person can control the way he deals with life's events.[2]

Let's take a look at professional sports for an illustration. The world record for running a mile was set at four minutes in 1945. It was not until 1954, nine years later, that Roger Banister broke that record. Since then, many other athletes have broken the four-minute record.

---

1. *Avos* 4:1.
2. Rabbi Yeruchom Levovitz, *Daas Torah, Bereishis,* p. 206.

For nine years nobody was able to break the record. Why? Psychologists theorize that the goal was not the problem; rather, it was the athletes themselves. They considered it impossible to run a mile in less than four minutes and did not make the attempt. But Mr. Banister did not impose limitations on himself. He believed it was possible and reached his goal. Once he demonstrated that it was possible, other athletes said, "If Banister can do it, so can I."

Until 1954, athletes behaved as thermometers, reflecting the negative opinions of what the world said about the impossibility of a four-minute mile. As a result, they could not beat the record. However, one thermostat by the name of Roger Banister took control of the environment and broke the record. The athletes who followed his example became winners because they broke their self-imposed limitations and, like thermostats, set new expectations for themselves.

FEARs that hold you back. What limitations do you impose upon yourself? What beliefs do you have that hold you back from succeeding? What experiences and educational principles do you refer to when you impose those limitations? What false evidence have you used to reinforce those limitations? What are your FEARs?

FEAR can be read as an acronym for False Education Appearing Real; False Experience Appearing Real; or False Evidence Appearing Real.

People often base their FEARs on false premises. One example is the person who once experienced a setback and was left with a lasting negative impression about himself. Another is the person who was once told that he was incapable of doing something, and believed it. Someone else's opinion, a single setback, or one's own distorted self-image do not make a strong enough foundation on which to base a lifelong attitude of inadequacy. However, the evidence appears real enough for a person to formulate lasting impressions.

Here are four FEARs that people often have:

1. *Fear of rejection.* We have all seen people who are in a position of power use their influence in deceitful and unethical ways — for example, the person who observes others dealing in a dishonest manner, yet stands on the side and says

nothing. Sometimes he is afraid of retribution; sometimes he simply doesn't care. But often he says nothing because the ones in power are part of the "in-crowd," and by ruffling their feathers the onlooker would be rejected.

Although the person who succumbs to this pressure knows he should act otherwise, he says, "I can't go against my friend. He is important to me and I want him to respect me. If I don't say anything, he won't have to know I disagree. But if he knows I disagree, he may reject me." He imposes a limitation on himself, and as a result acts improperly himself.

Fear of rejection is the reason that young people often remain members of gangs even after realizing that they should break the attachment. When their friends push them in an inappropriate direction, one in which they prefer not going, they feel compelled to cooperate for fear of being rejected by their friends.

2. *Fear of change.* People often become complacent in a familiar setting and avoid change. Although they realize that making a change at this time may be in their best interest, they maintain the status quo. They would rather stay in a comfortable environment, ineffective though it may be, than subject themselves to the tension and disorientation of shifting to an unfamiliar one.

Take, for example, a yeshivah student who is not learning well in the institution he is currently attending. He is familiar with another yeshivah and feels he would do better there. But he is wary of the unfamiliar setting and avoids transferring. He thinks, "I have a room and friends here. I am comfortable, and everything is so familiar. How can I switch to another yeshivah? What if it doesn't work out? Besides, the switch will cause me too much stress." This young man's self-imposed limitation will impede his growth.

Many people hold onto unsatisfying jobs, uncomfortable apartments or undesirable friends. They know they should make an adjustment but avoid it, because they fear the unknown. They say, "I don't know what the new situation will bring. I'm afraid to find out. So I will just remain with what I have." Their self-imposed restraints choke them off from success and happiness.

3. *Fear of failure.* Sometimes, people do not venture from their own familiar corner because they are afraid of failing. They avoid making new friends, saying, "What if they won't like me?" They avoid taking business risks, saying, "What if it doesn't work out?" And they avoid communal responsibilities, saying, "What if I don't do a good job?" They are bound by the gnawing fear of failing and the attendant humiliation. So they impose restrictions on themselves which prevent them from pursuing life-enhancing opportunities.

    When Rabbeinu Bachya ibn Pekudah first considered writing the *Chovos HaLevavos*, he found himself under the constraint of such a limitation. He felt he did not have the talent to write a perfectly organized work, and he was afraid of failure. This FEAR held him back, until he began to realize what it was doing to him. He reconsidered the project and produced a major ethical/philosophical work.[1]

    The very topic of fear of failure is one he addressed in his book:

> There are many intellectual gains that people forfeit because of their fear of failure. And there are many deficiencies that people retain because of this fear. It reminds me of the saying, "One rule about being cautious is not to be too cautious" (*Chovos HaLevavos*, Introduction).

    It is a good idea to be cautious; after all, nobody wants to make a mistake that can be avoided. But too much caution can be crippling. And when caution translates into unfounded fear of failure, it can hold one back from reaching many goals that are within his grasp.

4. *Fear of success.* Some people are apprehensive about success because they do not want the new reputation and set of responsibilities that come along with it. Sometimes they

---

1. *Chovos HaLevavos*, Introduction.

even worry that their old friends will feel intimidated and desert them. Other times they are nervous because they think they will have to carry themselves differently in public. Yet another concern is the voice of their poor self-image, telling them that they are not worthy of success.

We can illustrate the fear of success with the man who receives a promotion as a manager. He has mixed emotions about the promotion because he feels inferior to his new peer group of veteran managers and is nervous about meeting the standards of his new responsibilities.

Uncomfortable with his promotion, he begins to suffer emotional anxiety. He confides to his wife that, although this promotion reflects professional success, he really does not want it. As a result, he may even sabotage his success by doing something that will bring about a demotion.

As with all FEARs, this man's concerns are not well-founded; they are nothing more than self-imposed limitations which hold him back from fulfilling his potential. If he would recognize his fears for what they really are — that is, False Evidence/Experience/Education Appearing Real — he would be in a position to free himself from his self-imposed restrictions and to undertake new responsibilities.

Procrastination can be fear in disguise. People often delay a task by saying something like, "I'll do it some other time." Sometimes this is legitimate, and sometimes it is nothing more than an excuse to avoid an undesirable task.

There are still other times when people procrastinate as a way of pushing off a task that they are afraid of doing. Rather than saying, "I am afraid of change" or "I am afraid of failure" or "I am afraid of success," they say "I will do it some other time." In this case, procrastination is a disguise for fear, and if it persists, they may never get around to doing the task, because "some other time" may never come.

Every successful person was once a beginner. Did you ever see a novice ice skater? She clumsily holds onto the side rails, and whenever she releases her hold or a child zooms by, she loses her balance and falls. As uncomfortable as it may be, the only way she will learn to skate is to get up, fall again, and get up again. But once she learns to skate, she will begin to zoom along with the same children who knocked her off balance in the first place.

Every successful person, every winner, was once a beginner. Rabbi Akiva began learning the *aleph-beis* at the age of forty.[1] Rabbi Eliezer Ben Hurkenus first learned to recite *K'rias Shema* at the age of twenty-eight.[2] Observers may have jeered at them or expressed doubts about their success at these ages. But that did not stop Rabbi Akiva and Rabbi Eliezer. They also knew they were beginners. But they expected the best from themselves, put their FEARs to the side, and undertook a program that would bring them to their goal. They risked the chance of looking foolish, and they persevered. They went through the falling-down and getting-up process, and enjoyed the reward of success.

We all have hidden talents. Like Rabbi Akiva and Rabbi Eliezer ben Hurkenus, we all have hidden talents and abilities waiting to be uncovered. But we often suppress our growth by giving our FEARs center stage. This is not the way to live.

Chazal told us that we are obligated to ask ourselves, "When will my actions equal those of my forefathers?"[3] Rabbi Eliyahu Dessler deduced that since we are obligated to aspire to higher levels, it must be that higher levels are within everyone's reach.[4] Therefore, one should never believe that he is inept, because within each and every person lies a wealth of hidden ability. If he would only tap those hidden talents, he would accomplish more than he ever dreamed.

Chazal further told us, "The day is short, the work is great, and the workers are lazy."[5] This implies that people in general do not utilize their full potential and are capable of accomplishing much more than they are already doing.[6]

Secular thinkers agree. William James, the father of American psychology, said that people utilize only a fraction of their true abilities and that they are capable of a great deal of stretching. Another

---

1. *Avos d'Rav Nosson*, Ch. 6.
2. *Pirkei Rabbi Eliezer*, Chs. 1-2.
3. *Tanna d'Bei Eliyahu Rabbah* 25.
4. *Michtav M'Eliyahu*, Vol. 3, pp. 21-23.
5. *Avos* 2:15.
6. Rabbi Chaim Shmulevitz, *Sichos Mussar*, 5732:9.

expert put it this way: "What lies behind us and what lies ahead of us are tiny matters compared to what lies *within* us." Yet another student of behavior put it this way: "Everyone has the potential to be a winner, but some people are disguised as losers. Don't let their outside appearances fool you."

We are all created in the "image of G-d" and are endowed with "pure souls created by G-d."[1] Equipped with such powerful potential, one can never estimate how much he can accomplish.

There are fascinating stories of people who have used their physical potential to do the "impossible"; for example, the man who lifted a piece of heavy equipment to rescue a relative from harm. He never knew he had such physical strength until he had to use it. It is the same with all of us; we all have hidden physical and mental abilities waiting to be uncovered.

True to this idea, a teacher who withholds a Torah law from a student because he thinks the student will not understand it is called a thief. The student is *entitled* to that information and the teacher is required to share it with him, no matter how intellectually weak the student appears.[2] The question is: Why should the teacher waste his time trying to get the point across to a seemingly weak student? The answer obviously is that each and every person has abilities and talents that are unknown, just waiting to be tapped.

Rabbi Akiva is an example of a person who tapped his hidden talents. As we mentioned earlier, he was ignorant of Jewish knowledge up until the age of forty. It was believed that he had no talent for Torah learning, and when he married, his bride's wealthy father disowned her because he felt that Akiva was not a worthy husband. Nevertheless, Rabbi Akiva persevered and showed the world how high a person can go.[3]

Rabbi Eliezer ben Hurkenus is another example. He was also considered incapable. As we mentioned earlier, he did not even know how to read *K'rias Shema* until the age of twenty-eight. When he first decided to leave home to study Torah, his father wanted to disinherit him. But to his family's surprise, he became a towering Torah scholar.[4]

---

1. Said in the morning prayers.
2. Talmud *Sanhedrin* 91a, following Maharsha.
3. *Avos d'Rav Nosson*, Ch. 6.
4. *Pirkei Rabbi Eliezer*, Chs. 1-2.

Rabbi Yochanan ben Zakkai is another illustration of this phenomenon. At first, he showed such little promise that his colleagues disregarded him. One day before starting the lesson, Hillel, their teacher, asked if all the students were present. The students had such meager regard for Rabbi Yochanan ben Zakkai that they didn't even realize he wasn't there. One student, however, did take notice and told Hillel. Hillel responded, "Let the small one come. A generation of people will follow him." Rabbi Yochanan ben Zakkai eventually became a Torah giant.[1]

Chazal learned from this incident that "we should not push away the small ones from before the big ones, because lambs eventually become grown sheep."[2] Similarly, we should not push *ourselves* away, in our *own* minds, because we eventually can become "sheep," accomplishing more than we ever dreamed possible.

We are built for success. Our Creator is all-wise, all-loving and all-powerful. Such a Creator would not make a faulty product. Our Creator engineered us for success. He wants us to live to our full potential. He wants us to "choose life."[3] Just as a loving parent wants his children to be successful and derives satisfaction from their achievements, our loving Father wants His children to succeed, and He has great pleasure when they do.

The *mitzvah* of *bris milah* teaches us that "just as we have the power to perfect our physical bodies through *bris milah,* we have the power to perfect our spiritual beings through proper thoughts and actions."[4] The Vilna Gaon went one step further, saying that the reason we were created in the first place is to perfect our *middos.*[5] Obviously, our Creator built into our systems the capability to excel, or He would not expect us to try.

We mentioned earlier in the name of Rabbi Eliyahu Dessler that striving for higher levels of spirituality is more than an ideal — it is a requirement. Rabbeinu Yonah elaborated on this point:

> Where there are no other people greater than you in wisdom, try to be a great man. Continue seeking wisdom,

---

1. Rabbeinu Yonah, *Avos* 1:1.
2. Ibid.
3. *Devarim* 30:19.
4. *Sefer HaChinuch, mitzvah* 2.
5. Vilna Gaon, *Mishlei* 4:13.

although nobody in your city is wiser than you. And even if there is nobody as wise as you in your entire generation, imagine yourself living in the Talmudic days together with those wise people. And after you reach their high level, imagine yourself living in the time of the prophets or Moshe Rabbeinu, and try to reach their levels of spirituality and wisdom. With this attitude you will never cease learning. Every day you will correct your *middos,* which will add to your wisdom, and you will become an overflowing fountain (Rabbeinu Yonah, *Avos* 2:5).

Growth and the pursuit of perfection is a never-ending quest. With every level of wisdom and spirituality we reach, we should train our eye on the next level — and expect to succeed. This leaves us with the same conclusion: If we were not engineered with the capacity to excel, we would not be expected to constantly strive for higher levels of perfection. Obviously, we are built for success.

Even after all this talk of using our hidden talents to succeed, let us not forget that any result is ultimately in the hands of Hashem. The success that we achieve is decreed from Above; we only have to try our hardest to attain it, then leave the rest up to Him. If the final result is determined by Hashem, it must be that we can accomplish more than we would ever dream possible:

> Since a person does not create outcomes — rather, through his actions he is assisted from Above — the more effort he puts into achieving success, the more he will be assisted from Above. If so, there is no limit to the capabilities of man, because no matter what he does, the outcome is not from his effort itself. For this reason, we should not be surprised when someone accomplishes extraordinary feats (Rabbi Chaim Shmulevitz, *Sichos Mussar* 5732:13).

Chazal further said, "In the way that a person wants to go, they assist him."[1] "They" refers to angels who help a person reach his goals. Hashem's desire for a person to succeed is so great that He

---

1. Talmud *Makkos* 10b.

offers the assistance of His angels to anybody who has his eye on a goal.[1]

Our Creator wants us to succeed. He even gives us a guarantee that, under certain conditions, He will help. One condition is that we do what is correct in His eyes; as *Chazal* said, "A person's wishes should be consistent with His wishes, so that His wishes will be consistent with the person's wishes."[2]

Another condition is that we put our faith in Him and realize that whatever we do will only bear fruit with His assistance:

> Whenever you plan to do something, remember Hashem and hope that He will give you success. Put your faith in Him and turn your heart to Him, because the success of the activity is not in your hands . . . There are people who look to Hashem for the big things, such as when they are about to go to sea or travel a long distance for business purposes. But for the small things they do not remember Hashem, because the task appears easy and they are sure they will succeed, or because they will not lose much even if they do fail. For this reason King Shlomo said, "Know Hashem in all your ways," in both big and small matters. Since all successes are in the hand of Hashem, people must remember Him in all their activities . . . Know Him in all your ways, whether it is a voluntary matter or a *mitzvah* . . . "and He will make your ways straight" — excluding the reward for having faith, you will succeed in the matter in which you considered Hashem's influence (Rabbeinu Yonah, *Mishlei* 3:6).

We are built for success. We are endowed with the resources to succeed. When we use those resources and have the proper belief in Hashem, we receive His supernatural assistance, in both *mitzvah* and non-*mitzvah* matters. If this is the case, it makes no sense to impose limitations on ourselves that hold us back from reaching our full potential.

Crash through your self-imposed limitations. You have the ability to accomplish more than you think you can. But you some-

---

1. See Maharsha there.
2. *Avos* 2:4.

times avoid opportunities that would bring out your best. Go ahead — take the risk. Risk looking foolish. Risk the chance of experiencing a FEAR. Don't let negative perceptions get in the way of success. Go after the goals you have the talent to reach, and if you don't have the skill, seek training.

Take a positive attitude — even if it goes against your grain. Think of reasons for doing the task, not reasons for not doing it. Think of your competencies, not your incompetencies. Be optimistic and expect the best from yourself. There is no guarantee that you will perform well, but with a positive outlook the chance of success is greater than with a negative one.

When the daughter of Pharaoh stretched her hand across the width of a river to snatch Moshe's basket, she was exhibiting a positive can-do attitude.[1] Suppose she had said instead, "My arm is not long enough to reach that basket. There is no way I can do it. I will have to forget about it." She probably would not have accomplished her feat. Instead, she did not let physical limitations stop her from reaching her goal. Her attitude was positive and as a result, she succeeded. True, it was a miraculous event; however, it only happened because of her self-expectancy.

Forming a positive attitude and crashing through self-imposed limitations can be difficult. There are two strategies that can lighten the burden: imagery and affirmations. These strategies target the very root of a self-imposed limitation — perceptions. They can help enhance a negative self-perception by creating images of success. The new images strengthen one's self-expectancy, thus increasing the chances of success. We will discuss this next.

Succeed by Creating Images of Success

Dr. Denis Waitley, a noted researcher, once assisted a professional football player into a relaxed, hypnotic state. He then told the football player that an ashtray on the floor weighed five hundred pounds, and asked him to lift it. The football player bent down and tried lifting the ashtray, but he couldn't. Bystanders urged him, "Come on, you can do it. It's not that heavy," but he still could not lift the ashtray.

---

1. Rashi, *Shemos* 2:5, following one *midrash*.

An instrument to measure the football player's muscle pressure was attached to him. It measured the biceps pulling with 300 pounds of force and the triceps pushing with 301 pounds of force. The football player could not lift the ashtray because he was countering the pull with a stronger push!

What was the football player's problem? He had an image of the ashtray weighing five hundred pounds. He believed it could not be lifted, and he behaved accordingly. No matter how much encouragement he received from others, he was determined not to lift it, because this was not consistent with his image of reality.

The only way this man was going to lift the ashtray was to create an image of it as weighing only a few pounds. His actions would then be consistent with his perception of reality, and he would lift it.

It is the same with any task; the image you have of the task can either limit you or enable you to achieve it. By choosing a limiting image, you become limited; by choosing an achievable image, you become enabled. This is the way to deal with all of life's "ashtrays."

Images determine a person's *middos*. Rabbi Shlomo Wolbe wrote that a person's images help determine his *middos*. For example, a quick-tempered person has images of anger, so he is easily angered. A lazy person constantly conjures up images of impending danger, so he quickly pushes off responsibilities. A haughty person has images of honor, so he seeks opportunities that will give him honor. A person sees in his mind's eye how he is supposed to act. He then acts accordingly.

Rabbi Wolbe also wrote that a person can change a *middah* with images. A quick-tempered person can learn to control his anger by creating images of patience and tolerance. A lazy person can become industrious by creating images of diligence and persistence. And a haughty person can become humble by creating images of humility and submission. Since the tendency is to be drawn toward one's images, these people will be drawn toward their new images and will eventually behave consistently with them.[1]

Children behave according to the images their parents create. Children often act the same way their parents do. As the saying

---

1. *Alei Shur*, p. 144.

goes, "The apple doesn't fall far from the tree." Even if the child dislikes a parent's behavior, he or she often repeats it, not only as a child but even as an adult. Why does a parent have such a powerful influence on a child?

The reason is that parents' behaviors are the images that become implanted in the mind of a child. Without realizing it, the parents' behaviors are deposited into the child's "image bank." Whenever appropriate, the child calls on those images and behaves in the same way. Even as the child enters adulthood, he or she takes along those images and continues to be drawn toward them.

Take, for example, a child of critical parents. Every time the child makes a mistake, large or small, her parents criticize her. The child now has an image of being critical. So when an opportunity comes to criticize someone else's mistake, or even her own, she sees the image of her parent's criticalness and copies it. The image of her parents' behavior remains in her image bank, and she continues to be critical even as an adult.

So too, parents who are impatient and quick to anger leave the child with an image of anger and impatience. So whenever the child becomes upset, she calls up those images from her image bank and responds just as her parents would. Since these images become part of her very fabric, she will continue to behave this way even as an adult.

On the other hand, parents who perform acts of *chessed* by helping others, giving charity, and inviting needy people into their home leave their children with images of kindness. The children unknowingly deposit these images into their image banks and call on them when the time comes to help someone out.

Parents are well advised to be proper role models,[1] probably for this reason. In whatever way parents behave, images of their behavior are implanted in the minds of their children.

This is the reason that telling a child, "Do as I say, not as I do" does not work. As long as the child has an image of what the parents *do*, he will not do as the parents *say*. The child is more impressed by the image of his parents' *actions* than by their talk. The child will do as the parents do, no matter what they say,

---

1. Chazon Ish, *Emunah U'Bitachon* 4:16.

because an image of their actions is implanted in his mind and draws him toward it.

People trust their images and depend on them. People behave as though their images are the truth. They act and feel according to the images they have of themselves and the world around them, never questioning the validity of their perceptions. The following scenario illustrates this idea.

A man is walking on a lonely country trail and meets what appears to be a bear. It seems real, so he panics. But the "bear" is really an actor in a bear outfit. And once he reveals himself, the man turns calm.

Let us suppose that the man immediately thinks the bear is an actor dressed in a bear outfit. Would he panic? Of course not. As far as he is concerned, there is nothing to be afraid of.

In both cases, the man reacts to the image he has of the "bear." In the first case the image is distorted. In the second case the image is true. Real or distorted, he trusts his perception and accepts it as truth.

We relate to all our images in much the same way. Whether our images are true or distorted, we believe they are true and act accordingly.

Distorted images which appear real are the cause of many arguments and misunderstandings between people. For example, a husband and wife may be considering the purchase of a new home. The wife is enthused over the idea, but the husband is reluctant. After months of hunting, a house that interests the wife finally goes on the market.

The husband suggests that the price is too high. The wife listens to his position, then decides that he is only giving her a hard time. "After all," she thinks, "he has always been reluctant. Why should he be any different now?"

With this image in her mind, the wife feels insulted that her husband is disregarding her position. She tells him, "I am uncomfortable in our tiny apartment. I really want to move into a larger house. You obviously don't care about my feelings." After this comment, tempers flare and they end up arguing.

The argument is the result of the wife's image of her husband as not being interested in purchasing a home altogether. Whenever they discuss the issue, she has this recalcitrant image of him in front of her. So when he questions the fairness of the price, her image of him is immediately called up and she concludes that he is just being disagreeable.

In truth, however, he is not being difficult at all; he is just sharing a point that she might not have considered. Nevertheless, she has a less noble image of him. She trusts that image, although it is distorted. So she reads too much into his words and totally disregards the validity of his point. Her behavior is consistent with her mental image.

In anything we do, we pattern our behaviors after the image of how we think we are supposed to act. If our image is correct, we act appropriately. If our image is distorted, we act inappropriately.

It follows, then, that if a person's image of *himself* is correct, he will act appropriately, and if it is distorted, he will act inappropriately. We will discuss this next.

Images help shape a person's performance. Earlier, we said that a person only goes as far as he thinks he can go. We illustrated this with the story of the talented job-seeker who thought he was inadequate and with Rabbi Moshe Feinstein's example of the ignoramus. We explained that if a person expects failure, he will probably not perform well. But if he thinks he is capable and he expects to succeed, he will perform better.

Now we are adding a third ingredient to the formula for success: images. Images are not thoughts; they are mental pictures — vivid, detailed, and appearing real — which a person has of his successes, failures, competence and incompetence. Thoughts, on the other hand, are abstract and conceptual, representing a person's train of logic, reasoning, and any abstract idea he has about himself.

The language of images consists of pictures and imagination. The language of thoughts consists of logic and intellect.

Both images and thoughts play a role in shaping the opinion a person has of himself and his subsequent performances, but images have a stronger influence than thoughts. A person's mental picture of himself is the ingredient that really gives force to his self-perception and subsequent actions.[1] The impact of thoughts alone is

---

1. This is implied by Rabbi Simcha Zissel Ziv, *Chochmah U'Mussar*, Vol. 1, pp. 2-4. Also, by Rabbi Shlomo Wolbe, *Alei Shur*, p. 144, and Rabbi Eliyahu Dessler, *Michtav M'Eliyahu*, Vol. 4, p. 254.

limited. In combination with images, though, the impact is significant.

Here is a question: Since one's image of himself plays a pivotal role in the quality of his performances, could he improve his performances by improving his mental image of himself? Could a person accomplish more by creating positive inner images of himself?

Yes, a person can improve his performance and accomplish more in life by creating positive images of himself. Before discussing this point, we will elaborate a bit more on the important topic of imagery. We need a firm understanding of imagery to appreciate how it can affect one's performance.

Imagery transforms your state of mind. *Chazal* said that a wise person sees the outcome of his actions.[1] Notice the choice of words here: the wise person "sees." A wise person actually *sees* the outcome in his head before it happens. He creates a lifelike mental picture of the outcome, as if it were actually happening.

Why is it wise to create a mental picture of the outcome? Why isn't it enough to simply *think* about it?

Indeed, thinking about the outcome has its advantages. But seeing the outcome is a more powerful tool. When you see the outcome, it becomes more real to you. It becomes part of your life, and you can relate to it more effectively.

For this reason, the Chofetz Chaim said that we can deter ourselves from committing sins by creating mental pictures of the punishment. When we see the punishment with our eyes, as if it were actually in front of us, we relate to it more definitively.[2]

A person can transform his state of mind from the present to the future by seeing in his mind's eye an outcome as though it were already happening. Mentally viewing the result of this action allows a person to consider his options from a realistic viewpoint. Since it becomes part of his life, he is then in a better position to take into account the consequences of his action before he performs.

Rabbi Eliyahu Dessler made an interesting observation about the power of imagery:

1. *Orchos Chaim LeHaRosh* 46.
2. *Chovas HaShmirah,* Introduction.

Rabbi Simcha Zissel asked, "How did the forefathers and all the great people of the world reach their elevated levels? How were they stronger than us?" He answered that they knew the awesome power of imagery.

The *yetzer hara* knows this secret; it always uses imagery and imagination to defeat us. And we are only able to fight against it with its own weapon — creating images of holiness.

The righteous ones always saw images of *Gan Eden* and the tremendous pleasure in the ways of Hashem; this is how they triumphed over their *yetzer hara* and withstood all tests . . .

The Pesach *Seder* is founded on this concept — to sense the miracles of Egypt through lifelike images (*Michtav M'Eliyahu*, Vol. 4, pp. 252, 255).

This is how our forefathers reached their spiritual goals. This is how righteous people triumph over the *yetzer hara.* And this is why, on Pesach, we are supposed to draw lifelike pictures for ourselves of the miracles of Egypt.

Here is another example of imagery transforming our state of mind. There is a *mitzvah* to feel for the suffering of others. How can you feel what someone else is feeling if it is not happening to you? By creating mental pictures of that predicament. In your mind's eye, "see" the suffering of others and get a "feel" for it, as if it were happening to you. Then think about how you would expect others to relate to you under the same circumstances. This exercise transforms you from observer to participant, equipped with the ability to relate to others who are in that predicament.[1]

Rabbi Simcha Zissel Ziv said that you can lighten the task of studying a difficult topic by transforming your state of mind. Imagine in your mind's eye that you have only one page to study and that you will complete it today. Then imagine that once you have completed it, you will be free to do anything you want. Every day imagine the same thing, until you have completed the entire project. This energizes you to complete an otherwise difficult

---

1. Rabbi Simcha Zissel Ziv, *Chochmah U'Mussar*, Vol. 1, p. 2.

project, because every day you see yourself as responsible for only a small, accessible part.[1]

Images of past successes enable you to succeed now. As we have often mentioned, people often impose limitations on themselves because they think they cannot succeed. They may be correct, but they may be making a big mistake. How can they know? One way is to recall past successes that relate to the matter at hand. If they succeeded then, they should be able to succeed now.

I am acquainted with a man who, as a teenager, went on a self-guided tour of Israel. He and his companion always sought the most economical travel arrangements. In one city they noticed a building with a large sign that read, "*Hachnasas Orchim* (Free Guest Lodging)." This was an opportunity they could not pass up.

They knocked at the door, and an elderly man answered. He enthusiastically escorted them to a room and wished them a pleasant stay. When they entered the room, they were shocked. There were cobwebs across the entire ceiling and in every corner. The furniture was broken and dusty. The floor was dirty and the air was musty. But there were two beds and running water — and it was free. They stayed the night, and surprisingly enough, they slept quite well.

Little did my friend know that this experience would linger in his mind as an image of success for the rest of his life. From then on, whenever he was challenged with physical discomfort, he would call up the image of that experience. He would say to himself, "If I could stay overnight in that room and sleep well, I can tolerate this discomfort, too." That experience left an image in his mind which, when recalled, gave him the courage and confidence to withstand many challenges that he faced.

We all have success stories, but for some reason, we too often recall our failures. This in turn lowers our self-confidence and reduces our potential for success. But if we would follow the example of my economical friend and recall our *success* stories, it would provide the courage and confidence we need to move forward. By saying, "If I could do it then, I can do this now," we can transform doubt into a positive frame of mind.

---

1. *Chochmah U'Mussar*, Vol. 1, p. 176.

Suppose you are a computer expert and you are invited to give a seminar. Your first reaction is to become nervous. But as you recall images of past successful presentations, you become more relaxed.

Suppose you are asked to get involved in community affairs. You really want to help out, but you have many other obligations and are afraid that there will not be enough time for them all. You can boost your self-confidence by recalling a time when you were very busy and, with proper planning and diligence, you were able to fulfill all your responsibilities. This image should put you into a more relaxed, confident state of mind, better prepared to take on new responsibilities.

We have discussed how mental pictures of other circumstances can transform your state of mind, and how mental pictures of past experiences can give you the courage to move forward in challenging times. Imagery can do more than that. Creating images of *future* experiences — that is, performances that you have not yet had — can empower you to be a peak performer at whatever you do. Read on.

Imagery Is a Mental Rehearsal to Reach Goals

Our memories, as we have mentioned several times, are full of images of past events. We retain these images long after the events and recall them at various times throughout our lives.

Many people have "recalls" at the most peculiar times. They may be observing strangers, conversing with friends, reading or hearing about unrelated events. Some people are reminded of their grandmothers when they smell freshly baked bread. Some are reminded of peaceful summer days when they see a newly landscaped lawn. Something triggers the memory of a long-forgotten event, an image that may be totally unrelated to the activity at hand.

A dramatic illustration of the phenomenon of recall is the way a brain surgeon can trigger the remembrance of long-forgotten events in a patient. By touching certain parts of the exposed brain, the surgeon can induce the patient to recall events that were never really forgotten, but were stored deep in the recesses of his memory.

Just as we "*re*call" by bringing into our minds images of events that *already* happened, we also "*fore*call" by bringing into our minds images of future events *before* they happen. We "forecall" all the time; either it is automatic, with no effort, or it is planned, with conscious effort.

The newlywed in our example used forecall. She had a quick-tempered husband and felt that she would never be able to deal with him. She pictured her marriage soon falling apart. The school-teacher from an earlier example also used forecall. He saw himself as unable to address the needs of his weaker students before he had even begun to try. Both used forecall in a negative way, instinctively and without even realizing it.

Athletes also use forecall, but in a positive way. They commonly rehearse upcoming sporting events in their minds, creating vivid mental pictures of running, jumping or throwing, with grace, coordination and perfect timing. The result is that at the actual event, they perform with greater accuracy and coordination.

Scientists have found that visualization is more than a simple mental exercise. When they connect athletes to biofeedback machines and instruct them to rehearse the event mentally, the machines sense the correct muscles twitching as the athletes mentally go through the steps of the event. When they imagine putting the right foot out, the machine senses the muscles in the right foot twitching. When they imagine lifting the left arm, the machine senses the muscles in the left arm twitching. Their muscles, responding to the stimuli of their thoughts, are in effect rehearsing the upcoming event. With all these rehearsals, both their mental and physical reflexes are trained and coordinated. Neural pathways to success are created, and the athletes are better prepared for the actual event.

Athletes always succeed in their visual rehearsals. So by the time the actual event comes, they have already succeeded hundreds or thousands of times. They have succeeded so often that they are poised, relaxed, and properly prepared at the time of the actual event. This increases their chances of real success.

Rabbi Eliyahu Dessler told us that creating images of success indeed generates success:

> A wonderful suggestion for a person who wants to withstand tests is to do this: Frequently, before the

experience, he should create images of the experience and his success in it. He should think of all the reasons and arguments he will use to conquer his evil inclination, and how he will be happy with his success. Then, when he comes to the experience, it will be easier for him to succeed. This is a proven and tested method (*Michtav M'Eliyahu,* Vol. 4, p. 253).

While Rabbi Dessler recommended imagery as a technique to conquer the evil inclination, it can also be used to enhance any life experience.

With imagery, a person can even learn to endure discomfort and hardship. By creating mental pictures of *future* painful situations, he becomes prepared for such events. Then, when the event occurs, he is able to tolerate it.[1]

Rabbi Akiva used this strategy with remarkable results. He was one of the ten martyrs tortured at the hands of a heathen emperor. While his skin was being scraped off his body with a steel rake, Rabbi Akiva recited *K'rias Shema* and lovingly accepted Hashem as G-d. His students were impressed by this incredible show of faith and self-discipline. They asked him how he was able to behave with equanimity while undergoing such torture.

Rabbi Akiva told them that it was not so difficult, because he had already prepared himself for the event. For years, each time he recited *K'rias Shema* and came to the words "with all your soul," he created vivid mental pictures of sacrificing himself for the sanctity of G-d. By the time the event actually occurred, he was well rehearsed and fully prepared. He had already responded positively to torture many times in his mind, and it was not new to him now.[2]

Rabbi Akiva had forecalled an event. He visualized a future event and rehearsed it in his mind. By the time the event occurred, he had been there many times. Using the same strategy, anybody can visualize succeeding in any kind of event, large or small.

Create a setting conducive to visualization. Some people can visualize more easily than others, but with practice anybody can do

---

1. Rabbi Simcha Zissel Ziv, *Chochmah U'Mussar,* Vol. 1, p. 71.
2. Rabbi Eliyahu Dessler, *Michtav M'Eliyahu,* Vol. 4, p. 253; *Yesod VeShoresh Ha'Avodah,* Ch. 1:11.

it. Choose a peaceful, non-threatening atmosphere. Sit in a quiet place, relax and close your eyes. Soothing music sometimes helps. Then begin to imagine, in your mind's eye, every detail of the event you are anticipating and how you will feel after succeeding.

Expect success. Visual rehearsals can result in more successful performances only if you believe you have the ability to succeed. When you expect to succeed, you can accept as real the images that you create. But if you do not expect to succeed, thinking about it causes frustration and you begin to reject the mental images that you create.

Expecting success has another advantage: You become motivated to reach into your inner resources to find new ways and new solutions, even if it means seeking new training. But if you do not expect success, even if you desire it, you will not make the effort to achieve it. "After all," you say, "why put time and effort into a project that I cannot succeed at anyway?"

Examples of visualization. Let us put all this together and see how we can use visual rehearsal to reach everyday goals. Take the newlywed from our earlier example as an illustration. She was ready to give up on her marriage because she could not tolerate her husband's temper. How could she use visualization to help her keep the marriage intact?

First, she could take the attitude, "There is a solution, and I am going to find it. I am not going to let my husband's temper destroy my marriage." Expecting the best, she would be in the frame of mind to devise a plan of action.

After making a plan, she would then create mental pictures of implementing it successfully. She would picture every detail: her husband losing his temper and screaming, the angry expression on his face, the confident way that she would look at him, the assertive words she would use, her calm tone of voice, her attitude of courage and assertiveness, the surprised expression on her husband's face when he sees her response, her husband becoming subdued, and the satisfying feeling of success after it is all over.

The office worker that we mentioned earlier could use the same strategy. She was ready to look for a new job because she was not able to deal with her critical boss. Instead, she could adopt the belief that she has the ability to deal successfully with her boss. She could take the attitude, "Although I always avoided difficult people in the past, I know there are ways of dealing with them. It is about time I learn how to do it. I am going to get some advice and solve this problem."

After making a plan, she would create mental pictures of implementing it successfully. She would picture every detail: the physical layout of the office, her boss becoming critical of her performance, his harsh tone of voice, his poor choice of words, her courage in standing up to him, what she would say to him, her assertive tone of voice, and the feeling of accomplishment after the encounter is over.

The schoolteacher from our previous example could also use this strategy. He was ready to give up on several students because he thought that he did not have the skill to teach them successfully. Instead, he could take this attitude: "I have not taught such weak students *yet.* There is always a first time. I am going to find out how to do it, and I will succeed." Then he would devise a plan of action and create detailed mental pictures of implementing it successfully.

Is there a guarantee that this strategy will work? No, there isn't. However, as we have mentioned several times, one thing is guaranteed: The chance of success is greater with positive expectations and images of success than without them. Using the positive approach is self-enabling; using the negative approach is self-limiting.

Can the mind be drawn after images of success that have never actually happened? It certainly can. In the scenario of the bear and the actor, the person responded to what he thought he was seeing, whether it was true or not. We saw the same idea in the scenario of the couple purchasing a home, where the wife responded to the image she had of her husband even though it was not valid. And we saw how Rabbi Akiva felt well rehearsed for torture as a result of imagined torture. The mind entertains all types of images, whether they are distorted or real, whether they have happened already or may happen in the future. This is human nature. And as *Chazal* said, we can use this piece of human nature to our advantage.

Visualize through writing and role modeling. Visualization requires relaxation, imagination, concentration and self-discipline. Some people have difficulty mustering up all these forces to create detailed mental pictures. There are two variations of visualization that can ease the task: writing and role-playing.

Role-playing means assuming the role of the individual you want to become. It can be done in front of a mirror or with another person. Instead of creating images in your mind, act them out in an artificial setting.

Writing about the upcoming experience serves the same purpose. Instead of creating an image in your mind, put it onto paper by writing or drawing vivid pictures about it. In the process of both role-playing and writing, your mind creates pictures of the future performance.

Both approaches are physical and do not require the pure mental ability of traditional visualization. Using these approaches may help you concentrate for longer periods of time, leaving a strong impression of the image in your mind.

Practice makes permanent. You have heard the saying: "Practice makes perfect." This is only true if you practice properly; imperfect practice becomes a habit which is difficult to correct afterwards. Therefore, a more accurate version of the saying is: "Practice makes *permanent.*" If you practice performing a task correctly, you will make a *habit* of doing it correctly; if you practice performing a task incorrectly, you will make a habit of doing it incorrectly.

It follows, then, that visual rehearsal leads to successful performances only when you create mental images of *proper* performance. Therefore, if you do not know how to perform, don't guess. Don't mentally rehearse how you *suppose* it should be, because if it is wrong you become impressed with a bad habit. Instead, seek training from an expert. When you practice it in your mind the right way, you will be prepared to perform properly when you need to.

Use imagery to correct mistakes. When a professional golfer misses a shot, he doesn't kick the dirt and cry, "I missed!" Instead, he replays the shot in his imagination. He either swings his real club at an imaginary ball or, in his imagination, he swings an imaginary club at an imaginary ball.

The professional golfer uses his mistake as an opportunity to perform better the next time. When you miss a "shot" in life, follow the golfer's example and use the failure as an opportunity to do it better the next time. Create an inner image of the proper way and rehearse it in your mind.

Imagery reconditions your personality. We explained earlier that your perception of yourself and others determines, to a large degree, the amount of success you have in life. We also explained that your perception is a product of your conditioning, and that your conditioning is the product of all the images you have collected over a lifetime.

It stands to reason, then, that you can modify your conditioning by collecting new images. Through imagery, you can recondition yourself to produce different perceptions, thus increasing your prospects for success.

Suppose you have been negatively conditioned and have formed a negative self-perception. By creating instead many positive mental pictures about yourself, you will begin to believe them. Your conditioning then begins to conform to those images. Thus, through imagery, you can adjust your conditioning to be closer to what you want.

Imagery is a powerful tool that can recondition one's personality. With new positive input, a negative personality can become positively reconditioned. The "new personality," in turn, creates more positive perceptions and attitudes, which can guide one to more success and happiness.

Affirm Yourself Positively

Another method of putting images of success into one's mind is called affirmation, sometimes referred to as self-talk. With this technique, you repeat inspirational slogans about yourself. Over and over, you repeat slogans that affirm your ability to reach the goal you have set. The message leaves you with positive images and you begin to expect the best from yourself, increasing the chances for success.

Our newlywed could use this technique as well to her advantage. She could reinforce her ability to solve her marital problem by affirming positive things about herself. Over and over, she could say things like, "I am capable of dealing with my husband's temper. I can tolerate it. I know that I am worthy even when he becomes angry at me." Repeating these statements many times during the day would boost her feeling of worthiness and her ability to deal effectively with the situation.

The office worker could also use affirmations to create the attitude she needs to deal with her boss effectively. Over and over, she could say, "I deal with my boss very effectively. I do not become upset at his behavior." Drilling these statements into her own mind many times during the day will make it easier for her to stay relaxed and deal effectively with her boss.

The schoolteacher could also use affirmations to build his confidence. He could say, "I can teach to all levels of ability. I am capable because I am a good teacher." With self-talk, he affirms his worthiness and capability. This boosts his self-confidence and directs him toward success.

Affirming is closely related to visualization because whenever you say positive things about yourself, you also create coordinating positive images about yourself. With these new images, you begin to perceive things differently. Your self-expectancy is more positive and your prospects are improved.[1]

Some people feel awkward saying that they have attributes which they do not yet have. The newlywed, for example, may think, "How can I say that I deal effectively with my husband's anger if I haven't done it yet?" But this question should not stop her. As long as she allows the idea to sit in her mind and she doesn't fight it, it will have an effect.

Enable Yourself with Dominant Thought

High expectations and images of success, as we have explained many times, increase the likelihood of success. But there is more to the formula; you also have to be focused on the goal. The more focused you are, the greater your chances of reaching the goal.

This focus is your *dominant thought.* It is the underlying force that gives you the thrust and energy to expect success, generate images of success, and work to achieve success.

Dominant thought can be illustrated with the earlier example of walking the beam. In that example, some friends offer you a reward

---

1. Rabbi Yisrael Salanter, cited in *Tenuas HaMussar,* Vol. 1, p. 253; Rabbi Yeruchom Levovitz, *Daas Chochmah U'Mussar,* Vol. 1, p. 114; *Cheshbon HaNefesh,* Ch. 1.

for walking across a beam which is lying on the ground. After accepting the challenge, they raise the beam four feet in the air and offer a larger reward for walking across. After accepting this challenge, they raise the beam one hundred feet in the air and offer a one-thousand-dollar prize for walking across. You do not accept the challenge because you are afraid of falling.

Why are you able to walk across the beam when it is on the ground but not when it is raised high in the air? After all, it is the same beam and you are the same person. Earlier we said that when it is high in the air, you impose a limitation on yourself. But there is more.

When the beam is on the ground, there is nothing to be afraid of. You focus your attention on what you *want* to happen — getting to the other side — and also on the reward of success. But when it is high in the air, there is something to be afraid of. You focus your attention on what you *don't* want to happen — that is, falling to the ground, the penalty of failure. You become debilitated, even though a one-thousand-dollar prize is waiting at the other end.

Now suppose they raise the beam one hundred feet in the air and place your young child right in the center. Would you walk across to rescue him? Probably. What self-sacrificing parent wouldn't risk his or her own life for the sake of a precious child?

Why would you attempt to walk across the beam now if it seemed so dangerous just a moment ago? Because your focus is different. A moment ago you focused on the penalty of failure — falling and being injured. Now you focus on the reward of success — rescuing the child. The risk of failure is no longer important.

Whether the beam is on the ground or high in the air, it is the same beam and you are the same person. The only difference is your focus — your dominant thought. When the beam is on the ground, your dominant thought is to receive the reward. This enables you to walk across. But when the beam is high in the air, your dominant thought is the possibility of falling. This stops you, except when your child is sitting on it. Then your dominant thought is to save him, enabling you to cross the beam.

Depending on your dominant thought, you become energized or debilitated, expanded or limited, enabled or disabled.

Circus tightrope walkers use this idea to accomplish their daredevil feat. They love the challenge and thrive on the adventure of balancing themselves high in the air. Would you or anyone you know ever dream of walking a tightrope? Probably not. You may even say that it is a foolhardy thing to do. So why do professional tightrope walkers do it? Do they not value their lives? Do they need the money so desperately? Are they mentally unstable?

They are none of these things. They just live with a different focus from yours. First of all, they enjoy the adventure of tightrope walking and want to do it. But that alone does not enable them to perform such a daring act. What enables them is their dominant thought. They concentrate on the goal of getting to the other side, and they never allow themselves to focus on what they do *not* want — that is, the ground below.

Certainly they know there is a chance of falling, but they also know they have the skill to balance themselves. They say to themselves, "I can walk across the rope when it is two feet in the air, so why shouldn't I be able to walk across when it is one hundred feet in the air?" And if the thought of falling enters their minds, they replace it with the thought of reaching the other side. This becomes their *dominant thought,* which enables them to do something that others consider dangerous or impossible.

In anything we do, we can focus on what we want or on what we don't want. Whether the task concerns a job, hobby, social endeavors, character refinement, family relationships or business ventures, our focus can either be achievement-oriented or failure-oriented. The orientation we have is important because it represents our dominant thought, and it either energizes or debilitates us. Our dominant thought leads us to become winners or losers.

Winners focus on the rewards of success. They think, "People will be proud of me when I succeed, and I will be proud of myself, too," or "When word gets out of my success, I will be popular, and as a result, more people will want to be my friends," or "My future will be much brighter!" No matter what the task involves, they know there are risks; however, they seek the training and concentrate on the reward of success. Their dominant thought is achievement-oriented, and it energizes them to persist.

Losers, on the other hand, focus on the penalty of failure. They think, "What if I don't succeed? What will people think of me? What will it mean to my career? Will I lose my friends?" Their dominant thought is failure-oriented, and it debilitates them.

Winners focus on reaching goals; losers focus on relieving tension. Winners get involved in activities that give them a valuable reward over time; losers get involved in any activity that provides immediate pleasure. Winners, driven by a dominant thought of reaching goals, see opportunity in every event and utilize it to accomplish their goals; losers, driven by a dominant thought of pleasure and tension relief, do not see opportunities because they have few goals.

Dominant thought and imagery. As we mentioned earlier, a person creates images consistent with his dominant thought — whether for success or failure — and is drawn toward those images.

This is the reason you are not able to walk across the beam one hundred feet in the air. Your thoughts are focused on the penalty of failure and you create images of bodily injury, or maybe death. Your images are consistent with your dominant thought and they push you to withdraw.

The tightrope walker, on the other hand, creates images that pull him to succeed. He sees the other side of the rope and he creates mental pictures of his triumphant finale. If he would create images of the ground below, he would be drawn to it and probably lose his balance.

Our newlywed could use the idea of dominant thought to preserve or undo her marriage. If she focuses on a broken marriage, she would create images of failure. Pulled toward those images, she would behave in a way that would keep the cycle of failure going. But if she focuses on solving her problem and is determined to learn how to deal with her husband, she would create images of making her marriage work. Drawn toward those images, she would struggle to succeed.

Don't focus on what you don't want. In driver education courses, students are instructed never to gaze at something off the road, because the tendency is to steer toward it. Although the driver knows he should not go in that direction, if the object becomes his dominant thought it may pull him in its direction.

The tightrope walker focuses on getting to the other side, not on the floor below. The beam walker focuses on rescuing his child, not on the ground below. If they focus on what is below — the reverse of what they want — they may be drawn toward it.

I once saw an illustrated children's book whose objective was to teach good *middos*. Every page had a large picture portraying a child displaying a bad *middah*. Underneath, there was a short paragraph explaining why one should not behave this way and describing the proper way to act.

This book depicted *poor middos* with vivid pictures. It depicted *good middos* with wordy explanations. Which leaves the child with a stronger impression — the picture or the paragraph? Probably the picture. The problem is that the picture portrays what the child is not supposed to do, and once the child registers this negative image he may be drawn toward it. Although the author had good intentions, the child who reads the book may be more hurt than helped.

If you want to improve a relationship, think about what you will do *right* and how the relationship will *improve.* Don't focus on what you should *not* do and the negative consequence of that action. If you want to improve a *middah,* think of how you will *act* and the reward. Don't focus on how you *don't* want to act and the penalty. No matter what you do, put images of the *desired* performance into your mind. These are what you will follow.

Dominant thought and planning the future. During the Vietnam war, many American soldiers were captured and held in prisoner-of-war camps. Some were placed in maximum-security camps and others in minimum-security camps. Although the maximum-security camps had much harsher living conditions, the prisoners often outsurvived their counterparts in the minimum-security camps.

After the war, researchers began asking why these prisoners had often survived while those in the minimum-security camps had not. Dr. Denis Waitley found that the former had specific goals and ideals from the time they were captured until their release. They had philosophies and knew what they stood for. Even while they were in prison, they planned their future. They reviewed their business plans, practiced their golf swings, and made plans for their families and their personal lives. They did not want their visions of the future to suffer just because they were temporarily imprisoned.

They knew what they wanted and many even attempted escape, at the risk of severe punishment. They had dominant thoughts of survival and success which energized them to *make plans* for survival and success.

On the other hand, Dr. Waitley suggests that the minimum-security prisoners had no specific goals. They had no visions and no business plans, family plans or personal plans. They became demoralized and never attempted escape; after all, the penalty of being caught was too great. Their dominant thought was not to get out and build a future; rather, it was focused on their horrid living conditions.

The Vietnamese captors recognized the attitudes of their captives. They knew they had to watch the idealistic, goal-oriented prisoners. These prisoners had determination and would try to escape. Their thinking was dangerous; they had plans for the future and their captors saw it in their behavior. So they were sent to maximum-security camps. The other prisoners, however, were sent to minimum-security camps. Their thinking was not dangerous; they had no apparent goals or determination, and the Vietnamese assumed that they would never take the risk of escaping.

Like the prisoners in the maximum-security camp, a person will plan a future if his dominant thought is headed in that direction. An interest alone in a particular goal may not be enough to drive him to make meaningful plans; he may need a dominant thought focused on the goal to push him. Once he has it, he will naturally make plans to reach the goal.

Dominant thought and determination. A determined person, by definition, focuses his dominant thought on his goal. He persists and does not let obstacles or FEARs interfere with his plans.

The Me'iri said that determination and thoughtful planning usually result in success.[1] Rabbi Simcha Zissel Ziv discussed the importance of determination:

> A strong desire within a person generates power, enhances thought processes, helps overcome laziness and

---

1. *Mishlei* 21:22.

propels a person in the path of wisdom (*Chochmah U'Mussar*, Vol. 2, p. 172).

This is how our forefather Yaakov was able to learn Torah in the yeshivah of Shem and Ever every night, all night long, for fourteen years.[1] Although this appears to be a superhuman feat, it wasn't; it was the result of strong determination.[2]

Similarly, when Yaakov saw Rachel the shepherdess and rolled away the heavy stone cover from the well, a task that ordinarily required several people, it was the result of strong determination.[3] We can learn the following from Yaakov:

> If a person coordinates all his capabilities, he will be able to do wonders. We see this when a fire breaks out; one person lifts things that ordinarily require several people . . . Each and every person is able to roll off the stone from the wells of life through single-minded determination (Rabbi Chaim Shmulevitz, *Sichos Mussar*, 5732:9).

Here is a story that illustrates the power of determination. A man who loved birds once purchased a bird feeder and installed it in his backyard. He filled it with bird seed, and before the day was over he noticed that it was empty. The neighborhood squirrels had found it and helped themselves to the seed. So he built a fence to prevent the squirrels from reaching the feeder, but it did not keep them away.

The next day, he went to a hardware store to purchase a squirrel-proof bird feeder. He took it home and installed it. By the end of the day he noticed that the squirrels had helped themselves to the seed again. Now he was really upset. He took the feeder back to the hardware store and demanded a refund.

He asked the shop owner why he was selling a squirrel-proof bird feeder if it was not squirrel-proof. The owner said that there was really no such thing as a squirrel-proof bird feeder. The man was puzzled. "Why," he asked, "if we can fly a man to the moon, can't we manufacture a squirrel-proof bird feeder?"

---

1. Rashi, *Bereishis* 28:11.
2. Rabbi Chaim Shmulevitz, *Sichos Mussar*, 5932:9.
3. Ibid.

The shop owner replied, "I have two questions for you. How much time during the day do you think about a plan to stop the squirrels?" The man answered, "Fifteen to thirty minutes."

The owner asked, "How much time do you think the squirrels spend trying to get into that bird feeder?"

The man answered, "All day!"

"You see," said the shop owner, "the squirrels are determined. They focus on a single goal and concentrate all their efforts on reaching it, all day long. So they succeed."

The squirrels are determined — in effect, they have a "dominant thought" to reach the bird feeder. This energizes them and enables them to succeed in overcoming any obstacle.

The next time you consider doing something important, be determined to accomplish it. Be like the squirrel. Be like Yaakov our forefather. Create a dominant thought of reaching the goal and focus your attention on it. This will energize you to find the resources, both inside and outside yourself, to reach that goal.

Help Children Strengthen Their Self-Expectancy

The saying goes: "Give me a fish and you provide me with a meal. Teach me to fish and you provide me with food for a lifetime." If you always give another person food, he will not learn how to provide for himself, but will always be dependent on you. If you teach him how to provide for himself, though, he becomes independent. He will have "food for a lifetime."

Parents and teachers can teach children how to "fish" by making them feel important, encouraging them to expect the best from themselves, and taking them through visualization and affirmation sessions. Once the children internalize these skills, they have "food for a lifetime."

Help children expect the best from themselves. Once parents and teachers understand the power of self-expectancy and have practiced it themselves, they are in a position to share the "secret" with their children. They can help a child understand that his self-expectancy determines, to a large degree, the success he will have in any project. And they can teach the child that he can improve his self-expectancy.

If a child should ever say that he cannot do a task — whether it pertains to school, home, social life or a hobby — adults can help him recognize his real capabilities and become aware of his self-imposed limitations. They can also encourage him to crash through those limitations and create a realistic, positive attitude.

When a child fails at something, don't let him say, "I am a failure." Instead, teach him to say, "I failed at this task." As subtle as it sounds, there is an enormous difference between "I am a failure" and "I failed at this task"; one is self-indicting and puts images of inferiority into the mind, while the other simply reports the outcome of the event.

Teach children how to visualize. Parents and teachers can teach children the skill of visualization, too. Suppose a child has difficulty organizing her belongings. Like all skills, the best way to learn organization is to practice it. Along with real-life practice, adults can help the child achieve this competency by guiding her through mental rehearsals in which she would create detailed mental pictures of arriving at school on time, arranging her desk for class, keeping her supplies where they belong, coming home after school, putting her belongings away, completing assignments and gathering her belongings in preparation for the next day.

A child who has difficulty settling down at home to study can learn to become more diligent through mental rehearsals. Adults can guide the child in creating detailed images of the room she studies in, the desk, the chair, the books she uses, and the act of studying quietly and with concentration.

A child who thinks he cannot pass a test can build his self-confidence with visualization. Adults can guide him in imagining himself studying with persistence, going to school the next morning with a feeling of confidence, sitting at his seat, and taking the test with expectations of success.

Visualizing requires concentration and self-discipline, two traits that many children don't have. For these children, role-playing, writing and drawing about the experience can be helpful in holding their attention for longer periods of time.

Teach children to affirm themselves. Adults can also help children learn how to affirm themselves. The child who needs organizational skills would repeat slogans such as "I am organized" or "I always put my belongings in the proper place." The child who thinks he cannot pass a test would repeat slogans such as "I am smart, and if I study properly, I can pass any test." And the child who has difficulty settling down to study would repeat slogans such as "I study for all my tests" or "When I am studying, I don't let anything distract me." These affirmations create images of success which translate into better performance.

Tell the child what you want, not what you _don't_ want. When you instruct a child to do something, images of what you want him to do are created in his mind. But when you instruct a child not to do something, images of what you don't want him to do are put into his mind. This is why it is important to tell the child what you _want_ him to do, not what you don't want him to do. Then, when it is time to perform, the child calls on those desirable images and acts accordingly. You have given him an advantage by feeding positive images into his mind.

For example, you may want your child to stop biting his nails. Say, "Please keep your hands away from your mouth." This generates images of hands away from the mouth, exactly what you want. Don't say, "Don't bite your nails." This may generate images of nail-biting, exactly what you don't want.

Similarly, someone training a bed-wetting child should say, "When you wake up _dry_ tomorrow morning, I have a treat for you." This creates images of what you want. The parent should not say, "If you don't wet your bed, I have a treat for you." This creates images of what is not wanted.

Relate positively to children. Every time parents or teachers interact with a child, they contribute to his conditioning. When parents or teachers put a child down or make him feel inadequate in any way, they reinforce a negative conditioning. But when they make the child feel important, they enhance a positive conditioning. The child's conditioning, as we mentioned earlier, creates the attitudes and motivation that influence the degree of success he has in life.

And, as we mentioned earlier, the messages that parents and teachers convey translate into images that are recorded in the child's mind. When they make critical remarks, the child records a negative image of himself. But when they praise him, he records a positive image of himself. These images are stored in an "image bank," ready to be withdrawn whenever the child becomes involved in an activity that relates to that stored image.

Not only do parents' relationships with a child represent a deposit into his image bank, their actual behaviors become images, too. When a child sees a parent or teacher become angry, no matter what the cause is, an image of anger is recorded in his mind. Afterwards, when he becomes upset over something, he may unconsciously call up that image and duplicate it. The image of his parents and teachers becomes, to some degree, part of his automatic response system.

The behaviors of adults can work positively, too. For example, when a child sees a parent performing *mitzvos* with enthusiasm and joy, an image of joyful *mitzvah* performance is recorded in his mind and becomes part of his automatic response system. When it comes time to perform a *mitzvah*, he may call up the image and duplicate it.

Through their words, actions and attitudes, parents and teachers are a constant source of either positive or negative images which feed into the minds of children. If they relate to children with thoughtfulness, sensitivity and careful planning, they will be catalysts that motivate children positively.

When criticizing, be constructive. When children make mistakes, some adults automatically say, "Look what you've done. You did it all wrong. What's the matter with you?" They call attention to the mistake, show their dissatisfaction, and expect the child to correct himself. The problem is that a child may never make the correction because he does not know how to perform the task properly.

Putting a child down without providing correction is not a useful strategy for other reasons. Depending on its frequency, it may bring about any of the following negative results.

Non-constructive criticism may make a child feel inadequate. The child will then expect to fail in his endeavors, increasing the likelihood of failure. And when failure does occur, his feeling of inadequacy will again be reinforced, resulting in the likelihood of more failure. Caught in a vicious cycle, the child is set upon a road of failure.

When adults put a child down for making a mistake, they are teaching him that mistakes are terrible. Hearing this message, the child may never learn that a mistake has a positive value, that it is an opportunity to do it right the next time.

When adults put a child down, the child may learn from their behavior that it is appropriate to put people down when they make mistakes. With images of intolerance and criticalness now stored in his image bank, the child may call on those images as a guideline sometime in the future when someone upsets him.

This does not mean that adults should never criticize a child. Certainly, we want the child to realize he made a mistake. But more importantly, we want him to know how to perform properly and to feel good about himself so that he will be motivated to succeed in his future efforts. We want to put the child on the road to success.

We can do this by saying, "That is not like you. You can do better. This is the correct way, and I expect you to do better the next time." This is constructive criticism. It is corrective, sensitive, and leaves the child with a good feeling about himself and about the person offering correction.

When a child violates a rule, whether in the home or classroom, let him know that his action is unacceptable and tell him how you expect him to behave. Let him know that you expect more from him because he is capable of it. Tell him, "You know what to do, and you are capable of doing better. I expect you to live up to those standards."

Constructive criticism leaves a child with images of sensitivity and good *middos.* It also leaves the child with images of ability and success. His self-esteem remains intact, and his self-expectancy for future performances is positive. This increases the likelihood of success, which in turn reinforces a positive self-image and self-expectancy. A productive cycle is created. The child is now set on a path of success.

Chapter Three

Allow for Mistakes and Failure

Can you recall a time when you failed or made a mistake? Maybe you tried to learn a new skill or make a new friend. Maybe you tried to correct a bad *middah*, obtain a desirable job or achieve an academic pursuit. Whatever it was, you made the effort and missed the goal.

How did you react to the setback? Did you see it as yet another proof of your inadequacy, allowing it to reinforce an already low self-esteem? Or did you look it straight in the eye and rebound with resilience, not allowing it to bring down your self-esteem, but believing that you would do better next time?

Everybody responds to failure differently. Some respond positively, others negatively. Some see failure as an unnecessary evil; others see it as a useful part of growth.

Yes, there are differences in the way people respond to failure. But one thing remains the same; everybody experiences failure, without exception.

There is no person in the world who does not make a mistake (*Peleh Yoetz, Taos*).

You will certainly stumble, and you will fall in several areas (Rabbi Yitzchak Hutner, *Pachad Yitzchak, Igros U'Michtavim*, p. 217).

Indeed, failing is a fact of life over which we sometimes have no control. However, we do have control over the way we *respond* to the failure. This is important, because *the way we respond to failure sets a path for continued failure or renewed success.*

Failure is an attitude, not an event. Progressive people view failure in a positive way, and they come out ahead because of it. Even in the face of challenge and setbacks, they are able to maintain a proactive, positive mindset. Sometimes, the positive attitude comes easily; other times, they make a conscious effort to adopt one.

Let's look at Judy as an example. Judy purchased a used automobile from a dealer who impressed her as honest. After she brought the car home and showed it to her friends, she discovered that she had paid one thousand dollars too much. She also found out that the dealer had a reputation for being a swindler.

Judy felt horrible. She became depressed over the loss of money, and she felt it was her fault for not asking other people about the dealer's reputation before making the purchase. The tension and anxiety built until she lost her appetite and had trouble sleeping at night. Finally, after several weeks, she stopped dwelling on the incident and began to return to normalcy.

Many people react to their mistakes the same way. After realizing they made a mistake, they become depressed, feel guilty or beat themselves up for the error. But they need not respond this way. There is a positive way to deal with a mistake.

Although Judy's natural reaction was to worry and become depressed, she could have made a conscious decision to react with a positive attitude. She could have said, "Yes, I made a mistake. I should have first found out about the dealer's reputation. Now I have learned my lesson. Now I know to do research before spending my hard-earned money. I am not going to get too upset about it because this incident will save me from losing even more money in the future."

Failure is often a matter of attitude. And, like all attitudes, it is in the mind. It is not so much what failure does to people as what people do with events which they perceive as failure.

Events, by themselves, often have little meaning; what is important is the meaning that people attach to them. Thus, failure is a function of how one deals with events, not how events deal with the person. As with all attitudes, people have the ability to control their outlook on failure.

We will now look at some positive ways to view failure and mistakes. Although there is some repetition, each view depicts a slightly different angle. Depending on the situation, the reader may find one angle more useful than another.

Failure Is a Temporary Inconvenience

Some people think that their setbacks have a permanent effect. They think their mistakes are irreversible, and that even if they could be turned around, the distress that they cause cannot be removed.

Take Judy as an example. She felt defeated and took the attitude "Oh, no, I failed. I made a terrible mistake. What am I going to do now? I will just have to live with the terrible memory of my mistake forever." Only after the incident was far behind her did her anxiety begin to dissipate.

Indeed, Judy made a mistake when she purchased the car; however, she made another mistake by keeping her anxiety close to heart. Instead, she should have learned a lesson from the mistake and realized that life can still be productive afterwards. By taking the attitude that her mistake was only temporary, she would have been able to dismiss the anxiety produced by the error.

> When you can correct a mistake, it is not proper to suffer over the past; rather, make the correction for the future (*Sforno, Bereishis* 4:6).

With this attitude, Judy would have seen failure as a temporary inconvenience, not as a permanent condition. She would have realized that failure is nothing more than an obstacle, never a defeat.

King Dovid broke the *aleph-beis* pattern in *Tehillim* 145 by omitting a passage beginning with the Hebrew letter *nun*. He did not include this letter because it represents the word *"nofel"* (which means *fall, failure* or *defeat*), and according to King Dovid, there is no such thing as total failure or defeat. He believed that failure is never permanent; rather, it is followed by progress and advancement.[1]

It is interesting to note that in the passage following the omitted *nun,* King Dovid wrote, "Hashem supports all those who fall." The omission of a passage about failure and the inclusion of a passage about Hashem helping people who fall imply that failure and mistakes are only temporary; when people fail, they do not have to stay that way. Hashem helps them back onto their feet.[2]

Judy, too, should have seen her mistake as a temporary inconvenience. Yes, it was her own fault that she had lost the money, but she did not have to give the mistake center stage, nor did she have to live with her pain continually. Instead, she could have learned the lesson of the missing *nun* and felt secure that her failure would be followed by better decision-making in the future. Who knows? If she had not learned her lesson now, she might have lost more money in a future deal! This is what we mean by temporary inconvenience; when it is followed by growth and success, its negative effect is not long-lasting.

Let us look at an important historical event as a dramatic illustration of this point:

During World War II, the British army was defeated in the Battle of Dunkirk. Having lost one-third of its troops, the army retreated, leaving all its arms and munitions behind. This was one of the gloomiest days in the history of England.

While England was nursing its wounds, Winston Churchill delivered a public address. He spoke about the defeat, but he did not treat it as a permanent condition; rather, he saw it as a temporary inconvenience. He made this point, boldly proclaiming, "We shall not flag or fail. We shall go on to the end. We shall fight in France, we shall fight on the seas and oceans, we shall fight with growing confidence and growing strength in the air, we shall defend our island whatever the cost may be . . . we shall never surrender."

---

1. Talmud *Berachos* 4b, following Maharsha.
2. Ibid.

Even as England sustained daily air raids, sending its citizens to shelters wondering if they would survive the day, Churchill's encouraging words lived on. The people followed his lead and endured the air raids. They refurbished their military supplies and persisted with courage and determination — until they ultimately achieved victory.

Churchill did not dwell on gloom and doom. Nor did he succumb and say, "Oh, no, what are we going to do now? The enemy is winning and we stand no chance. We'd better surrender." Instead, he realized that the gloomy situation did not have to be permanent; it could be changed if they would only try. He took a positive attitude and inspired his countrymen with an unrelenting drive for victory.

This story illustrates how viewing failure as a temporary inconvenience enables people to continue striving toward their goal. You can do the same. Whenever you make a mistake or fail, say to yourself, "This, too, will pass. Yes, I failed, but the failure is not here to stay. I can improve and enjoy a better future." View the event as a temporary detour, not a dead end. Then boldly make plans for the future and put yourself on the path of success.

Take, for example, a businessman who is negotiating an important deal. After weeks of discussion, negotiations stop. He certainly has reason to be upset; he has put a great deal of time and effort into a deal that fell through. But he doesn't have to let the result become permanent or stop him from pursuing other business ventures. He can change his situation by looking for new opportunities.

Another example is a mother who is trying to teach table manners to her children. After weeks of instructing, guiding and imploring, the children still slouch and eat with their fingers. The mother has put hours of time and effort into training her children, and since she has seen no progress, she surmises that she has categorically failed.

Instead, she can view her apparent failure as a temporary inconvenience and reset her goal. Refusing to give up, she can look for new ways to teach her children table manners.

Don't let the *yetzer hara* keep you down. When a person consistently exhibits a bad *middah* or does not perform *mitzvos* properly, the proper course of action is to recognize the error and search for ways to correct it. The improper response is to rationalize the erroneous position or to become depressed, thinking that successful performance is impossible.

The *yetzer hara* is the source of both these improper responses. The *yetzer hara* is not satisfied when a person neglects a *mitzvah*; it wants the person to continue his dereliction or to become dejected over it. Either way, the mistake becomes permanent and keeps the person from growing to his full spiritual height.

For example, Shimon had a tendency to become angry. In an effort to correct that *middah,* he decided to respond calmly to any person or event that upset him. The next time a person said something to annoy him, he held his temper. But after several seconds, he blew up as usual.

Shimon realized he had not lived up to his commitment. He really wanted to improve, but instead he became dejected and said to himself, "I am just not a strong person. I obviously cannot control my temper. I will just have to live with this bad *middah* for the rest of my life."

Shimon's *yetzer hara* prevailed upon him to become angry that day, but it also did much more than that. It tried to keep him down by generating self-defeating thoughts, thus making his bad *middah* even more deeply ingrained.

Shimon should have realized that one failure does not guarantee another. Since he had been able to control his temper for a few seconds that day, he should have understood that he might be able to control it for a few more seconds tomorrow. Just because he had made a mistake today did not mean that the bad *middah* would become permanent. On the contrary, he could change it if he tried hard enough.

The same principle applies to any failure. No matter what the setback is, you do not have to allow the *yetzer hara* to control your future by succumbing to the permanence of the outcome. You can make it temporary by gathering your strength, making the correction and bouncing back.[1]

Another strategy to fight the *yetzer hara*'s attempt to keep you down is to realize that a substandard performance can still be

---

1. Rabbi Yeruchom Levovitz, *Daas Torah, Bereishis*, pp. 26-27. Also see *Tenuas HaMussar*, Vol. 3, p. 273, citing Rabbi Nosson Tzvi Finkel.

considered successful as long as you put effort into it. Is effort so important? Yes, because every performance related to a Torah ideal has two goals: good performance and effort.[1] If you focus on your effort and realize that although you did not reach the goal of a good performance, you still reached the goal of exerting effort to achieve it, your spirits may be lifted, giving you renewed strength.

Another strategy is to realize that no matter how good your performance is, the final outcome is in Hashem's hands:

> A person should not be concerned with the outcome of his actions. He is only expected to do what he is required, and the outcome is in the hands of Hashem. The one who thinks that he himself brings about the outcome through his actions is saying, "My power brought about this success,"[2] and it is forbidden to say this in both spiritual and mundane matters (Rabbi Chaim Shmulevitz, *Sichos Mussar*, 5732:13).

Failure Is Natural to Progressive People

Before Thomas Edison discovered the incandescent light bulb, he experimented with thousands of ideas. After the discovery, he said, "I knew the end was near because I was running out of bad ideas."

Edison's experiments were costly in both time and money, but he did not let this deter him. He understood that it was only a matter of running out of failures before he finally succeeded.

This is how medical researchers discover cures for diseases. They think of an idea, experiment with it, and if they do not find the cure, they try out more ideas until they succeed. Sometimes it takes years, but researchers appreciate the trial-and-error process as a way to understand what does not work and what may work. They realize that each failure brings them one step closer to the cure.

If medical researchers would allow failure to deter them from the goal, they would never succeed. They would feel so awful about making mistakes — mistakes that are only natural to progress — that they would stop pursuing the goal as soon as they encounter

---

1. Rabbi Moshe Feinstein, *Darash Moshe*, p. 111.
2. *Devarim* 8:17.

too much failure. One stub of the toe would stop them from trying new ideas or taking risks.

A yeshivah man once fell upon this faulty pathway when he experienced a setback in his spiritual growth. He wrote a letter to Rabbi Yitzchak Hutner, recalling his previous aspirations to become a *talmid chochom* and expressing how his setbacks had caused him to give up all belief in himself.

In his response, Rabbi Hutner wrote about a common "sickness" — preoccupation with a goal's outcome while still trying to reach it. He wrote that this kind of thinking leads a person to believe that being "planted in the house of Hashem" means living peacefully on "lush pastures of tranquil waters." Anything short of this seems to be an indication of failure.

Rabbi Hutner dispelled this notion. He wrote that failure is an integral part of success and is built into the very system from which success emerges. Here are some excerpts from his letter:

> You will certainly stumble, and you will fall in many areas. But I guarantee that after you lose on all those fronts, you will emerge from the war with the crown of victory on your head . . .
>
> The wisest of all men said, "A *tzaddik* falls seven times, yet he stands up."[1] Foolish people interpret this to mean that although the *tzaddik* falls seven times, he nevertheless rises afterwards. Wise people, however, know that it really means that the *tzaddik's* ability to stand is only *through* falling seven times . . .
>
> My friend, if your letter described the *mitzvos* and good deeds you have done, I would say that I received a good letter. But now that your letter tells of failures and obstacles, I say that I received a *very* good letter . . .
>
> When you picture in your mind the heights reached by our great people, realize that these are best described through their fierce battles with all the base instincts. Whenever you sense a conflict inside yourself, you must know that in this aspect you are more similar to great people than when you find the tranquility which you seek.

---

1. *Mishlei* 24:16

It is only in those places that you experience the greatest setbacks; only in those places do you stand the possibility of becoming a figure of excellence . . .

I am together with you in your bad predicament, but this predicament is the very womb which gives birth to greatness . . .

The honorable path is not straight; rather, it is circuitous, like a snake on the way . . . (*Pachad Yitzchak, Igros U'Kesovim*, pp. 217-219).

Nobody deliberately makes a mistake or tries to fail; nevertheless, mistakes and failure are an inevitable part of life. Progressive people therefore accept occasional failure as part of the natural sequence of events in their lives. They are willing to make some mistakes, knowing that in the long run these experiences will lead them to success.

Progressive people know that "you have to climb the mountain if you want to enjoy the view." They realize that those who are afraid of making mistakes say nothing and do nothing — and become nothing. They know that the only ones who make *no* mistakes are in the cemetery. Progressive people take reasonable risks and try new ideas. They know that a chance of failure lurks in every risk, yet they are not afraid of it.

As with the discovery of the incandescent light bulb and the search for medical cures, success is a numbers game; there are always failures before success. It is only a matter of time, patience, persistence, and sometimes money, before success comes. As the wise saying goes, "There is no difference between a big shot and a little shot, except that every big shot was once a little shot who kept on shooting."

Abraham Lincoln knew this. In 1831 he failed at business. In 1832 he lost the race for the Illinois legislature. In 1834, however, he won the election. In 1838 he was defeated in the race for the Speaker of the Illinois House of Representatives. In 1843 he was defeated for Congress. In 1846 he was elected to Congress, but in 1848 he was defeated once again. In 1850 he was defeated for the Senate. In 1856 he was defeated for Vice President. In 1858 he was defeated again for the Senate. In 1860 he was elected President of the United States and became one of the most prominent leaders the country has ever known.

Mr. Lincoln progressed in his career by tenaciously pursuing his goals even after multiple failures. He accepted those failures as the natural course of reaching his goal. He knew that if he could not bear the failure, he would never live to enjoy the success.

Babe Ruth, the baseball superstar holding the record for the most home runs, also holds the record for the most strike-outs. He did not let his many failures interfere with his pursuit of success.

Did you ever write a speech, newspaper article or school report? The first draft is rarely the final one; it has too many mistakes in grammar, sentence structure and overall clarity. So you rewrite it. The second draft is better, but still not good enough. So you write a third draft. Sometimes you have to write more than three drafts before you are finished.

Professional writers have been known to write ten or more drafts before they are satisfied. If, after the first, they would say, "This is not good; I am not a writer," they would never be published. They *expect* to go through several unsatisfactory versions before they get the one they want.

Did you ever have a conflict with a new friend? Often this seems to indicate a breakdown in the relationship. Experts disagree. They say that all good relationships go through some sort of conflict, particularly in the early stages. It *must* be this way; only through unpleasant encounters can each person learn about the other's sensitivities and how to deal with them.

Thus, conflict — what appears to be failure — is really a natural forerunner to a healthy relationship. It is part of the normal sequence of events in establishing any meaningful relationship.

Success is a continuum. At one end is what we call failure; at the opposite end is success and satisfaction. Success begins with failure and ends with accomplishment. Seen this way, failure is an integral, anticipated part of the success process.

From all this, we can conclude that failure itself does not hold us back from reaching our goals; rather, our *fear* of failure and *reaction* to failure are what hold us back. This means that our own attitude can either choke us off from success or propel us forward toward our goals.

We have a choice. We can choose to become dejected, give up, and allow the failure to stop us in our tracks, or we can get back onto our feet and proceed with a new plan. If we react to the failure with an unproductive attitude, we will remain at the negative end of the success continuum. But if we react with a positive attitude, we will come one step closer to our goals.

Failure Is an Opportunity To
Do it Right the Next Time

When you fail, there is a cause. Either you have made an error in judgment, or you simply lack the skills to succeed. Whatever the reason, the setback is an indication of some sort of weakness. Doesn't it make sense, then, to find out what the weakness is, so that you can perform better next time?

This means that if your skills are deficient, it would be advisable to seek more training. And if your judgment is impaired, you would try to rectify it. It means that instead of giving up, you would do something to correct the problem.

As reasonable as this sounds, some people sink into a depression, lamenting, "I blew it. It's all over now." They lose all hope for the future.

Let us look at Ari as an example. Ari was fired from his job because he did not get along with his manager. He then became depressed, feeling that he was incapable of holding onto any decent job. He even had visions of standing in the welfare line for the rest of his life. Ari saw his failure as the undertaker who buried his life's aspirations. He surrendered himself to the idea that he would never achieve what he really wanted.

There are others who would react to Ari's predicament differently. Instead of becoming depressed, they would immediately begin to look for another job. But if they still defend their original actions and never find out how to improve, they will naturally repeat the same mistake when they find another job.

Still others react to Ari's predicament in a third way. They blame themselves for the mistake and beat themselves up for being so foolish. They say, "I *should've* done it this way" or "I *could've* done it that way" or "If only I had thought about it more carefully, I *would've* done something else altogether." Although they learn a lesson, their self-condemnation drags them down into a depression and holds them back from making the kind of improvement of which they are capable.

A more productive way to deal with this problem is to analyze the mistake to see how it could have been avoided. One can seek the opinions of friends and professionals, and even read a book or two about the topic of his mistake. After learning some lessons, he can then stand up straight, put on a smile, look for a new job, and apply the lessons he has learned.

Failure should be a teacher, not an undertaker. There is a lesson in any failure, and one can use it to do a better job next time. Understood properly, failure is a real opportunity; it is a chance to do it right the next time.

Chazal said that "a person does not fully understand the words of Torah unless he first stumbles in interpreting them."[1] While this is in reference to Torah study, the same rule applies to any endeavor. For a person to grow and become an expert at anything, he must first make some mistakes; innovation only comes through mistakes.

Rabbi Simcha Zissel Ziv said, "Failing teaches an intelligent person the proper way, whereas 'a fool walks in darkness'[2] and never learns the proper way."[3] Rabbi Yisrael Salanter put it this way: "The benefit of stumbling is great light."[4] For this reason, Rabbi Nosson Tzvi Finkel always exhorted his students never to become depressed over a mistake, but rather to learn from the experience and to become a better person because of it.[5]

A business expert once said that he could imagine a group of young executives discussing a candidate for a top job and saying, "This person once had a big failure. That's a bad sign. Maybe we should look for someone else." If the same group of executives, twenty years later and with twenty years more experience, were

---

1. Talmud *Gittin* 43a.
2. *Koheles* 2:14.
3. *Chochmah U'Mussar*, Vol. 1, p. 144.
4. Cited in *Tenuas HaMussar*, Vol. 1, p. 307.
5. *Tenuas HaMussar*, Vol. 3, p. 273.

interviewing a candidate who had never failed, they would probably say, "What worries us is that he has never failed."[1]

Understanding the instructive value of failure, Microsoft Corporation, the computer software giant, prefers hiring people who have made mistakes during their career.[2]

A wise man once said, "A person of character can appreciate difficulty, for it is through difficulty that he can realize his potential." A man of character first recognizes the problem and discovers his weakness. He then makes the necessary improvements. He appreciates the event for exactly what it is: a chance to improve and perform better next time.

It is not enough to feel bad about a mistake. The Chofetz Chaim once stopped his congregation in the middle of *Selichos* and reminded them that it is not enough to feel bad about their sins; they have to make plans and take action to improve their ways, too.[3]

While the suggestion is quite obvious, people do not always follow it. They may feel bad about their failure, and they may even understand what went wrong. But that is where it often stops. Without taking steps to correct their shortcomings, they will never improve.[4]

Ari, whom we discussed earlier, felt bad about losing his job; however, he did not make any plans to improve. Instead of sitting back and feeling sorry for himself, he should have been solution-oriented and sought training to improve his skills. He could then have reentered the job market with renewed anticipation of success.

Admit to a mistake. King Chizkiyahu was informed of a prophecy that his children would become sinners. He did not want to father bad children, so he refused to marry. The prophet Yeshayahu informed the king that he should have married anyway and that the punishment for his mistake would be an early death.

King Chizkiyahu quickly admitted to his mistake and immediately made plans to marry. But Yeshayahu told him that it was too late;

---

1. Patricia Seller, *Fortune*, cited in *Reader's Digest*, "What's So Good About Failure," August 1995, p. 108.

2. Ibid.

3. Compiler's notes on *Chofetz Chaim Al HaTorah*, *Vayikra* 26:40-41.

4. Chofetz Chaim, ibid.

the decree could not be changed. The king did not accept this; he believed that he could learn from his mistake and make the necessary improvements. He said, "I learned from King Dovid that even when a sharp sword is at a person's throat, he should not stop praying for mercy."[1]

Had King Chizkiyahu defended his position or beat himself up for the error, he would have never made the improvement. Instead, he admitted to his mistake and took the constructive approach of *teshuvah*.

By learning from a mistake and making the necessary improvements, it is possible to correct even the most troublesome predicament. For this reason, one should never deny a mistake or make it appear that he is holding on to his error.[2]

If you offend another person and he tells you how badly he feels, don't deny or justify your action, and don't become dejected or distressed over it. Accept it and begin to treat that person differently. Let your mistake become your teacher. And while you are at it, consider how you may be able to improve your overall treatment of other people.

If you have a conflict with your son or daughter, don't mourn over your awful relationship or look for someone to blame. Instead, ask yourself if you helped bring about the fight; you may have been offensive or overcritical, causing the child to react defiantly. Talk to the child about it, and pay attention to what he says. If he blames you, he may be right. Then use this information to improve the relationship.

If a manager talks to you about a task on which you have performed poorly and suggests ways to improve, don't become insulted or defensive. Instead, welcome the suggestion and consider its validity. If it makes sense, apply it. Even if it does not make sense, you can still apply it, as long as it will not cause any harm. You may be surprised to find out that the suggestion is a good one. Unless the manager has an ulterior motive, he only has your success in mind, and his suggestion may bring you closer to that goal. Even if it doesn't lead to success at the task itself, it can leave you with the benefits of a better working relationship.

---

1. Talmud *Berachos* 10a.
2. *Peleh Yoetz, Taos.*

Failure Is Not a Reflection
of Intelligence or Capability

After making a mistake, some people come to all kinds of conclusions about their physical and mental abilities. For example, a teacher who wrote an article for a local newspaper about an innovative school program noticed after it was printed that it contained some errors. She confided to a friend, "Just look at this article. It is quite obvious that I am a poor writer. I will never write another newspaper article again."

Another example is the man who, after starting a new business, realized that his shop was not attracting customers because it was in a bad location. When he closed the shop, he said to himself, "I am not a good businessman. I will never start another business again."

The teacher and the businessman failed just once, yet they considered themselves failures. Yes, they made mistakes. But they made an even bigger mistake by thinking that failing once or twice meant that they were failures.

The word "failure" is an all-encompassing label. It says something about a person's general capabilities. The word "fail," though, only describes a particular action. It tells us how well a person performed a specific act, not about his overall capabilities.

This distinction is important; if one attributes a setback to a personal deficiency, he will plan his future with this flaw in mind and may never reach his true potential. But if he views his setback as a performance still in need of improvement but unrelated to personal inadequacy, he will make the appropriate effort to succeed in his future endeavors.

Instead of calling herself a failure, the teacher should have concluded that she failed in this instance. She could have said, "I made a mistake this time. But I learned an important lesson about writing. I will do better next time." She could have concluded that the article did not necessarily reflect her true capability.

The businessman, too, should have concluded that he failed to choose a good location for his shop, not that he himself was a failure. He could have said, "I picked a bad location. Now I know a few things I didn't know before. I will do better next time." The fact that he once chose a bad location does not mean that he cannot operate a successful business.

> If a person commits a sin, he is forbidden to become discouraged and lose his feeling of importance, because there is no greater danger than this. Rather, he must strengthen himself and elevate himself above the transgression, and move forward to meet his great potential (*Tenuas HaMussar*, Vol. 3, p. 273, citing Rabbi Nosson Tzvi Finkel).

While Rabbi Finkel discussed the topic of sinning, the same principle applies to any failure. After failing or making a mistake, a person should never come to a negative conclusion about his intelligence or capabilities. Instead, he should turn his focus to the ways in which he will meet his potential in the future. He should accept the blunder and raise himself above it.

When to conclude that you are incapable. Does all this mean that a person who constantly fails to reach a goal should continue pursuing it? Should a person ever conclude that a particular goal is beyond his reach?

It depends. If he improves with each incident, Rabbi Finkel would probably suggest that he continue pursuing the goal. But if he never improves, he should probably stop pursuing that goal and begin looking for a new one.

For this reason, during biblical times the men of the tribe of *Levi* had to serve for five years in the *Mishkan* before they could become tenured attendants. For five years they were given numerous opportunities to make mistakes and perfect their skills. If during that time they perfected those skills, they would remain at their jobs. But if they continued making mistakes, they were deemed unfit for service and were removed from their positions.[1]

Similarly, *Chazal* said, "If a student has not succeeded in his Torah studies after five years, he will not succeed."[2] Five years is enough time to experience failure, learn from the mistakes, and develop expertise in Torah. But if a student continues making mistakes, it is an indication that he will not succeed at the task.

---

1. Talmud *Chullin* 24a.
2. Ibid.

The Way One Deals with Failure Builds Character

In the Appalachian lumber country, there is a saying: "Rough weather makes good timber." Trees that are perched high on rugged mountaintops are constantly pounded by brutal winds and persistent rains. Yet year after year, they continue growing in spite of the harsh treatment. After surviving such a harsh environment, these trees become the finest quality lumber, used for the sturdiest construction projects.

Periodic failure is the "rough weather" that constantly pounds away at a person's character. The way one responds determines, to a large degree, his strength of character. If he responds negatively or helplessly, his character takes on the same weakness. But if he responds positively and creatively, he becomes resilient and persistent. Instilled with a strong character, he will be able to stand up to more challenges.

Whenever you are faced with a setback, look at it straight in the eye and say, "I am bigger than you. You will not defeat me." If you respond positively, aggressively and creatively, and use the event as an opportunity to refine your character, it will be a stepping stone for future successes.

The traits one employs influences character. Even if one fails to reach a particular goal, the *effort* he expends has a significant influence on his character. If he is diligent and responsible, if he acts with dedication and commitment, these traits become part of his total character even if he failed to reach the goal.

> When a person does a small *mitzvah* one time, he brings Hashem close and he becomes accustomed to His service. He then finds it easier to do another *mitzvah* that is equally or more difficult, because he is already accustomed to doing *mitzvos.* So when he does the second and third *mitzvos,* even if they are more difficult than the first one, he will perform quickly because habit takes control of him. He will eventually do all the *mitzvos . . .* And once he commits a sin and distances himself from the service of Hashem, it becomes easy for him to commit another

sin even if he has a weak desire for it, because he has already developed a tendency toward sins . . . and he will do all the sins, because his nature is accustomed to doing wrong things (Rabbeinu Yonah, *Avos* 4:2).

Rabbeinu Yonah is saying that performing *mitzvos* inculcates a general tendency toward *mitzvos,* while committing sins inculcates a tendency toward sins. In other words, your actions influence your attitude. If you want to have tendencies toward the good, pursue acts of good; if you want to have tendencies toward the bad, pursue acts of bad. Through action, your attitude and character become consistent with the action.[1]

Take, for example, the man we discussed who tried to start a business. He was committed and dedicated, and he put a great deal of effort into the project. He employed many valuable character traits in his venture, which were reinforced as part of his total character. With a stronger character, he will find it easier to employ the same traits the next time he has a need for them.

In summary. Progressive people have a positive, creative attitude toward mistakes and failure. Even as they suffer setbacks, they continue toward their goal. They believe that failure is a temporary inconvenience which is a normal part of any process, as well as an opportunity to learn how to perform better next time. Instead of dwelling on the failure and allowing it to affect their self-image, they immediately look for a lesson and focus on the solution.

Help Children Deal with Failure

You can help your children cope with failure by teaching them to understand the value of mistakes and encouraging them to persevere in the face of any challenge.

Be a role model. The most powerful way to guide a child is to be the kind of person you want the child to become. As a role model, the child looks up to you and copies your behavior. In other words, you can preach more with your life than with your lips.

Therefore, whenever you suffer a setback, admit it and continue to move in the direction of the goal. At times, it may even be

---

1. See also *Sefer HaChinuch, Mitzvah* 16, and *Mesilas Yesharim,* Ch. 7.

appropriate to tell your child about the failure, the lesson you learned from it, and how you plan to improve. You can share with the child your expectation of occasional failure and your view of failure as a temporary inconvenience.

Allow for failure. Inform the child that in your home, or in the classroom if you are a teacher, periodic failure is natural. Create a "laboratory environment" in which children can analyze their mistakes without guilt or criticism, then use the lesson to perform better next time. In this environment, children get hands-on practice in dealing with failure.

Encourage risk-taking. Thomas Edison took risks because he viewed failure as the beginning of the success continuum. You too can encourage children to try new ideas, then to analyze why those ideas did or did not work.

Do not cover up the penalty of failure. What motivates people to avoid failure? The ensuing penalty. If not for the negative consequence of failure, people would not be deterred from repeating mistakes. Therefore, adults should not cover up the penalty of a child's mistake. They should instead allow the child to experience the consequence and learn to avoid more mistakes.

Let's say, for example, that a child receives a failing grade on her report card. The mother does not want her daughter to feel badly, so she denigrates the teacher for giving the failing grade. She may even accuse the teacher of giving unfair tests or picking on her daughter.

Assuming the teacher is competent, this child deserves the failing grade. But now that the parent is covering up for her, it is unlikely that the child will ever take the proper steps to improve. Additionally, when the child sees the parent shifting the blame onto the teacher, she may also learn to shift blame and never to take responsibility for her own mistakes.

Create an atmosphere conducive to success. While failure has its benefits, too much failure is unhealthy. A child who constantly fails may not be motivated to excel at anything. Why should he? According to him, failure is the most likely outcome.

You can break a cycle of failure by creating goals that the child can surely reach. As the child becomes familiar with the good feeling of success, he will try to perform better in all his tasks. Success itself becomes a motivator for good performance and generates continued success.

Teach children to make positive affirmations. When a child fails, she may stop pursuing the goal. The child must therefore learn that when she fails, it does not mean she is a failure.

You can help the child internalize this message by guiding her to repeat positive affirmations about herself. She would say, "I am on my way to success" or "I learn from all my mistakes" or "This is only temporary. Tomorrow I will improve."

Offer advice and encouragement. When a child fails, adults should obviously encourage him to continue trying to succeed. But the rules of *chinuch* tell adults to go one step further by helping the child understand the *meaning* of failure. They should remind the child that a setback is not a reflection of capability or intelligence; rather, it is a normal event in a person's life, and anyone who wishes to succeed will have to accept occasional failure, too.

Provide training. When a worker performs unsatisfactorily, the manager does not fire him immediately. A wise manager first provides the worker with more training and more opportunities to try, in the hope that he will improve and contribute to the growth of the company.

Wise parents and teachers should do the same. When a child acts inappropriately or makes a mistake, they do not ignore him or give up on him. Instead, they provide the child with training and further opportunities to practice so that he will improve.

Chapter Four
Understand Success

I magine for a moment that you are an athlete, preparing to compete against five others in a race. You spend weeks training for the event. Finally, the big day comes. You try your hardest and run your fastest, but by the time you reach the finish line, someone else has already crossed it. Coming in second place, are you a winner or one of four losers? Would you say you are successful or unsuccessful?

Suppose you are a student in a class of thirty. As the year comes to a close, the teacher is about to choose two students for the honor roll. Although you have worked your hardest during the year, you are not chosen. The teacher explains that since you rank third in the class, you do not qualify. Are you a winner or one of twenty-eight losers? Would you say you are successful or unsuccessful?

What is success? Is it coming in first? Is it the fastest? The strongest? The richest? The smartest? The most knowledgeable? Is there only one winner — and everyone else is a loser?

Or does success mean something else? Maybe it means trying your hardest and performing to the best of your ability. When you run your fastest, even though you do not come in first place, you are a success. When you study your hardest, even though you are not at the top of the class, you are still a success. To be a success, maybe you don't have to be the richest, strongest, smartest, fastest or most knowledgeable. Maybe you just have to do your best with your own abilities.

According to this interpretation, you are a success if you live up to your potential — even if you place last. But if your performance is anywhere short of your potential, you are not fully successful — even if you place first.

We will see shortly that *Chazal* defined success the second way. They said that success is determined by comparing one's performance to his or her own set of abilities. According to *Chazal,* one could have lost the race and still have been successful.

Confusion about the meaning of success. There are many people who are misguided about the meaning of success. They profess the Torah view, yet they glorify the single winner who comes in ahead of everyone else. They preach to their children that the most important part of any task is effort; they say things like, "What's important is not if you win or lose, but how you play the game." But at the same time, they fail to applaud those who try their hardest and only place second or third. And when these people fail to reach the top or get what they want in their own lives, they consider themselves unsuccessful even if they put all their effort into the task.

These people are obviously misinterpreting the meaning of success, and they don't even know it. Are you acquainted with anyone like this?

In this chapter we will discuss the reason people are caught between the "win-or-lose" attitude and the Torah view. We will also discuss the demotivating effects of the "win-or-lose" attitude and the motivating effects of the Torah view.

The Win-or-Lose Attitude Is Part of Our Culture

Take a look at the way people in our society typically interpret success. They are of the opinion that one either wins or loses; if one does not win, he is a loser, and if he does not lose, he is a winner. From their point of view, there are only two options.

Let's look at professional baseball as an illustration. A baseball team plays an entire season with the goal of competing in the World

Series. Only the two teams who distinguish themselves as the best in the nation make it to the big event. Even then, only one wins. The winning team collects the prize money and all the accolades that come along with victory.

How do the players and fans of the losing team react? With sad, sunken, defeated faces, they bemoan, "We failed. We are losers." Cameras have actually caught fans and players — mature adults — crying over the loss. Although the team made it all the way to the biggest event of the season, they are considered total failures and are not even appreciated for the outstanding achievement of reaching the World Series in the first place. Why? Because in the end they did not come in first. Anything less than number one is losing.

The win-or-lose concept is an integral part of our society. There is only one victor in a political election; one top-prize winner in a lottery or any other contest; and one winner in a camp color war, school spelling bee or sports tournament. Whatever the event, what do people say about the ones who do not win? "They lost. They didn't succeed."

There are two other attitudes which are closely related to the win-or-lose point of view; the *make-it-to-the-top* and the *get-what-you-want* attitudes. Here, the ones who are recognized are the people who make it to the top or simply get what they want, even if they stand alongside others who have made the same achievement. Take the millionaire and the president of a company as examples. Although there are many other millionaires and company presidents in the world, each one is put on a pedestal for making it to the top and getting what he or she wants.

Since we are part of the culture around us, its prevailing beliefs become part of our way of thinking.[1] Dragged along with the world's pattern of thinking, we begin to interpret success by the win-or-lose criterion. For this reason, many of us applaud those who come in first, make it to the top or get what they want. We consider anything else as inferior even if we have an intuition that the Torah approach recognizes people for realizing their potential. Because of our society, we become confused between the win-or-lose approach and the Torah approach.

---

1. Rambam, *De'os* 6:1.

We are influenced from a young age. When children are growing up, parents often compare the performances of one child and another instead of looking at each child's capabilities separately. This treatment is often the first exposure a child has to the world's interpretation of success. They too begin to compare themselves to others; if others do better, they see themselves as losers, and if others do worse, they see themselves as winners. This is the either/or attitude; either they win or lose, regardless of their own set of talents.

The win-or-lose focus becomes even more prevalent as a child enters the competitive environment of school. He is exposed to honor roles which salute the few "best" performers, while disregarding those who make a noble effort to meet their own potential. In schools, children participate in all sorts of competitions — talent shows, spelling bees, and an assortment of other athletic and creative contests — which clearly separate the less competent children from the more competent, without meaningful regard to personal capability or perseverance.

And what happens after these competitions come to an end? Teachers typically say, "Congratulations to the contest winners. But really, you are all winners, because you all had fun and learned something." While the intent here is to dispel the win-or-lose notion, some less sensitive teachers mean it only as lip service. And every astute child knows the difference.

They know it from the way those teachers separate the winners from the losers in many subtle and not-so-subtle ways. For example, they smile at the winners, shake their hands, pat them on the back and extend special privileges to them. With this differential treatment, why should the "losers" feel proud of their efforts? Deep down, they sense that they are really not recognized as true success cases — and they begin to believe it, too.

Even in the absence of formal competition, every child knows which students are the "best in the class." They notice the ways that teachers recognize the students who earn the highest grades. This gives children the sense that being on top has real value, and anything else misses the mark even if they reach their own full potential.

The win-or-lose attitude is further reinforced when the children go home at the end of the day, if insensitive parents reprimand them for receiving C's and D's, without even finding out if they worked to their full capacity or why they received those grades in the first place. After being lectured for not receiving A's and B's, these children get the feeling that if they fall short of reaching the top they are considered failures, even if they worked hard to succeed.

Some parents do tell their children how proud they are of their efforts. They say, "We know that you studied hard and put a lot of effort into it. We are very proud of you for that." But their noble message may become fuzzy if they loudly applaud a brother or sister who received A's. The low achiever compares the way he is recognized for studying hard to the way the sibling is recognized for reaching the top. This once again reinforces the win-or-lose point of view.

After completing twelve or more years of formal schooling, many young adults enter the competitive world of business. In this environment, they not only see more of the same attitude, but they are often forced to live by it. They may even take "win-or-lose" to its furthest extreme; we call it "dog eat dog," where each person, in his or her pursuit for first place, pushes others aside, steps on them, or deliberately causes them a personal or professional loss.

We can see that the very system in which we live instills in us the win-or-lose attitude. Indeed, we are victims of our culture and therefore cannot be blamed for having confused beliefs. But once we become aware of the proper attitude — and this chapter will describe it — we can train ourselves to view success differently. Not only will we be living by Torah values, we will be living a happier life, too.

The Win-or-Lose Attitude Demotivates

If success means coming in first, being on top, or getting what you want, the vast majority of the world's population will never succeed. After all, only one person can be first, and very few can make it to the top or get exactly what they want. This may be the reason so many people do not even attempt to excel; they must compete against others who are more skilled, so they say, "Why bother trying! I'll never come in ahead of them."

Furthermore, if people who do not come in first do not receive recognition for their accomplishments, they never receive the motivating effect that recognition can have.

Recognition is an important motivator. As the rule goes, the behavior that is rewarded will be repeated. When a person is rewarded for a particular behavior, he is motivated to repeat it. But when he is not rewarded, he may not want to repeat it. Recognition is rewarding and has the power to motivate people to repeat behaviors.

Recognition is rewarding because it satisfies a person's need to feel important, the strongest force within the human psyche.[1] Thus, recognizing a person's progress can motivate him to continue progressing and reach goals he would otherwise never attempt, whereas withholding recognition may result in a lack of interest.

Withholding recognition may result in even more than a lack of interest. As the low achievers see the high achievers being recognized while they are ignored, they begin to think that their accomplishments are worthless, even though they performed as well as they possibly could have. They may even begin to doubt their capabilities or consider themselves inferior. These attitudes inhibit them from putting full effort into future projects.

The anticipation of success motivates. People desire the good feeling that comes along with success. This is why success itself motivates people to succeed even more. But if they know that only a few will ever succeed — that is, by the win-or-lose interpretation — they lose their incentive. As they constantly fall short of what they perceive as success, they may begin to believe that success is unattainable. The prospect of success, then, loses its motivational power.

However, when we put success on a standard that compares one's performance to his or her own ability, everyone can attain it. Because it is both attractive and attainable, people look forward to it and become motivated to achieve it.

The Torah View of Success

What words would you use to describe a successful person? Wise? Strong? Wealthy? Honored? This is what popular opinion

---

1. *Mesilas Yesharim*, Ch. 19.

says. In fact, many people go so far as to say, "If only I had these four qualities, I would feel truly accomplished."

How does popular opinion characterize these four qualities? Typically, *wisdom* is characterized by the extent of one's knowledge; *strength* by one's ability to control and dominate others; *wealth* by the material fortune one has amassed; *honor* by the degree of positive recognition one receives from others.

Chazal had a totally different view:

> Who is wise? The one who learns from others . . . Who is strong? The one who controls his emotions . . . Who is rich? The one who is happy with his share . . . Who is honored? The one who honors others (*Avos* 4:1).

In the Torah view, wisdom, strength, wealth and honor — four signs of success — are characterized by the way you use your mind and express yourself, not by what you have or how you are treated. Learn from others instead of amassing knowledge, and you are wise. Control your emotions, not other people, and you are strong. Be happy with what you have instead of collecting material possessions, and you are wealthy. Honor others instead of receiving it, and you are honored. Train your mind in these traits, and by Torah definition you are successful.

Success in the Torah view has nothing to do with coming in first, getting what you want, or reaching the top. It is unrelated to other people, other things or external circumstances. *Success is how you look at life and how you use your own talents to deal with life's challenges and opportunities.*

> The *ben Torah's* (yeshivah student's) dream of greatness must be to achieve his own full potential — which, if pursued diligently, is really above and beyond whatever he may have dreamed possible. But if his whole concept of success is based on what others consider success — being a *rosh yeshivah* or a *rosh kollel*, or at the bare minimum, a *maggid shiur* in a *beis hamidrash* (otherwise why bother?) — he may be in for a disappointment . . .
>
> For sure one may think of position and prestige — if this motivates the person to learn. But one must remember that this is only a *means*, at best — not a real end.

Confusing the incentive with the goal is fraught with the danger of frustration and despair (Rabbi Chaim Dov Keller, "Of Identity and Success," *The Jewish Observer*, May 1982, p. 7).

While Rabbi Keller was concerned with yeshivah students, his rule applies to anyone in any situation. Success is how you look at life and how you use your own talents to deal with life's challenges and opportunities. True success comes from within; it is generated within a person and finds its way out. This is very different from the popular view.[1]

Additionally, people who understand success according to the Torah view do not need recognition from others to keep them motivated. When they do their best, they know it and are proud of it, regardless of how their performance compares to that of others. Since they do not compare themselves to others, they never say, "Why bother trying? I will never come out on top." On the contrary, they compare their performance to their ability, and are therefore motivated to try their hardest even when others perform better.

At this point, we can ask an important question: How can this interpretation of success be applied to *mitzvah* observance? No matter how much effort you put into keeping the *mitzvos* of *Shabbos* and *kashrus*, for example, there is only one way to fulfill them successfully: total observance. Two more examples are the prohibitions of *chometz* and *lashon hara.* No matter how much you try to avoid them, total abstinence is the requirement for the *mitzvah.*

In regard to these *mitzvos*, success is not a function of effort or ability. There is only one way, and anything short of it is failure. How, then, can we apply the Torah view of success to *mitzvah* observance?

Two categories of *mitzvos*. *Mitzvos* can be divided into two categories. The first category includes those which must be performed exactly as they were mandated. *Shabbos, kashrus, chometz* and *lashon hara* are examples. To succeed, we must keep these *mitzvos* exactly as they were designated.

---

1. See Rabbi Abraham Twerski, *Let Us Make Man*, CIS Publishers, 1989, pp. 92-102, on this point.

However, there is a second category. *Tzedakah, parnassah, chessed,* Torah study, character development and loving one's fellow Jews are examples. There is no single way to keep these *mitzvos*; they can be performed at various levels, beginning with nominal performance and going all the way up to doing as well as one's individual talents allow. While one receives a Heavenly reward for performing them even at a lower level, one cannot be considered a truly successful *mitzvah*-performer until he meets his potential. With these *mitzvos,* success is determined by comparing one's performance to his own ability.

Take Torah study as an example. One is only required to learn as much Torah as his intellect allows; there is no requirement to outdo or even match the achievements of others. Therefore, if one meets his potential, he is a success — even if others learn more and attain a greater level of wisdom than he. But what if he only learns a fraction of what he is able to? Is he a success? No. Although he performs the *mitzvah* of Torah study at a low level and even receives a Heavenly reward for it, he cannot be called a *success* until he meets his potential.

Tzedakah is another example. One is only required to give as much *tzedakah* as his bank account allows; there is no requirement to outdo or even match the generosity of others. Therefore, if one gives as much as he can, he is a success — even if others give more. But what if he gives only a fraction of what he is able to? Is he a success? No. Although he performs the *mitzvah* of *tzedakah* at a low level and receives reward for it, he cannot be called a *success* until he meets his potential.

Loving one's fellow Jews is another example. A person's ability to fulfill this *mitzvah* depends on his emotional makeup. But as long as one loves others as much as he can, even if it does not match the achievement of others, he is still considered a success.

With the *mitzvos* of the second category, there is no clear standard for achievement; rather, each person performs according to his or her own talents and abilities. It follows, then, that whenever we define success in terms of personal ability and progress, the *mitzvos* we are concerned with are those of the second category.

This difference is also true regarding success in other areas. Certainly, there are times that success is achieved by doing our personal best. Often, however, there are tasks whose standards are evaluated by the attainment of specific objectives. Take, for instance, a professional widget maker who is hired to produce 50 widgets each day. If he falls short of this goal, even if he produces as many widgets as he possibly can, he cannot be called a success. Unlike the *mitzvos* of the second category for which there is no clear standard of achievement, this widget maker did not satisfy the conditions of his employment.

What Is Success? What Is Winning?

People who have the Torah view of success and winning may find that they are able to cope more effectively with life's challenges. They may find that their lives are enriched as a result. We will now list some definitions of success and winning that exemplify the Torah view. The definitions may seem repetitive, but each has a different nuance.

1. *Winning is doing your best with the strengths you have.*
We mentioned earlier that the world judges success by comparing one's performance with the performance of others. You are called a success only if you reach the top or do better than everyone else.

This is not fair, because you can only do as well as your potential allows. The fact that someone else can do better is irrelevant. He was born with that capacity. You, on the other hand, can only do what your innate strengths allow. Therefore, "reaching the top" for you is different from "reaching the top" for him. You have "reached the top" if you do the best you can possibly do with the strengths you have, even if others perform better.

> . . . there is more than one definition of success . . . each person's success must be in accordance with his own unique talents, his own strengths and weaknesses (Rabbi Chaim Dov Keller, "Of Identity and Success," *The Jewish Observer,* May 1982, p. 5).

The Talmud relates an incident which demonstrates the futility of comparisons. Rabbi Yosef, the son of Rabbi Yehoshua ben Levi, became ill and passed away. He subsequently came back to life, and his father asked him what he had seen in the other world. He answered, "I saw an upside-down world; people whom we consider important are on the bottom, while people whom we consider unimportant are on the top." His father responded, "My son, what you saw was the clear world."[1]

Rabbi Yehoshua ben Levi was teaching his son that the people whom we consider successful may, in truth, be failures, and the people whom we consider failures may actually be successful. The reason for this confusion is that we, in the "unclear world," define success differently from the way the "clear world" of the Torah defines it. We therefore frequently give honor to the wrong people.

Take, for example, the wealthy philanthropist. Because of his charitable support, he attains fame and wins the admiration of his community. People respect him because, as compared to others, he gives more money to worthwhile institutions. But what if he has the capacity to give more? Would he still be eligible for the same fame and admiration?

Rabbi Yehoshua ben Levi answers this question. With his interpretation of success, this philanthropist, since he did not live up to his potential, would not be considered successful.

A Torah scholar, too, often becomes renowned for his erudition and rabbinical expertise because he has the greatest mastery. But he may be capable of even greater expertise! If this were the case, Rabbi Yehoshua ben Levi would not consider him successful.

While we must honor the philanthropist and the Torah scholar because of their deeds and achievements, since they could have achieved even more than they did, they would occupy a lower position in the "clear world."

On the other hand, ordinary people who work to their capacity really deserve more honor than they get. Because they meet their potential, they would occupy a higher position in the "clear world."

This means that if your knowledge is commensurate with your capacity to learn, you have reached the top, even if there are others who are more knowledgeable. If your business has grown to the level that your capital and acumen allow, you have made it to the top, even if there are others who have built more lucrative businesses. If you have done all you could possibly do, you have made it

---

1. Talmud *Pesachim* 50a, and Rashi there.

to the top, even if others appear to have accomplished more. You are a winner as long as you do your best with the strengths you have.

When Rabbi Meir Shapiro founded the Yeshivah Chachmei Lublin, someone asked him, "Why are you building a yeshivah for five hundred students? Where will you find enough cities to provide a position for five hundred rabbis?" Rabbi Shapiro answered, "Who says all five hundred will become practicing rabbis? I will make two rabbis and 498 others who understand what a rabbi is."

Rabbi Shapiro did not imply that only the two students who emerged as rabbis would be considered successful in their course of study, while the others would be considered failures. Rather, all five hundred would be successful, each according to his own potential. This is the way to measure the yeshivah's success.[1]

2. *Success is progressive movement toward a goal.*

A crew of dedicated workers once began clearing a raw mountainside for the construction of a new settlement. As they were clearing the stones and bushes, the supervisor climbed a tree, looked around, and realized that they were on the wrong mountain. He announced, "We are on the wrong mountain. We'd better stop working and move over to the right one." One enthusiastic worker yelled back, "Why should we do that? Can't you see how much progress we are making here?"

There is a similar story of two friends who were driving from New York to Miami. They had only a few days vacation time and planned to make the trip in record time. After several hours of driving, they began noticing signs to Boston. The passenger told the driver, "I think we should stop and make sure we are going in the right direction." The driver responded, "What for? We are making great time!"

The two travelers and the crew of workers were active. They were fully engaged. But they were unsuccessful because they were not making any progressive movement toward their goal.

Progressive is the key word here. Success does not mean activity; rather, it is the *progressive movement* toward a goal. The travelers were unsuccessful not because they were far from their

---

1. Explained by Rabbi Chaim Dov Keller, "Of Identity and Success," *The Jewish Observer,* May 1982, p. 6.

destination, but because they were not making any progressive movement *toward* their destination. Had they been steadily traveling in the right direction, their efforts would have been considered successful even before they arrived.

The crew of workers was also unsuccessful, not because they had not yet cleared the mountainside, but because they were not working on the right mountain. Had they been steadily clearing the proper area, we would consider their efforts successful even before they finished the job, because they would have been making progressive movement in the direction of their goal.

Did you ever see the way some people are busy, busy, busy — always active in some sort of project, but not getting much accomplished? For example, a manager may spend hours of time making plans for a new project. He speaks to a lot of people and gets more information than he can possibly use, but he never gets around to implementing the project. Or he may get the project going, only to discover that it is not beneficial to anyone.

The manager is active. He is fully engaged. But he is unproductive. He is unsuccessful because he is making no progressive movement toward a goal.

An experiment once performed with processional caterpillars illustrates this point. A processional caterpillar follows the path of the caterpillar in front; hence, the name "processional." Scientists once placed several processional caterpillars, one behind the other, in a circle. They placed some pine needles, the food these caterpillars eat, in the middle of the circle. Day after day, the caterpillars followed each other in a circle. Then, one day, they all died from starvation. Although their food was just a few inches away, they never veered from their activity to nourish themselves.

These caterpillars were active. But they were not achieving anything. Some people are the same; they are active but make no progressive movement toward any kind of achievement.

Chazal suggested, "Say a little and do a lot."[1] In other words, don't spend your time involved in activity. Rather, get involved in goal-oriented action. It is not enough to be busy; there has to be some sort of accomplishment.

---

1. *Avos* 1:15.

Concerning Torah mastery, *Chazal* told us, "Your duty is not to complete the task, but you do not have the freedom not to try."[1] Although perfect performance — that is, total mastery — is impossible, we must still try to achieve it. But if the goal is unattainable, why should we try to reach it? It will never happen anyway! The answer is simple. As we have mentioned before, there are two goals in any action consistent with Torah ideals: good performance and effort. While good performance — in this case, total mastery of Torah — is out of our grasp, *effort* to reach mastery is within our grasp.

Chazal told us that the effort to reach a goal — any progress we make toward it — is also important. We should not focus solely on good performance; we should also focus on effort — *progressive movement* in the direction of good performance.[2]

There is a special prayer recited before Torah study. In this prayer, we say, "I toil and they [non-Jews] toil. I toil and receive a reward, while they toil and do not receive a reward."[3] The words of this prayer suggest that as long as we pursue Torah ideals, we are rewarded for our effort, even if we do not reach the final goal.

Toil is the important factor here. Toil means the progressive movement toward a goal. *Chazal* told us here that if we toil, we are rewarded, because this is considered success.

A Talmudic sage, Rabbi Shimon Ha'Amsuni, knew this. Rabbi Shimon spent a great deal of time explaining the purpose of dozens of seemingly superfluous words in the Torah. When he came across a word which he felt had no explanation, he abandoned his entire thesis and declared all his previous explanations erroneous.

He could have done as most people in his predicament would do — close his mind to the notion that he had made a mistake, remaining loyal to the principles that he had spent so long developing.[4] Or he could have become dejected and said, "I wasted my time. I should never have started this project in the first place." But he didn't behave in either way. He quickly changed his thinking and said instead, "Just as I received a reward for my explanation, I will

---

1. *Avos* 2:16.
2. *Darash Moshe*, p. 111.
3. Talmud *Berachos* 28b.
4. Rabbi Simcha Zissel Ziv, cited in *HaMeoros HaGedolim*, p. 94.

receive a reward for my reversal."[1] Since he had been toiling and was making progressive movement toward a worthy goal, even though he erred and did not reach it, he considered himself successful and expected a reward for his work.

So if you have been working on a project for a long time and have not yet completed it, don't say, "I haven't reached my goal. I am not successful"; say instead, "I am making progressive movement toward my goal. I am therefore succeeding."

Suppose you are a student studying for an exam, and after several hours of study you still do not understand something. Don't throw your hands up in despair and cry, "I have spent all this time studying, and I still don't understand it." Say instead, "Yesterday, I knew nothing about this topic, and today I know something. True, I do not fully understand it, but look how much progress I have made. As long as I am progressing toward my goal, I am successful."

Suppose you are a parent trying to motivate a child to share household duties. Although the child is fulfilling many of his duties, he is still neglecting some. Don't become frustrated and say, "I have been trying to get him to take on his share of household work, but he is just not cooperating. I am obviously not a very effective parent." Say instead, "Look how much progress he has made. Last month, he did nothing but eat, play and sleep. Now, he is also helping out with some household work. True, he has not yet reached the goal I have set for him, but he is making progress. In time, he will do more."

3. *Success is the journey, not the destination.*

When you travel, you no doubt have a destination in mind. Reaching that destination is the end of a long process. First comes the journey, then the destination. It is the same with any goal; first you make the preliminary steps, then you reach the goal. All the steps in between are part of a long process called "success."

So whenever you set a goal and fall short of reaching it, or you miss the deadline to complete it, you can still be proud of your accomplishments, because as long as you are making progress, you are traveling on the road of success. You are not a failure if you miss

---

1. Talmud *Pesachim* 22b.

a goal, but you are a failure if you stop trying, because once that happens you have brought the journey to a close.

4. *Success is a process of growth and improvement.*

According to the Torah view, one is successful even if he does not reach his goal, as long as he is steadily growing and improving. The Torah sees success as a *process* of growth and improvement, not as a single achievement. Let's explain.

When you make a mistake and miss a goal, you can react in various ways. You can kick your foot against the wall in frustration, or learn from the mistake and continue moving forward. *Chazal* said that the second way is appropriate.

> A person does not fully understand the words of Torah unless he first stumbles in interpreting them (Talmud *Gittin* 43a).

While *Chazal* said this regarding Torah study, it applies to any endeavor. Blundering and faltering provide the opportunity to sharpen one's skills. With improved skills, one can perform better the next time. This is what we mean by growth and improvement. If a mistake is used for the purpose of improvement, it is a productive event. Thus, there is no such thing as failure as long as the experience is used in a beneficial way. It then becomes part of the success process.

5. *Success is coming in second when last year you came in third.*

Suppose you are a salesperson. You set a goal to acquire fifteen new accounts. After working your hardest, you only get ten. While this is three more than last season, it still does not meet the goal of fifteen. Would you dwell on the ten you have or the five you don't have?

If you dwell on what you do not have, you may become frustrated and lose interest in building your accounts. But if you highlight what you do have — three more accounts than you had last year — you begin to appreciate your accomplishment, and you may even become motivated to continue acquiring accounts.

It is the same with any goal. As long as you make serious improvement over your previous efforts, even if you do not reach your final goal, you are still a winner. Don't focus on the fact that you came in short of first place. Instead, focus on the fact that you came in closer to first place than ever before. This is real progress and is something to be proud of.

6. *Success is coming in "last but best."*

Pete Strudwick was born with only partial hands and no feet. Yet, at the age of forty-one, Pete had special boots made and ran up Pikes Peak in the 1971 Pikes Peak Marathon. Although he knew he would arrive at the finish line hours after the first contestant, he considered himself a serious competitor. And when he finally reached the finish line, he was proud of his achievement. Why? Because he conquered his disability and did the "impossible." Yes, there were others who reached the finish line before him, but he reached it *best.*

Even before he began the race, it was clear that he would lose. But Pete did not see it that way. Disabled though he was, he did not let it interfere with his plans. He was motivated because he did not see coming in last as a contradiction to success, as long as he gave it his best effort. So he ran. And he succeeded, because he ran "better" than anyone else.

There are many disabled and elderly people who compete in all types of tournaments. Although they may come in last, they are winners. Why? Because they come in *best.* They don't let their handicaps stop them, and they are proud of it.

Another example is the twenty-year-old dyslexic who, after years of instruction, finally learns to read. Indeed, other people learn to read at a much younger age, but he is not deterred. Although he cannot take pride in coming in first, he can take pride in coming in best.

Chazal said, "Righteous people do not stand in the same place that *ba'alei teshuvah* (penitent people) stand."[1] This means that people who have recently committed themselves to a Torah-true life-style have a higher status than those who have been religious for years.

The question is: Why should righteous people, who have been observing *mitzvos* their entire lifetime, be considered on a lower level than those who are just beginning? The answer is simple.

---

1. Talmud *Sanhedrin* 99a.

Ba'alei teshuvah have already become accustomed to a non-Torah way of life. Exchanging this life-style for a new one is a major undertaking, requiring great courage and commitment. People who are "*frum* from birth," on the other hand, have never made such a drastic change. True, they may come in first, but *ba'alei teshuvah* come in *best.*

So the next time you find yourself not performing as well as others, ask yourself what you are up against. If you are overcoming a deficiency or a disability, take pride in being a winner, because your performance is *better* than anyone else's.

7. *Success is a way of life, not a specific achievement or personality type.*

A person with the Torah view of success appreciates his efforts and improvements as part of the success process. He does not need a specific achievement to feel successful; with each development in the right direction, he sees himself as a winner — even if he falls short of his goal. He is always competing against himself, not others. He takes pride in every new development, and his self-esteem is bolstered. This is what we mean when we say that success is a way of life, not a specific achievement or personality type.

Success and Persistence

Persistence is part of any success story. It is not enough for a person to make progress toward a goal; he must stand resolute against opposition, discouragement and temporary failure. As the old saying goes, "Winners never quit, and quitters never win." Persistence keeps the wheels of progressive movement going.

> What was the origin of Rabbi Akiva? He was forty years old and he had not learned Torah. One time he was standing near a well, and he asked, "Who carved out this stone?" They answered, "Isn't it the water that constantly falls on the rock, day after day?" Rabbi Akiva immediately reasoned, "If soft water can carve its way into a hard rock, Torah, which is hard as iron, certainly can make an impression on my human heart." He immediately went to learn Torah . . .

To what is he compared? To a stone cutter who chisels out mountains. One time the stone cutter took his chisel in hand, sat on a mountain, and began chipping small pebbles. People asked him, "What are you doing?" He answered, "I am removing the mountain and putting it into the Jordan River." They replied, "You are not able to remove the entire mountain." He nevertheless continued chiseling until he reached a boulder. He got underneath it, smashed it, removed it, and placed it in the Jordan River. He then said, "This is not your place, but that is" (*Avos d'Rav Nosson,* Ch. 6).

Rabbi Akiva was forty years old and had never learned Torah; even by the Torah interpretation of success, he was not successful. But once he made the commitment to learn, his ambition created an inner drive to overcome all the obstacles he met along the way. There is no doubt that Rabbi Akiva had some discouraging moments, especially in the beginning, yet he faced those challenges like the persistent stone cutter. And like the stone cutter, Rabbi Akiva also "moved mountains."[1]

The Torah tells us how our forefather Yitzchak dug many wells. At first glance, this information may seem trivial, but it isn't. It teaches a powerful lesson in persistence. When Yitzchak dug a well and found no water, he went on to dig another. When he was forced to abandon it on account of a quarrel, he went on to find another. On several occasions he met up with difficulty and opposition, yet he did not become discouraged, nor did he feel he was incapable of the task; instead, he persisted until he found a useful well he could call his own.[2]

Helping Children Understand Success

You can help instill the Torah view of success in children by creating an atmosphere that dissolves the "win-or-lose" attitude and emphasizes the Torah view.

First of all, always compare the child's performance to his own

---

1. Rabbi Chaim Mordechai Katz, *Be'er Mechokek,* pp. 21-22.
2. *Chofetz Chaim Al HaTorah, Bereishis* 26:19.

ability, not to the performance of others. Look carefully at all the talents that help him toward his goal and at the difficulties that hold him back, and show him how he used or failed to use them.

For example, if a child receives several C's on his report card, don't say, "What is the matter with you? Your brother didn't get any C's!" Instead, try to understand why he received those grades. Maybe he was ill while the class was learning the topic. Maybe he has a learning disability which impedes his growth. If you can attribute his low grades to a factor that is out of his control, and if you can be sure that he tried his hardest — because there is, of course, no substitute for hard work — assure the child that he did as well as he could and that he is therefore a winner.

Second, encourage children to persist even in difficult times. Let them know that success and achievement are the results of failure and hardship. Imbue them with the idea that life always presents obstacles, and overcoming these challenges is an integral part of any success story. Let the child know that if he made his best effort, he is a winner.

Suppose a child wants to play a guitar. He goes to his first music lesson and learns the proper way to hold the instrument. At the next lesson, he begins to read music. He then learns to play a few notes. By the tenth lesson, all he can do is hold the guitar, read some music and play a short, simple tune. He thinks that he is a failure because he is not learning fast enough and he finds it difficult. So he loses interest.

This is where parents can be helpful. They can encourage the child to persist. They can teach him that challenges arise in the course of pursuing any goal. They can tell him that all beginnings are difficult, and that after time things will get easier.[1] They can help the child understand that an occasional failure is to be expected, and that he will never learn to play guitar unless he continues taking lessons.

Third, help a child feel proud of his progress, even before he reaches the final goal. By recognizing his progress, you send the message that success is movement, not necessarily the end result. Once the child learns to appreciate the growth process and the

---

1. Rashi, *Yisro* 19:5.

journey toward the goal, he will not let one or two setbacks stop him from reaching it.

While these three suggestions are helpful, the most effective way to teach children the Torah view is to live it yourself. If your children see you become excited after performing as well as you can, even if others do better, they are left with a powerful impression.

There is one problem with all this: Our culture uses a different criterion for success. As we mentioned earlier, people typically judge success by comparing one's performance to the performance of others, without giving ample recognition to effort and progress.

If we are going to create an environment conducive to the Torah view of success, we will have to change this. We will have to tell children, "Here, success means progress toward a worthy goal. You don't have to be the 'best in the class'; you just have to work to the best of your ability and make steady progress." With this understanding of success, children will begin to realize that it is attainable. They will anticipate success and will be motivated to take action.

Parents and teachers will have to avoid comparing one child's performance to another's. Even if another child performs better, there is no need to highlight it. And when praising the low-achieving child, they should do so with the same enthusiasm with which they recognize the high-performing child.

Even before the child reaches the final goal, adults can praise him for his efforts. By acknowledging his success before the final achievement, he gets an important message: As long as there is effort and progress toward the goal, there is success.

How can teachers and parents overcome the obstacles they face in a competitive society? Unfortunately, there is no way to overcome the problems totally. However, to some degree, teachers have the power to make adjustments in their own classrooms. Even within the parameters of the system, they have enough freedom within their own classrooms to implement policies that reflect the Torah view.

One thing they can do is emphasize student-to-self comparison. They can praise and reward progress, and they can create an honor roll which salutes effort and improvement. Even when they mark tests and assign grades for report cards, they can highlight the effort and improvement the children have made.

With this treatment, children get a feel for the Torah view of success. They know that in their classroom winning is possible for anyone who is willing to make the effort to move steadily forward. If they occasionally miss their goal, they can appreciate the progress they have made and will not become dejected. With this attitude, they will be motivated to continue trying and to achieve their goals.

Chapter Five

Succeed Through Goal-Setting

here was once a salesman who would think about how he ought to be home with his family whenever he was on the road. Then, when he was home with his family, he would think about how he ought to be on the road selling his goods. This salesman did very little business. Is it any wonder? When he was on the road, his mind was at home; when he was at home, his mind was on the road. At any one time, he wasn't really anywhere!

It is very likely that this salesman did not set clear goals projecting the number of prospects he would approach and how much he would sell. Even if he did, he may not have made a plan for how and when he would make the sales, or he did not make a serious commitment to the plan.

Many people are like this. They do not set goals for themselves — and even if they do, their goals are unclear, unplanned, or they are just not committed to them. And like the salesman, these people don't get anywhere.

Then there are people who do set clear objectives and relentlessly pursue them. When it comes to business, they decide how much they will sell, and they don't stop selling until they have met their quota. They decide to improve a bad *middah* or get involved with a *chessed* project, and they stick to it until they reach the goal. Whatever they decide to do, they see it through to the end.

What gives these people the ability to reach their goals? Are they successful by nature, born with good luck? Do they have goal-oriented personalities? Or have they mastered a skill that can be learned by anyone?

Their success is actually the product of a skill that can be learned by anyone. The name of this skill is goal-setting.

Goal-setting is a necessity. *Chazal* said, "A person is obligated to say, 'When will my actions equal those of my forefathers, Avraham, Yitzchak and Yaakov?' "[1] Concerning this, Rabbi Chaim Shmulevitz commented:

> This obligation is directed to every person. Even if one's actions are far from those of the forefathers, he must still have a strong desire to reach the level of their actions; then he will merit growth according to his talents (*Sichos Mussar*, 5733:21).

Every person, without exception, is obligated to set a goal of top performance, in the style of the forefathers. Every person must aspire to greatness, even if he or she thinks it cannot be done.[2] With a goal-oriented attitude, he or she will grow and succeed.

While *Chazal* emphasized the importance of goals in regard to spiritual growth, the same idea applies to any project. If a person sets a goal and has a strong desire to reach it, he stands a greater chance of achieving the goal than if he would never have set it in the first place.

Plan goals. Setting a goal and aspiring to reach it is not enough; there has to be a *plan* and a *commitment* to attain the result. King Shlomo said it this way:

> [If] the thoughts of a person take into account the end, whatever he does will be profitable. But [if] one does not look toward the end, all his work is lost (*Mishlei* 21:5).

---

1. *Tanna d'Bei Eliyahu Rabbah* 25.
2. See Rabbi Chaim Shmulevitz, *Sichos Mussar*, 5732:28.

Here, King Shlomo compared the one who plans goals to the one who does not. He called the planner "a person who takes into account the end." This person knows what he wants and finds a way to get it. But the one who does not look toward an end result — that is, he does not plan goals — is unproductive and will not succeed.

From the words of King Shlomo and Rabbi Chaim Shmulevitz, we see that success is the result of setting a goal, making a reasonable plan to reach it, and — obviously — following the plan. To the degree that a person sets a goal and lives by it, he or she will see success in life. Simply speaking, you get what you set.

In a discussion about reaching spiritual goals such as correcting bad *middos* and improving the quality of *mitzvah* performance, Rabbi Shlomo Wolbe wrote:

> We must be aware of this extremely important fact: Whatever a person truthfully wants, he will get in his lifetime. And what a person gets in his lifetime is a reflection of what his will has always been (*Alei Shur*, p. 121).

You get what you set. If you truly want to correct a bad *middah*, you will. If you truly want to improve your *mitzvah* performance, you will. And if you do not succeed, it is an indication of a deficiency in the desire to make those improvements in the first place.

Some people, instead of blaming their lack of success in spiritual matters on themselves, blame it on Hashem. As if they did everything in their power to bring about the desired result, they say, "I failed because Hashem did not offer His help."

Rabbi Wolbe warned against taking this attitude: "The lack of success is testimony either to his weak will or his not using his will altogether."[1] If a person misses a goal, it means his will was never strong enough in the first place. In other words, he never really committed himself to the goal.

You get what you set. Did you ever think about the specific kind of family, social and spiritual life you want to have — and devise a way of achieving it? Did you ever think about the kind of career you want to have, the home you want to live in, how much money you want in your bank account — and make a plan to get it?

---

1. *Alei Shur*, p. 122.

When you commit yourself to a specific set of goals and make a plan to achieve them, you increase the chances of a good outcome. But if you do not have any specific goals, you have nothing to strive for, and you may never reach your potential or get what you want out of life. King Shlomo said it this way:

> An intelligent son gathers in the summer. An embarrassing son sleeps soundly during the harvest (*Mishlei* 10:5).

The embarrassing, or foolish, person has no goal. He sleeps soundly, plans nothing, and does nothing. The result? He becomes nothing. The wise person, on the other hand, "gathers in the summer." He had specific goals beforehand and made an effort to reach them. Because he *planned* for something and *did* something, he *becomes* something.

If the only reason you go to work today is because that is what you did yesterday, you are not coming any closer to a goal which you probably never had anyway, and if you have no goals you will not achieve as much as you otherwise can.

Setting new goals involves risk-taking. Esther had a tendency to become impatient. She wanted to correct this bad *middah,* so she decided to remain patient whenever the situation called for it. If in the end she succeeds, she can say that her efforts were put to good use. But if in the end she still continues to lose her patience, all her work will have been in vain. There is a risk in trying to reach the goal, because keeping patient can be very difficult, and only with a great deal of effort and determination can it be done.

Moshe wanted to open a clothing store. Before reaching this goal, however, he had to obtain the capital to purchase a shop, and he also had to learn the business. If the business succeeds, all his efforts will have been put to good use. But if it fails, he will have lost a great deal of time, effort and start-up costs. It is a gamble, and the only way to win is by taking the risk.

If Esther and Moshe do not like to take risks, they may avoid their goals altogether. This is understandable. However, they may be taking a greater risk by *not* setting these goals, because without them, Esther will retain a bad *middah* and Moshe will remain financially insecure. The risk they are taking by avoiding the new goal may be greater than the risk of taking it on.

We can illustrate this point with the captain of a ship who plans a route to get to his destination. He knows that there will be risks and dangers throughout the voyage, but he still goes ahead with the plan. Why? Because if he does not make a plan and allows the ship to go in the direction of any wind, he may end up on some uninhabited, rocky shore. True, his plan involves some risk, but if he were not to make the plan he would be taking a *bigger* risk.

Are you hesitating to make some sort of personal or professional change? If you are, take a moment to consider the consequences of *not* making the change. Ask yourself if you are prepared to stay the way you are. Like the captain with no plan, you may be taking a greater risk by maintaining the status quo.

Project the outcome. When you hold a stick at one end and raise it from the ground, what happens to the other end? It rises too. It is one stick, and you cannot expect the other half to remain behind. Knowing that a stick has two ends, your decision to raise one end is also a decision to raise the other.

Every action has a logical reaction. It is one of life's natural laws. Choose an action and you concurrently choose the outcome, the other end of the stick. The consequence of the action is just as much a part of your decision as the action itself.

Take, for example, an overweight person who chooses to eat too much. (After all, nobody eats by accident!) Whenever he decides to eat a cream-filled pastry or a second portion at dinner, he also decides to remain overweight — the other side of the stick. But when he chooses not to eat it, he is also choosing to weigh less.

Your choice of an action is simultaneously the choice of a reaction. Therefore, it is important to project the outcome of your decision:

> "Which is the good way to which a person should cling? . . . He should see the outcome (*Avos* 2:9)." He looks carefully at everything and sees all the outcomes before they happen. When the thing is rewarding in the beginning but leads to a loss in the end, he avoids it. By doing this, he will never sin because he considers the reward of a sin in relation to its loss. Therefore, a person should cling to this way, to think in the beginning what will be in the end, and to plan all affairs with this idea (Rabbeinu Yonah, ad loc.).

Your decision to pursue a new goal is a decision to improve your set of circumstances. Your decision to refrain from the goal is a decision to stay the way you are. You only have yourself to blame for the consequence of your decision.

Goals Motivate

When you recognize your responsibilities and commit yourself to them, an inner drive emerges.

> "Have you seen a man quick in his work?" (*Mishlei* 22:29). This refers to Yosef, as it is written, "And he came to the house to do his work."[1] It was theater day . . . and all the people went to watch, but Yosef went to his work, overseeing his master's finances (*Midrash Rabbah, Shir HaShirim* 1:1).

Yosef was called "quick in his work" because he did what he was supposed to do while everyone else was at the theater. The question is: Just because Yosef tended to his duties, why was he called "quick in his work"? What is the relationship between dedication and quickness?

Rabbi Chaim Mordechai Katz explained that when a person has a clear perception of his mission and is committed to it, he does his work quickly and without hesitation. In other words, clarity of mission motivates. Yosef's mission was clear — to oversee his master's finances. Once we see that Yosef had a clear goal, we can deduce that he was quick in his work, too.[2]

Nobody would have stopped Yosef from going to the theater or from pursuing any other activity. But Yosef chose to fulfill his duty instead. Why? Because he was committed to it and always steered himself in its direction. His strong commitment to reach his goal created an inner drive. *Just by having a goal, he was motivated to reach it.*

Motivated goal-setters find solutions. Once a person is motivated to reach a goal, he will naturally go in its direction. And when challenges arise, he finds ways to overcome them.

---

1. *Bereishis* 39:11.
2. *Be'er Mechokek*, p. 22.

The lazy person says, "An old lion is in the way, and a young lion is between the streets" (*Mishlei* 26:13).

Why is this person called lazy? If there is a lion, he is not lazy; he is justifiably scared. And if there is no lion, he is also not lazy; he is a liar.

Indeed, there is a lion outside; nevertheless, if this person were motivated — that is, if he had a clear mission — he would avoid the lion by digging a tunnel or climbing the rooftops. He would tap into his resources, search for a solution, and find a way to reach his goal.

However, this is not the case. This person is not committed to a mission and does not even try to avoid the obstacles that get in his way. Instead of looking for solutions, he looks for excuses. So when he sees the lion outside, he excuses himself from his duties — as any lazy person would do.[1]

A lazy person looks for excuses, but a motivated goal-setter looks for solutions. A lazy person justifies his inactivity by saying, "I am not able to do it. It is way above my capabilities. Why should I even bother trying?"[2]

But a motivated goal-setter says, "If there is a problem, I will find a solution." He constantly asks, "How am I going to solve the problem and get what I want?" Even when there are no apparent solutions, constantly asking this simple question to himself may lead to a solution.

There is a fascinating story of a man who found a solution to his problem by constantly asking himself how he was going to get what he wanted. During the Holocaust, this man was a prisoner in a concentration camp. He desperately wanted to escape and always shared his dream with others. Their only response was, "Stop thinking such nonsense. There is no way out." But this was not enough for him. He was obsessed with the idea of escaping. He kept asking, "How am I going to escape?"

One day he noticed a pile of corpses in a truck, waiting to be taken outside the camp for burial. Here he found an answer to his question. He would climb into the pile, pretending that he was also dead, and leave the camp along with the others. So he quickly

---

1. Ibid., p. 21.
2. *Sichos Mussar,* 5732:28.

undressed himself and jumped into the pile. As more corpses were loaded into the truck, he felt their weight, coldness and stench pressing in on him, but he knew he had to stay until he could safely break away.

The truck finally started its motor and began to cart its load to an open grave outside the camp. As the driver dumped the corpses into the giant hole, he had no idea that there was one live person among them.

The escapee stayed in the open grave until night, when he felt sure that he could run away unnoticed. Still undressed, he made his way through the pile of twisted human limbs and ran twenty miles to freedom.

This man had a single goal: escape. He kept asking, "How am I going to escape?" He was obsessed, and because of his obsession, he found the answer — in a pile of corpses. He had a mission, and he kept asking how he could accomplish it until he found a solution.

Goals can motivate a lazy person. How can the lazy person raise himself out of his lethargy and become motivated? Is there a strategy? Yes, there is. King Shlomo, the wisest of men, told us what it is:

> Lazy one, go to an ant, observe its ways and become wise. Without a chief, overseer or ruler, it prepares its bread in the summer and gathers its food in the harvest (*Mishlei* 6:6-8).
>
> What lesson did King Shlomo want to teach a lazy person? The Rabbis said that the ant has three chambers [in its dwelling]. It does not use the upper one because of moisture; it does not use the lower one because of mud; it uses the middle one. The ant only lives six months . . . and its total life intake is one and a half kernels of wheat. Yet in the summer, it gathers all it finds . . . Why does it do this? Because it says, "Maybe Hashem will give me long life and I will be prepared to eat" (*Midrash Rabbah, Shoftim* 5:2).

The ant recognizes its responsibility — to prepare for the future — and is committed to it. Because of its strong sense of mission, the ant is motivated to collect all the food it finds and to create an elaborate system of chambers to protect the food.

Here, King Shlomo offered the lazy person a strategy to emerge from his lethargy and become motivated: Set a goal and become committed to it. Once this is accomplished, a strong inner drive develops and motivation replaces laziness.[1]

Goals Give Direction

Did you ever wonder how a missile is able to locate and strike a target thousands of miles away? Let us look at two missiles employed during the Persian Gulf War, the Patriot, used to intercept Scud missiles, and the Tomahawk, used to strike targets deep within enemy territory. The Patriot detects a reflected radar signal from the Scud and is directed toward it, while the Tomahawk has the target's coordinates and a "road map" programmed into its guidance system. Like a lighthouse that guides ships at sea toward the shore, the targets guide the missiles in their direction.

As elementary as it sounds, reaching the target is not so simple, because a missile usually veers off course while in flight. It must therefore be equipped with a mechanism that will bring it back on course. This is where the target comes in. The missile is equipped with an "eye" that is always trained on the target. Whenever it goes off course, it "sees" the target and makes the necessary adjustment. In effect, then, the target guides the missile in its own direction.

Now, what if the missile would have no specific target? Aimed at nothing in particular, it would self-destruct in the air or simply fall to the ground whenever its fuel was depleted.

Similarly, a goal leads a person in its direction. This means that whenever a person goes off course, he can bring himself back by focusing on the goal and making the proper adjustment.

Take for example, a yeshivah student who has made a commitment to master a specific area of learning. He sets a deadline, then he immerses himself in the project. After several weeks, a friend invites him to spend a few days in his mountain vacation home. The student considers the offer, but then he asks himself a key question: "Will this trip help or hinder my plan?" He realizes that the trip will keep him from reaching his goal, so he declines the offer. Just as a

---

1. *Be'er Mechokek,* pp. 21-22; *Sichos Mussar,* loc. cit.

missile uses its target to help it come back on course, this student has used his goal to help bring him back on course.

Suppose this student did not have a specific objective or deadline. He may have been serious about his studies, but as long as he did not have a specific goal, he might have justified the trip, saying, "Oh, the trip won't interfere with my plans. I can always learn when I return." After all, the trip does not interfere with anything since he has no goal anyway. The Vilna Gaon put it succinctly:

> The person who learns Torah for an end result will always see a benefit, because he constantly reviews what he learns and finds new meanings . . . But the aimless person who does not look forward to an end result and instead tries to grab too much at once loses everything (Vilna Gaon, *Mishlei* 21:5).

This rule does not apply only to Torah scholarship; it is the same for learning a trade, doing business, making friends, raising children or refining a character trait.

For example, a salesman who sets a goal of making twenty sales by the end of the month has an advantage over the salesman without a goal, or one whose only goal is "to sell as much as conveniently possible."

The salesman without the goal may waste his time in idle conversation or other unproductive activities. When his wife tells him that there is no milk in the house for the next day, he may run off to the store instead of waiting until evening or borrowing from a neighbor. When he hears a *thump thump* sound from his tire, he may immediately drive over to the mechanic and, without asking the mechanic to hurry, leave the car there for the entire day. Why shouldn't he? The milk and the mechanic cannot possibly interfere with his plans, because he either has none or they are not clear.

The salesman with the goal, however, does not waste time in idle activity, nor does he think of reasons to stay home or become involved with other matters. When his wife tells him that she needs milk, or when he hears a sound from his tire, he deals with the problem in a way that interferes with his business as little as possible. His goal is always in front of him and he avoids any activity that will distract him from reaching it.

Similarly, the parent of a child who has been failing math may set a goal of motivating the child to improve his math grade by fifteen points before the end of the month. This parent has an advantage over the parent with no goal at all, or whose only goal is "to motivate the child to do better."

The parent with the specific goal does not stop after a few failed attempts or any other obstacle. Instead, she seeks ways of helping her child improve and continues her efforts until the improvement occurs. The parent without the clear goal, however, has nothing specific to strive for and may stop coaxing the child after several failed attempts, or perhaps after the child improves by just a few points.

Serious goal-setters are like missiles with a target; *because* they have a specific destination, they can reach their potential. On the other hand, people who do not set clear goals are like missiles without a target; without a clear destination, they may "fall to the ground."

The ant in King Shlomo's lesson illustrates this idea. The ant is fixed on a goal of gathering huge quantities of food. Because it is constantly aware of its goal, it does not get involved with unrelated activities and is always drawn toward its mission.

Our forefather Yaakov modeled the same idea. When Yaakov was instructed by his father to go to Lavan's house, he hesitated. He wanted to avoid Lavan because he was afraid that Lavan's evil lifestyle would interfere with his goal of righteousness. Yaakov's internal guidance system, so to speak, sent his feet a message that going to Lavan's house meant going off course, so he instinctively made the adjustment to stay on course. Yaakov followed the direction of his goal — he went to the yeshivah of Shem and Ever.

However, when he dreamed of the ladder and received a guarantee from Hashem that he would be protected from physical and spiritual harm, he willingly embarked on the journey. With Lavan no longer a threat to his welfare, Yaakov was able to make the adjustment to include Lavan's house in his set of goals. His "heart" sent a message to his feet to take him there.[1] Once again, Yaakov followed the direction of his goal.

---

1. See Rashi, *Bereishis* 28:15 and 29:1.

There are people who say, "Life offers me nothing." Their problem may really be that they lack a meaningful goal. Without a goal they have no direction, so they think they have nothing to live for. But if they had a meaningful goal, they would be drawn in its direction, and life would take on a different cast.

Now the question is: How does a goal have the power to draw a person in its direction?

You become what you think about. Whenever you make a serious commitment to reach a goal, it takes center stage in your mind. Constantly aware of your objective, you almost automatically make sure that all your actions are consistent with it. Pursuing the goal then becomes second nature.

> If a person has a commitment, all his senses act as instruments which bring out his thoughts and commitments to action . . . [because] after a commitment, nothing more is needed (Rabbi Dovid Bleicher, *Divrei Binah U'Mussar,* pp. 141-142).

After committing yourself to a goal, you instinctively use all your powers to reach it. Like the squirrel, who is unstoppable in its search for food, reaching the goal becomes second nature.

Concerning spiritual goals, Rabbi Shlomo Wolbe wrote:

> When a person succeeds in his aspiration to come close to Hashem and His service, he does so because of his will, because his will is occupied with only one thing — to become close to Hashem. His will draws all his physical and mental powers to be directed toward this goal . . .
>
> The one who wants to serve Hashem with the *middah* of *chessed* only needs to be strong in his will to do *chessed,* and Hashem will help him see where and how to do acts of *chessed . . .*
>
> This is all we need to do: to constantly strengthen our will . . . (*Alei Shur,* pp. 120-121).

You become what you think about. Both your mind and body become focused in the direction of your thoughts and attitudes. Whether your thoughts are clear and directed, or unclear and chaotic, they dictate your pattern. This means that you can become more like the person you want to become and increase your chances of getting what you want by focusing on your goal and following a plan to reach it.

Goals Energize

On the street corners of major cities, you can observe thriving grocery stores owned and operated by Asian immigrants. When these immigrants arrived on the shores of the United States, they came with little more than the clothes on their backs, yet after several years they built successful businesses and became financially independent.

On the same street corners you can observe homeless men and women who spend their days begging, searching through trash, and traipsing aimlessly down the avenue. After many years, they continue to depend on public funds for their very existence.

At one time, both the immigrant and the homeless person had no income. But after several years, the immigrant came out way ahead. What was his secret?

The immigrant was driven by a burning desire for financial independence. With this desire pushing him forward, he generated the energy needed to reach his goal. He got a job and earned an income. He then took his small savings, opened a grocery store, and worked to make it successful. All his daily activities were directed toward his goal; he woke up in the morning and went to sleep at night thinking about it. He never gave up; whenever a problem arose, he always found a solution.

The homeless person also had a goal — simply to get through the day. And that is exactly what he did. All he wanted was to find enough food to stay alive and enough clothing to protect himself from the elements. He had a simple goal, and he generated just enough energy to reach it.

There is a saying: It is not so much what we do for our goals as what our goals do for us. We all generate enough energy to reach our goals. If our goal is to get through the day, we generate that much energy, which is not very much. Like the lazy person in *Mishlei*, we would think of excuses instead of solutions. But if we are committed to a higher goal, we generate the right amount of energy to reach that as well. Like the motivated ant in *Mishlei*, we would always be thinking of solutions instead of excuses.

Why do goals energize? In Chapter One, we showed how actions influence attitude. With this, we can understand why goals are able to energize. When one is committed to a goal and actively tries to reach it, his mind becomes aligned with the activity. With his mind "breathing" the same excitement as his hands, he becomes energized to pursue the goal.

Suppose a person wants to sew a dress but hesitates and delays. How can she become more excited and energetic about the project? By beginning to sew. Once she gets involved in the activity, the activity itself draws her in its direction. The activity creates the excitement and attitude needed to see the project through.

Another example is *Daf Yomi. Daf Yomi,* meaning "one page a day," is a fixed schedule of daily Talmudic study. With a long-term goal of completing the entire Talmud every seven years, the *Daf Yomi* plan calls on its followers to learn just one page each and every day. Although there are some days when it is very difficult to complete the page, dedicated followers always fulfill their daily commitment with no excuses. Instead of dozing on the bus or subway, they voraciously learn the *daf.* Even on busy days, they squeeze some learning in between appointments or late at night, even if it means losing some sleep.

What gives these people the extraordinary energy and willpower to pursue their goal? The answer is the goal itself. Once they are committed to finishing the *daf,* they generate the right amount of energy to do it.

The power of the *Daf Yomi* plan is that it obligates its followers to reach a daily goal. One just has to commit himself to that goal, and somehow he finds the inner resources to achieve it. But if he would only be committed to learning as much of the *daf* as is conveniently possible, he would not have the willpower to complete the page on busy days. He would feel justified in postponing the day's learning session whenever it becomes inconvenient.

Did you ever attend a wedding and see a man sitting in a corner, hunched over a pocket-size *gemara* and lost in thought, while all the other celebrants mingle nearby? You may have thought, "Why is this man doing such an odd thing? Is he antisocial? Or is he simply introverted?"

This man is probably neither. He simply has a goal. He is driven to complete the *daf*, knowing that if he does not complete it then, he will have to do it when he gets home after midnight. His goal keeps him focused and energized, even if everyone around him is doing something else.

Every serious yeshivah student knows that when he sets a goal to complete a topic of Torah by a certain deadline, such as before an upcoming vacation, he finds time that he would otherwise not "have" to do the work. While waiting for a lecture or *davening* to begin, he grabs the chance to study a few lines. While waiting in line at the bank, supermarket or cleaners, he pulls out his pocket edition and learns a few more lines. His goal gives him the drive to transform "dead time" into "opportunity time." The student with no specific goal or deadline, however, uses this time to think about his summer vacation, home repairs or any other item that crosses his mind. For him, "dead time" holds no real value or opportunity.

This rule applies to any goal, whether it is related to Torah study, business, character development, making friends or raising children. Armed with a commitment, you find the strength to perform in a way that would not have been possible otherwise.

Serious goal-setters do not procrastinate or get side-tracked. Procrastinators think there is no reason to do a task today if they can just as well do it tomorrow. They don't even need an excuse — the possibility of doing it tomorrow justifies the plan. For them, "tomorrow" is the greatest time-saving device of all times!

A person with a serious commitment to a goal thinks differently. Because he wants to reach the goal, he does not look for excuses to avoid it. Nor does he need the motivation of *Chazal*'s suggestion, "If not now, when?";[1] rather, his *commitment* and *desire* to achieve the goal energize him to complete the project.

Similarly, a serious goal-setter does not become side-tracked, allowing other interests to divert his attention, because he realizes that changing gears may leave him short of the goal. On the other

---

1. *Avos* 1:14.

hand, an uncommitted person may shift gears and start something new every time an interesting diversion comes his way.

Eliezer, the servant of our forefather Avraham, is an example of a serious goal-setter. He had a mission — to find a wife for Yitzchak. When he found the fitting wife, she introduced him to her family and invited him for a meal. But he declined the invitation until he received their permission to take Rivkah back to his master. Once they gave her permission to go, they invited Eliezer to stay a few more days. But he insisted on returning immediately to Avraham with Rivkah.

Eliezer had the opportunity to procrastinate or become sidetracked by accepting the hospitality of his host before taking care of business. Instead, he quickly finished his business and did not allow himself to become distracted.[1]

Similarly, when Avraham and his father Terach traveled from their native country to Canaan, Terach stopped in Charan and never reached his ultimate destination. Avraham, however, continued to travel; he did not stop until he reached Canaan. Avraham understood the importance of seeing a project through to the end.[2]

Goals Give You an Identity

What concerns you? What excites you? This is important, because your interests are a reflection of who you are. By discovering what is important to you, you can discover the real YOU. And the way to discover what is important to you is to look at the goals you have set for yourself. Used in this way, goals are a looking-glass into your personality.

Take, for example, a successful businessman who neglects his family, working twelve hours a day at the office. His wife complains that making money is obviously more important to him than his family, but he disagrees.

How can he discover who is right? He can analyze what it is that truly occupies and concerns him. He may begin to realize that making money is actually more important to him than his family. He will

---

1. Ralbag, *HaDe'os V'HaMiddos, Sha'ar HaCharitzus* 12.
2. *Chofetz Chaim Al HaTorah, Bereishis* 12:5.

then be in a position to make the appropriate adjustments in his life-style, if he so desires.

Setting Clear Goals

In the work place, managers do not always clarify an employee's job description. One reason is that they themselves do not have a clear idea of what the employee is supposed to do. It is easier to give general instructions, leaving responsibilities open and vague, rather than narrow down a specific set of expectations.

Another reason some managers avoid clear job descriptions is that they believe that any job is forever changing. They say, "Why should I tell the employee exactly what he is supposed to do when it may change next week?" Once again, it is easier to avoid a clear job description altogether.

The problem is: How can an employee possibly be successful when he does not know exactly what he is supposed to do? And how can a manager even *expect* an employee to fulfill a task about which he himself is not clear?

Furthermore, without a clear set of goals, an employee always stands the chance of being reprimanded for not doing something he did not know he was supposed to do, or vice versa. With different sets of expectations, the employee thinks he is doing his job properly — but the manager may not see things that way.

It is not enough to do things *right*; a person has to do the right *things!* That is why it is so necessary to have clear, specific goals. An employee will then know what he has to do, and a manager will know what he has to supervise. And when it comes time to criticize an employee, the manager can go back to the list of goals to see if the expectations were clearly defined.

It is the same with any goal. Whether it is between an employer and an employee, a parent and a child, a husband and a wife, or you and yourself, the rule is: You get what you set. Set a clear goal, and you stand a strong chance of achieving a good performance, satisfactory to all parties involved. Set an unclear goal, and you stand a strong chance of turning out a poor performance. The quality of a performance is often a reflection of the clarity of the goal.

Clear goals are a basis for evaluation. Try this experiment one day. Ask a worker to rate his performance on the job. Some typical responses are "I *think* I am doing okay"; "The boss did not criticize me today"; "No news is good news."

Why can't this person evaluate himself without the input of his manager? One reason, among many, may be that he is unclear about his goals. He is not really sure what he is supposed to accomplish. Therefore, he cannot evaluate his own performance.

Not only is he unable to evaluate himself, his manager would also find it difficult. With unclear goals, neither has a standard on which to base the evaluation. But with a clear set of goals, there *is* a clear standard. Both would know how the employee is doing by comparing his actual performance with that required by the previously set standard. The manager would also be able to use that standard as an anchor for praise or criticism.

Reaching clear goals motivates. Success breeds success. A person who performs successfully is motivated to perform well the next time, too. But if he is not sure what is expected of him, he will not be motivated, even if he does perform well.

Suppose you are bowling. Every time you roll the ball down the alley, you hit some pins. But there is one problem: you cannot see how many pins you knocked down because a thick cloth hangs down in front of them. So every time the ball clears the cloth and hits the pins, you never know if you hit seven, nine, or maybe even all ten. How excited would you be? How motivated would you be to bowl another game?

Now suppose you are baking a cake. You prepare a batter and put it into the oven. Then you walk away, never to see or taste the finished product. How excited would you be about the cake? How motivated would you be to bake another one?

In both cases you would probably not be excited about the performance or motivated to repeat it, because you never see the end result. You don't know how many pins you have knocked down or how the cake tastes. You have no idea if you have succeeded or not. But if you knew how well you bowled and how the cake tasted, and you were satisfied with it, you would probably be more motivated to repeat those performances.

Anybody trying to reach any goal can only become excited about his performance when he knows how well he is doing. And the only way he can know is by having a clear picture of the goal he is supposed to reach. He can then see if his performance meets the standard of the goal. Only with clearly defined goals can he evaluate his own performance. Then, after he evaluates himself well, he will become motivated to repeat the performance.

Take One Step at a Time

Suppose you are learning how to type. Your goal is to type sixty words per minute. But after four weeks, you can type only thirty. Would you be justified in becoming frustrated over the slow progress?

Suppose a first-grade teacher is teaching her class how to read. After three months, the students are still having difficulty forming small words. Would the teacher be justified in becoming frustrated over the slow progress?

Although many people do become frustrated in these circumstances, if the progress made is within reason, this feeling is unjustified. To explain this, let us look at the job of a bricklayer. When a bricklayer begins to construct a building, he has little to show for his work. But as time goes on and the building begins to take shape, his achievement is obvious. If he did a good job, in a timely fashion, he can look at his product and be proud of his accomplishment.

Reaching goals follows the same principle. Some goals need hours or days, and some need weeks, months or years to achieve. However, each step in the direction of the goal is a small incremental achievement which, after time, takes on the shape of the finished product. Like a bricklayer, the only way to reach the end is to take one step at a time.

Chazal recommended such an attitude for a person who is learning Torah:

> A foolish person says, "When will I learn the entire Torah?" A wise person learns one section every day until he finishes the entire Torah (*Vayikra Rabbah* 19:2, *Devarim Rabbah* 8:3).

Torah is too extensive to learn quickly — or even in a lifetime. But when a person takes one step at a time — that is, he learns a little every day — it adds up, and he becomes a *talmid chochom.*

This idea applies to all areas of life — whether one is learning Torah, learning to type, or teaching a class. When a person takes one step at a time, and he is progressing reasonably, there is no reason to become frustrated if the progress is slower than he would like. As long as he is doing the right things and is making reasonable progress every day, he will eventually reach the final goal.

Setting Attainable Goals

Suppose you have a temper and you decide to control it. You set a goal: to remain completely calm whenever you feel angry. Starting immediately, you prepare to suppress your anger totally instead of blowing up.

On that very same day, something triggers your temper. Realizing that you did not keep the commitment, you recommit yourself to the goal. But after several days, you once again lose your temper, and after several more days, you lose your temper again. It is becoming obvious that you are not achieving your goal.

This scenario is not farfetched, because your goal is unattainable. You cannot possibly suppress your anger totally just because you decide to. Your temper is so ingrained that it is nearly impossible to crush it in one abrupt effort. One who saw his inability to make such a sweeping change might easily become discouraged and give up altogether.

For this reason, the anger should be diminished in small, gradual, attainable steps. The first time something triggers your temper, try counting to twenty before blowing up. The next time, count to fifteen. Continue gradually, until you have taken control of your temper. By making the goal attainable, you become motivated to reach it.

It is the same with any goal. People are not motivated to work toward a goal they perceive as inaccessible. Even when they appreciate a goal's benefit, they may decide they are incapable of reaching it if the goal is too difficult.

It is especially important to consider the feasibility of a goal for children. Rabbi Shlomo Wolbe wrote, "Any demand that is above the age level of the child is likely to have a negative impact on his soft heart."[1] This means that expecting a child to reach an unattainable goal is not only ineffective, it can be damaging.

Sometimes a goal is within reach, but you lack confidence, or experience what is called "a mental block." Although you have the ability to do it, you think you cannot succeed and impose a limitation on yourself.

If you realize that it is only a lack of self-confidence that is holding you back, you can take measures to overcome the limitation. One strategy is to work toward the final goal in small incremental stages. Another is to try to reach the goal at a lower level of performance. Yet another strategy is to achieve just one portion of the goal.

As you make small steps in the right direction, you come closer to the end goal and begin to see it as a reality. Then, as it comes within reach, you begin to believe that you can actually achieve it.

Short-Term and Long-Term Goals

I am acquainted with a computer programmer who worked on a single project for an entire year. The company was sold, and before the new program was even put into production, the new owners dropped it and went on to other projects. After working for an entire year on a project that was rejected, the programmer felt dejected. She had intended to produce, but looking at her short-term productivity, she saw a total lack of accomplishment.

Now suppose this programmer had a long-term goal — for example, to gain experience so that she could open a consulting business of her own. If this were the case, she may have felt productive even after all her work was rejected. Why? Because she was getting the experience she needed to move onward. As far as her long-term goal was concerned, she was very productive.

When you only have short-term goals, every setback is significant. Since you focus on the current performance only, you feel the impact of any failure. But when you have long-term goals, you do

---

1. *Alei Shur*, p. 263.

not perceive every setback as a failure. You tolerate those difficulties because your focus is on something bigger and better. What you see in the present pales in significance to the factors that really make a difference to you in the future.

Setting High Goals

Once you decide to reach a goal and are committed to it, you reach into your resources and do what you can to achieve it. The bigger the goal, the deeper you reach. The deeper you reach, the greater your personal achievement. For this reason, setting high goals makes you a better person; it forces you to reach deep into your resources, drawing out the "Big You."

Some people, however, only set small goals. They think they have weak potential and will not be able to reach the big goals. They are like the fisherman who throws back all the big fish because he only owns a small frying pan.

How do people form their expectations of themselves? Many simply observe themselves and instinctively derive conclusions about their abilities. If they decide that they have strong abilities, they form high expectations for themselves. If they decide they have weak abilities, they form low expectations.

The problem is that they may have hidden talents and abilities waiting to be uncovered. They may be able to reach the big goals but instead rely on their instincts and form negative conclusions. They lower their expectations and allow their hidden talents to go untapped. They suppress their own growth.

There are many examples of people who developed their hidden talents by reaching deep into themselves to become paradigms of excellence. In Chapter Two, we illustrated this idea with Rabbi Akiva and Rabbi Eliezer ben Hurkenus, who began their Torah careers late in life and excelled beyond anyone's wildest imagination.

King Dovid is another example. When Shmuel the prophet asked Yishai, Dovid's father, to present all his sons so he could designate the one Hashem had chosen to be king, Yishai did not even bring Dovid in from the fields. When Shmuel finally met Dovid, Shmuel was still unsure that Dovid was the chosen one until Hashem confirmed that he was, in fact, His choice. Dovid had already worked on himself, quietly, and he went on to become one of our greatest leaders.[1]

Everybody has hidden talents waiting to emerge. That is why big goals are so important. Big goals tap those resources and subsequently bring out the "Big You."

The Goal Must Be Yours, Not Someone Else's

Some people get involved with goals that are not of their own making. One example is the young man who has an interest in business but goes to medical school because his parents tell him, "You are going to be a doctor." Another is the budding *talmid chochom* who stops his program of intensive Torah study because his rich uncle tells him, "You have to get a job."

In each case, one person sets the goal for the other. The problem is that the one who is trying to reach it is working toward a goal that is not his own. He will probably have minimal interest and limited motivation.

Whenever others tell you what to do and you listen, if you are not entirely persuaded that the goal they proposed is correct and beneficial to you, you may quickly lose interest and never succeed. How *can* you succeed? You don't really want it in the first place! You may ask yourself the key motivating question, "What's in it for me?" and the answer may be, "Not too much." With little personal gain, you naturally may not work to your potential. This principle applies to all areas of life:

> A person does an action to receive a benefit or to avoid a loss, and if not for this, the action is meaningless to him (Rambam, *Pirush HaMishnayos, Sanhedrin,* Ch. 10).
>
> A person only learns from a place that his heart desires (Talmud *Avodah Zarah* 19a).
>
> Every person is interested in his own needs more than yours (Rabbi Eliyahu Dessler, *Michtav M'Eliyahu,* Vol. 4, p. 244).

When you try to reach someone else's goal, the likelihood is that you will see little or no personal benefit in it. Your commitment will

---

1. *Shmuel 1,* Ch. 16, and *Yalkut Shimoni* there.

be weak, and you will not make the appropriate effort to overcome the inevitable obstacles that will face you. However, when the goal is yours and there is a personal gain, you will be motivated to succeed and determined to overcome anything that gets in your way.

A Goal-Setting Formula

Some people do not know *how* to set a goal or make a plan to reach it. For this reason, success often eludes them. If they had a formula to plug into and follow, they would possibly find success. If you share this problem, you may find the following seven-step formula helpful.

1) *Determine the goal(s).* Ask, "What results do I want to see?" Then ask, "What's in it for me?" and "Am I proud to pursue this goal?"

Before you are able to make a plan to reach any outcome, you first have to know the result you want to see. You will then be able to pursue it most effectively, and the chances of reaching it are greater. You also have to derive a benefit from the goal and be proud of achieving it; otherwise, you will lose interest in it.

It is a good idea to list the goals and their benefits on paper. This clarifies your objectives and may motivate you to pursue them.

2) *Establish priorities.* Did you ever set multiple goals, with the intention of reaching them all? There is nothing wrong with this, as long as you are able to reach them and do not find yourself pulled in too many directions.

However, if there are too many to reach, you may begin to focus on the least important objectives while overlooking the most important ones. And if you feel overburdened by the load, you may surrender to the pressure and quit before fulfilling even one objective. Although you wanted to accomplish a great deal, the number of tasks lying ahead actually holds you back from progress. What can you do about it?

Establish priorities. Make a list of all your goals and assign a level of importance to each. Then pursue the most important ones. After reaching those goals, begin to pursue the less important ones.

3) *Make a plan of action.* Before embarking on a sea voyage, the captain of a ship plans a route. He then uses the ship's controls to

navigate the ship along the planned route. As rough seas and strong winds take the ship off course, the captain uses his navigational equipment once again to bring the ship back on track.

What if the captain does not plan a route or use his navigational equipment to reach his destination? He is looking for trouble. The ship will begin to go in the direction of any wind and will probably beach on some rocky shore, never to reach its destination.

The captain has a goal — his destination. But this will not help him unless he also has a plan of action. The same rule applies to a business person, parent, student, or anybody with a goal; along with the goal, there must be a clear plan of action. Otherwise, that person may end up on a rocky shore, empty-handed.

When making a plan of action, ask these key questions: What? When? Where? Who? . . . *What* steps must I take to achieve the goal? *When* must I take each step? *Where* will each step take place? *Who* will be involved in each step? Answering these questions may be tedious and time-consuming, but one thing is certain — a few hours of planning *now* can save hours or days of unproductive activity *later*.[1]

Don't be surprised if you are not able to follow the plan as designed. At any point, unexpected snags and hurdles may arise, in which case the plan must be modified to meet the circumstances.

4) *Decide how to manage time efficiently.* Ask, "How much time is needed to achieve the goal? What must be done first? What can wait? When will I work at it?"

There are only twenty-four hours in a day, and using that time wisely will result in optimal success. Therefore, decide carefully how to manage your time, and avoid getting sidetracked by unrelated activities.

5) *Determine how achievements will be measured.* There is a simple formula to measure success: Look at what you have actually achieved compared to the result you wanted. To the degree that it matches, you are successful.

As simple as this is, many people choose a vague standard of measurement. Without knowing exactly how they are doing, they may never reach the goal they set in the first place.

---

1. *Mishlei* 21:5: "The thoughts of a person who plans are worthwhile" (following Rabbeinu Yonah's translation).

Suppose your goal is to lose weight. The proper way to measure the achievement is to look at the result you want and compare it to the number of ounces you actually took off, rather than looking at the vague fact that you weigh less this week than last week.

Suppose your goal is to excel in an academic pursuit. The proper way to measure success is to look at the grade you planned to receive and compare it to the grade you actually received, rather than looking at the vague fact that you are "doing better."

Suppose your goal is to refrain from *lashon hara*. The proper way to measure achievement is to look at the number of times you resolved to refrain from *lashon hara* and compare it to the number of times you actually refrained from *lashon hara*, rather than looking at the vague fact that you are "becoming more careful."

When you know exactly how successful you are, you will either continue at the same rate of progress or make adjustments. If you are progressing well, the success itself motivates you to continue performing at the same level. If you are progressing poorly, you can make the adjustments that will bring about the desired results.

6) *Set a target date.* Have you ever noticed how people often complete most of their work immediately before a deadline? Take, for example, the April 15 deadline for income tax preparation. Many people wait until the first or second week in April to do their taxes, although they had the ability to do them two or three months beforehand. Many people even wait until April 15, the actual deadline. This practice is so prevalent that post offices all around the country keep their doors open until midnight of April 15 to accommodate the people who wait until the very last minute.

Another example is the student who is assigned to do a book report. She does not even begin reading the book until three days before the deadline, although she was given the assignment four weeks earlier.

There are numerous other examples of people who wait until the last minute to do what they could have done days, weeks, even years earlier.

What if there would be no deadlines for taxes, book reports or anything else? Would students complete their book reports *this* year or *next* year? Would the taxpayer prepare his taxes four *months* or four *years* after the end of the tax year? How many people would fulfill their obligations in a timely manner? You know the answer.

Imagine for a moment that you receive a telephone call from friends who invite you and your spouse to an all-expenses-paid vacation on a private oceanfront villa. They tell you that the plane leaves the next morning at eight, and they need an answer now.

You really want to go, but as you consider the offer you realize that you have numerous things that have to be taken care of. You finally turn to your spouse and say, "I'm sorry. I don't think we can go. If we had more time, we would be able to tie up all the loose ends. But I just don't see how it is possible to do it in less than twenty-four hours."

Your spouse has other ideas. He quickly pulls out a sheet of paper and begins to take notes. What must be taken care of by tomorrow morning? What can wait until next week? What can we ask someone else to do? You and your spouse begin to make plans to meet the deadline.

Do you think that in the next twenty-four hours you will accomplish more than you would in any other twenty-four-hour period? Of course. Why? Because you have a deadline. If you miss it, you lose the vacation. The deadline is motivating, forcing you to find a way to do more than you would ever think possible in such a small amount of time.

Without a deadline, people delay, procrastinate, or push off the task indefinitely. With a deadline, however, people are forced to reach their goals within a specified time frame. They are motivated to meet the deadline because they know that missing it will result in an undesirable consequence. If you would make each day the day before an all-expenses-paid vacation, you might find that you are accomplishing more than you ever dreamed possible.

7) *Visualize reaching the goal.* In Chapter Two, we discussed visualization and the effect it has on successful performance. When you plan a goal, even before implementing it, visualize yourself going through each step. Also visualize the good feeling you will have after reaching the goal.

An illustration of the seven-step formula. Mordy was a forty-year-old man who weighed 235 pounds. He was always feeling weak and tired, so he visited his doctor. The doctor told him he was fifty pounds overweight and suggested that he go on a diet. He said, "Lose the weight slowly; it took years to put it on, so it makes no sense to take it off in a few months." Mordy accepted his doctor's advice.

Using the seven-step formula, he first asked himself, "What results do I want? Fifty pounds less fat." Then he asked, "What's in it for me? Will I be proud of my efforts?" He answered, "I will feel stronger, and I will no longer be embarrassed over my size." Answering these questions clarified his goal and motivated him to begin his weight-loss program.

The next step was to look at all his commitments and establish priorities. He learned *Daf Yomi* daily, and he volunteered his free time for important community projects. He was afraid that he would not be able to manage a new weight-loss program since he was already feeling the pressure of his job combined with his other commitments. Additionally, he had many *simchos* to attend, making it difficult to watch his diet.

Mordy knew that if he felt healthier he would be able to be more productive in general. So he looked at all his commitments and determined which he had to fulfill and which he could temporarily disregard. He prioritized his job, *Daf Yomi* and attending *simchos*, and put community involvement at the bottom of the list. "After all," he reasoned, "once I am healthy, I will be able to get involved again. And at that time my contribution will be even more meaningful."

As part of his action plan, he decided to attend his friends' *simchos*, but he would not eat at the reception and he would leave before dessert. He also decided to snack on fresh fruits and vegetables instead of junk food, and not to take a second portion at dinner.

He then set a deadline of one year to reach his goal. This meant that he would have to lose 4.2 pounds per month for twelve months, the equivalent of 2.13 ounces per day.

Mordy was still concerned about the pressure of the new commitment, so he decided to manage his time differently. He would attend the *Daf Yomi* class at night instead of early in the morning; this would give him a little more time to sleep in the morning and less time to snack at night. Managing his time in this way would help him reach all his goals with minimal pressure.

The next decision was how to measure his achievement. He decided to weigh himself every two days; this would give him an accurate assessment of his progress. If he saw he was not taking off 2.13 ounces per day, he would make sure to consume less calories every day.

After completing his action plan, Mordy visualized going through his daily activities while on a diet. He created images of walking away from fattening foods. In his mind's eye, he saw himself going to wedding receptions and not eating. He saw himself refraining from desserts, seconds and junk foods. He also visualized himself weighing fifty pounds less and feeling proud of it.

Putting Goals into Writing

Some experts recommend writing the goal, action plan and performance standards in 250 words or less, short enough to read in one minute. They recommend looking at it every day as a reminder of the goal and as a check on progress. They call this "one-minute goal setting."[1]

Some people object to this process. They say, "I know what my goal is. There is no need to write it. And even if I do write it, there is no need to review it daily. I am not going to forget."

This may be true, but for many people it isn't. Most people are involved in a variety of daily activities and often forget, delay or ignore the things they once considered important. But by reviewing the goal daily, they remain aware of it and continually pursue it.

A $25,000 Suggestion: Prioritize

Charles Schwab, a former president of the Bethlehem Steel Company, once had a problem. His managers were not meeting their steel production quotas. Mr. Schwab met with Ivy Lee, an efficiency expert, about increasing productivity in his company.

After visiting the company and talking with the managers, Ivy Lee had a suggestion. "At the end of each day," he told Mr. Schwab, "write down all your objectives for the next day. Then pick the six most important and prioritize them on paper. After that, put the

---

1. Blanchard and Johnson, *The One Minute Manager,* William Morrow & Co., Inc., 1982.

paper aside. When you come to the office the next morning, look at the paper and focus on the first objective. Do not go to another objective until you have completed the first. Once done, go to the second. Do the same for the third, fourth, fifth and sixth objectives. Whatever is not completed one day should go to the top of the next day's list."

Ivy Lee then met with the company's managers and recommended the same plan. At the end of the day, Charles Schwab asked about the fee for his services. Ivy Lee responded, "Try it out and send me whatever you think it is worth." After a short time, he received a check for $25,000.

Many successful people use Ivy Lee's advice, finding that it helps them to be more productive. They have made the same discovery as Charles Schwab — and it did not cost them $25,000. What is the secret of Ivy Lee's advice? It seems so simple; why does it bring about such success?

To answer this question, let us look at some of the reasons people do *not* reach the goals they set. One reason is that their goals are not clear. Another reason is that they have too many goals and are not able to reach them all, leaving them unmotivated to reach any. A third reason is that they allow unrelated and unimportant activities to distract them. Yet another reason is that they do not know how to prioritize. They start working on the second goal before completing the first, then go to the third before completing the second, and so on until they end up with a collection of half-fulfilled objectives.

Ivy Lee's plan addresses all these problems. It forces people to clarify all their goals; now they know precisely what has to be done. The plan also narrows any set of goals to six attainable units per day. With a reasonable number of goals, there is greater motivation to reach them all. Following the plan also forces a person to complete one objective before beginning another; now objectives are fulfilled, not half-fulfilled. Finally, the plan highlights the important tasks while disregarding the unimportant ones. This is the secret of Ivy Lee's advice. Is it any wonder people succeed with the plan?

Other efficiency experts add two more suggestions to Ivy Lee's plan: 1) Do the least enjoyable task first; and 2) delegate someone else to do all the tasks that you do not have to do yourself. With the unimportant tasks out of the way, you can pay attention to the things that count most.

Help Children Set Goals

Adults can help children understand how goals give direction, motivate and energize. They can encourage children to set high goals, both for the short and long term. And they can guide children through the seven-step goal-setting formula.

To illustrate helping a child through the formula, we will look at Tzipi, a ten-year-old girl who usually does not complete her homework assignments. Her problem is that she has other interests that distract her.

Suppose you are her parent and you want to help her succeed. What should you do? First, help Tzipi understand that she must fulfill her school obligations. Then show her how goal-setting can help her succeed. Once she agrees to this — and it is critical to get her agreement — you can guide her through the seven-step formula:

1) *Determine the goal.* Encourage Tzipi to ask the key questions: "What results do I want to see? What's in it for me? Will I be proud of reaching the goal?"

The answer to the first question is obvious: "The result I want is to complete my homework." The answer to the second question may not be so obvious. She may say, "What's in it for me? Higher grades." Or she might want the continuation of all privileges at home and in school, some kind of special reward, or the satisfaction of knowing that her parents will be proud of her. Whatever the answer is, Tzipi should be the one to offer it.

The answer to the third question may be, "I will feel proud of my improvement." This is important, because if she is not proud, she may not be properly motivated to reach the goal altogether.

2) *Set priorities.* First, direct Tzipi to make a list of all her required schoolwork and all her other interests. Then guide her in prioritizing those activities.

The reason Tzipi is not meeting her homework obligations is that she has too many other interests. Along with her daily homework assignments, Tzipi does household chores, practices the piano, studies with an older friend, and volunteers at the local nursing home. She also enjoys reading and playing with friends.

Tzipi has so many interests that she lacks the stamina to satisfy them all. For this reason, the goal-setting formula is important, especially the step of prioritizing. But she could do better. She could use Ivy Lee's $25,000 suggestion. First, she would list all her goals on paper. Then she would list the six most important ones. Finally, she would begin to pursue each goal, one at a time. Since her homework assignments will be different each day and her interests will probably change depending on her mood, she would have to make a different list every day as soon as she comes home from school. As the urgency of her commitments varies from day to day, so will her list of priorities.

3) *Make the action plan.* Direct Tzipi to ask, "What steps must I take to reach the goal?" As she searches for the answer, make yourself available for guidance.

If she is properly motivated and thinking reasonably, she may say something like, "I will do all my homework in my room, taking no breaks except to eat dinner. If I receive a telephone call, my parents will take a message and I will return the call later."

When she has several assignments to complete, she may say, "Tonight, I will complete the math and science work due tomorrow. I will also start studying for Thursday's *Chumash* test, and I will begin to read the book assigned for the book report. Every night for the next two weeks, I will read ten pages of that book."

4) *Time management.* Help Tzipi devise a time-management plan. She may block out certain times for homework and certain times for other activities.

She may say, "I will begin homework at five, eat dinner at six, and finish all my work by seven-thirty. I may do other activities before five or, if there is time, after I complete all my homework."

5) *Measurement.* Here, Tzipi decides how to measure her progress. She may say, "I will look at my assignment pad to see if I completed all my assignments. After studying, I will ask myself if I understand the work. If there is a test assigned for the next day, I will ask my mother to test me, and if I do well I will be confident of doing well on the test at school."

6) *Target date.* Direct Tzipi to make a deadline for herself. Typically, the deadline to complete any assignment is the night before it is due. If it is due in several days or weeks, the target date may be the night before it is due, or Tzipi can choose an earlier deadline.

7) *Visualize.* Here, Tzipi creates images of completing all her projects, disregarding other activities until after the assigned work is completed.

Role modeling. Another way adults can help children learn how to set goals is by role modeling. At home, parents can share their own goal-setting decisions with their children. They can show their children how they use the seven-step formula to set their goals.

In school, teachers can write on the chalkboard the day's objectives and the schedule for meeting them. Writing this on the board at the beginning of the day shows how goals have to be planned, and it organizes the day into attainable units. The teacher can say, "I am putting all our goals on the board as a goal-setting model. You should be using the same method at home with your assignments and other interests."

Delegate results, not process. There are many goals that children *must* reach — for example, household chores and schoolwork. After parents tell their children what must be done, the children must be expected to comply.

Indeed, when it comes to goals such as these, parents are obligated to tell a child what has to be done. However, they do not always have to tell the child how to do it, especially if he or she is capable of figuring out a way of doing it without assistance. By taking away the child's choice of how to achieve the goal, they may be choking off the child's own creativity and taking away his inner drive to achieve it.

If results must be delegated, by all means delegate them. But you don't always have to delegate the *process* for reaching them. Even if you think the child cannot accomplish the goal on his own, give him the independence to figure out a way. Who says your way is the best? Maybe the child will devise another way that is equally, or even more, effective.

Set Goals and Look to Hashem for Help

Whatever your endeavor, look to Hashem for assistance and He will help you in some form:

> In the way that a person goes, he is assisted (Talmud *Makkos* 10b).
>
> "In all your ways, know Him" (*Mishlei* 3:6). In every activity, remember Him and impress upon yourself that you do not have the power or ability to succeed without the hand of Hashem. Put your hopes in Hashem . . . "And He will make your ways straight" (*Mishlei*, ibid.), and you will succeed in the activity in which you remembered Hashem (Rabbeinu Yonah, ad loc.).
>
> The one who comes to purify himself receives Heavenly assistance (Talmud *Shabbos* 104a).

Even if your goal is to correct a bad *middah*, a task which Rabbi Yisrael Salanter said is more difficult than mastering the entire *Shas*, there is a guarantee that Hashem will help you:

> Whenever a person sincerely seeks the truth to follow Hashem, Hashem helps that person by correcting his *middos* and helping him recognize his fallacies . . . Hashem changes a person's bad nature and repairs his heart whenever that person makes the commitment to go after Hashem and to serve Him (Rabbeinu Yonah, *Mishlei* 21:2).

Indeed, some goals are difficult and may seem impossible to reach. Nevertheless, to the degree that one puts forth the effort to reach them, that person will receive assistance from Hashem.[1]

This is how Moshe Rabbeinu was able to erect the *Mishkan*. The pieces of the *Mishkan* were too heavy for any person to lift single-handedly, but Moshe Rabbeinu did it. He received assistance from Hashem — because he made a sincere effort to do it.[2]

Similarly, Aharon the high priest performed a waving ceremony with thousands of new priests, all in one day. It was humanly im-

---

1. *Sichos Mussar*, 5732:13, 28.
2. Ibid.

possible to do all this in a single day, but Aharon received assistance from Hashem — because he made a sincere effort to do it.[1]

Obviously, we will not receive such para-natural assistance from Hashem every time we try to accomplish something. However, one thing is guaranteed; the only way He will offer His assistance is if we make a sincere effort.

One more thing is guaranteed; we will accomplish more by setting goals and working toward them than by sitting back and waiting for good things to happen. Because Hashem will not do His part if we do not do ours.

---

1. Ibid.

Chapter Six

Improve Your Self-Esteem

he Chassidic master Reb Zushe of Hanipol once told his followers, "After I pass away and I stand in judgment before the Heavenly Court, I will not be asked, 'Why didn't you use your talents to become like your *Rebbe* or like Moshe Rabbeinu?' Rather, I will be asked, 'Why didn't you use your talents to become *Zushe*?' "

Reb Zushe's point is clear: None of us is expected to meet the potential of another person. We all have our own virtues which we must develop and use. We are all very different from one another, and each of us has a special value.

The problem is that many people believe that they have no special worth. They have a negative self-image and think that their deficiencies outnumber their attributes. They have a distorted view of their personalities, which leads them to have little respect for themselves and little confidence in their abilities. The result is that they doom themselves to a life of mediocrity at most and never live up to their potential.

If you or someone you know is like this, there is good news: You are not stuck with this attitude. If you want, you can change. In this chapter we will show you how to do it. But we must first discuss one fundamental idea — the fact that you have a special value. This is important because when you recognize it, your life becomes affected in a very positive way.

You Have a Special Value

> A person is in this world only once; there never was another person like him and there never will be, through the end of time.
>
> I, with my blend of talents, a son to a particular set of parents, born in a specific time period and in a specific place — certainly there is a special service which I must perform, and there is a portion of Torah personalized for me, and creation waits for me to do what I am obligated to do, because my service cannot be exchanged with anyone else (Rabbi Shlomo Wolbe, *Alei Shur,* p. 168).

You are a one-time phenomenon. You are unique.[1] You are valuable. Throughout time, there has never been another person like you and there never will be. You have a special set of strengths that nobody else has or ever will have. You have the potential to make a special contribution to the world, a contribution that only you can make.

You may ask: "But I have weaknesses, too. Doesn't this diminish my value?" Indeed, every person has weaknesses. But this does not minimize the value and importance that Hashem bestowed upon you when He endowed you at birth with a unique set of abilities. Nor does it take away from your value and importance as a *human being.* Your value is unfathomable:

> . . . in the image of Hashem He created him [man], male and female He created them (*Bereishis* 1:27).
>
> Man is cherished, for he was created in the image of Hashem (*Avos* 3:14).

---

1. See also *Berachos* 58a: "Their thoughts are unalike and their physical features are unalike."

He [G-d] blew into his nostrils the soul of life, and man became a living being (*Bereishis* 2:7).

Not only did Hashem create you in His image, He breathed His spirit into you. Your body and soul, with all their physical, mental, emotional and spiritual strengths, became sparked by Hashem. Every fiber of your mind, body and personality is woven by Hashem. You are special. You are holy. You have the power to make use of everything in the universe because of the inner resources that G-d gave you.[1]

Hashem created you in His image and with His spirit because He cherishes you. In His eyes, you are special.

Rabbi Nosson Tzvi Finkel constantly spoke about the greatness of mankind, inculcating in his students the notion that man is even more elevated than the angels. He would emphasize that a person remains in his elevated position even when he sins, and that with every sin a person has the opportunity to learn a lesson and climb even higher.[2]

In addition, Hashem told the Jewish nation, "You are children of Hashem your G-d."[3] This is not an allegorical comment or an exaggeration; you are a true child of the Creator in every sense of the word.[4]

For this reason, Moshe Rabbeinu was commanded to take a census of the Jewish nation. By counting each and every Jew separately, the message was sent that each and every Jew has a unique importance. Yes, there are smarter people and wealthier people, famous people and talented people. But one thing remains constant: Each and every Jew has individual importance. Each Jew is counted as one, no matter how talented or successful he or she is.[5]

Rabbi Chaim of Volozhin also discussed the special value of a Jew:

A Jew must never say in his heart, "What am I worth? What value do my actions have in the world?" Instead, he

1. Rabbi S. R. Hirsch, *Nineteen Letters,* Feldheim Publishers, 1995, p. 55.
2. *Tenuas HaMussar,* pp. 270-273.
3. *Devarim* 14:1.
4. Rabbi Aharon Kotler, *Mishnas Rabbi Aharon,* Vol. 1, p. 157.
5. Rabbi Moshe Feinstein, *Darash Moshe,* Introduction, p. 4.

should understand and know and internalize that each and every deed, word and thought of each and every moment of time is never wasted, Heaven forbid. How lofty are his deeds, for they all go to the Upper Worlds and have a meaningful effect (*Nefesh HaChaim* 1:4).

The Ba'al Shem Tov compared the Jewish nation to a star. Stars appear in the distance as tiny specks, but in reality they are gigantic. The Jewish nation is the same; although it may seem to have an insignificant appearance in the world, the world exists because of it.[1] So if you should ever compare yourself to other people or things and conclude that you are small, think of yourself as part of a gigantic star. As with a star, far off in the distance, you may have to come close to realize the greatness that you have.

Your value also lies in your physical attributes. Take a moment to look at your hand. Examine its intricate anatomy and all the complex things it can do. Look at your legs and feet, and think about their complexity and what they can do. Think about your eyes, ears, breathing apparatus and digestive system, and about the magnificent brain that coordinates it all.

There was once a woman who lost her eyesight as a result of taking a wrongly prescribed medication. She sued the doctor and won a million dollars in a court settlement. Would you give her your eyes in exchange for the million dollars? Of course not, because your eyes are worth more than that. And your eyes are just one small part of your body.

How much do you think your body is worth? More than a million dollars? More than a billion dollars? You cannot put a price tag on your body; it is beyond assessment. Now think about that for a moment — your value is in excess of billions of dollars!

Hillel the Sage appreciated the value of his body. Once he told his students that he was going to bathe. They inquired, "Is this a *mitzvah*?" He answered, "Yes." Then he added, "Whoever is appointed to take care of the statues of kings that are placed in theaters must polish and clean them, and for this he receives payment, and he even becomes distinguished [enough] to be among the

---

1. Ba'al Shem Tov, cited in *Mayanah Shel Torah, Bereishis* 15:5.

king's dignitaries. I, who was born in the image and form of Hashem, certainly [must honor my body]."[1]

Of course, Hillel did not imply that his body was created in the exact form of Hashem. This is impossible, for Hashem does not have a form. Rather, he meant that his *mind* and *spirit* were created in the image of Hashem, and that his body served as the sanctuary which held them. This sanctuary must be treated with at least the same dignity as the king's statues.[2]

"Okay," one may protest, "we can prove that each person has special worth. But I don't feel it. I feel inadequate, inept and inferior. I do not consider myself valuable. The ivory tower academicians can philosophize about the value of man, but as for me, I have no such philosophy."

This is a mistake. Every Jew must have such a philosophy, because the Torah requires every Jew to consider himself or herself valuable. Read on.

The Obligation To Consider Oneself Valuable

> Each and every person is required to say, "The world was created for me" (*Sanhedrin* 4:5). This means to say that I am considered as an entire world (Rashi, ad loc.).

The entire world was created for me, and I have the value of an entire world. Mind-boggling, isn't it? And it doesn't stop there; I am expected to *say* it and, obviously, to *believe* it.

This expectation is more than just a proper thing to do; every Jew is *required* to be aware of his or her special greatness. This can be deduced from the fact that every Jew is *required* to say, "The world was created for me" and "When will my actions equal those of my forefathers Avraham, Yitzchak and Yaakov?"[3] One can make these statements only if he feels that he is indeed valuable; otherwise, he would not be able to think of himself as an entire world, nor would he be able to truly aspire to the greatness of the forefathers.[4]

---

1. *Midrash Rabbah, Vayikra* 34:3. See *Yefei To'ar* there.
2. *Yefei To'ar*, ibid.
3. *Tanna d'Bei Eliyahu Rabbah* 25.
4. *Toras Avraham*, p. 49.

Similarly, Rabbi Aharon Kotler said, "A person is obligated to contemplate and recognize the great value that lies within himself."[1] Along these lines, Rabbi Avraham Grodzinsky wrote, "How great is the obligation for Jewish people to recognize their greatness."[2] And as we mentioned earlier, Hillel said that it is a *mitzvah* to treat our bodies honorably; in other words, we are required to recognize our own value.

Before the Torah was given, Hashem told the Jewish people, "You will be for Me a kingdom of *kohanim*."[3] According to Rashi, *kohanim* means officers with the stature and responsibility of state dignitaries. The same value was conferred on the nation after the Torah was given. Moshe Rabbeinu told the people, "Do not fear, for in order to elevate you Hashem came."[4] This means that Hashem came to the people in a prophecy for the purpose of elevating their stature in the world.[5]

Why did the people have to be elevated both before and after the Torah was given? Rabbi Shlomo Wolbe explained, "If they had remained small, they would never be able to reach the intent of the Torah."[6] The feeling of importance — that is, high self-esteem — is a prerequisite to Torah living.

What Is Self-Esteem

The feeling of value that we have been discussing does not connote vanity, conceit, haughtiness or an artificial sense of greatness. This would be *ga'ava*, which is clearly prohibited by Torah ethics. Rather, we are referring to a healthy feeling of worthiness and competence, the feeling of being fundamentally valuable and capable of achievement.[7] This is what we mean by high self-esteem.

High self-esteem is the feeling of being high, but not higher than others. It is the security of being capable, but not necessarily better than others. It is the confidence that you can do a good job, but not necessarily more skillfully than others. It is the feeling of being wor-

---

1. *Mishnas Rabbi Aharon*, Vol. 1, p. 157.
2. *Toras Avraham*, p. 3.
3. *Shemos* 19:6.
4. *Shemos* 20:17.
5. Rashi, ibid.
6. *Alei Shur*, p. 168.
7. Rabbi Abraham Twerski, *Let Us Make Man*, CIS Publications, p. 57.

thy, but not more valuable than others. It is self-acceptance, but not to the exclusion of others.

As we said, high self-esteem is not vanity or conceit. Whereas vain and conceited people flaunt their good qualities, people with high self-esteem have no such need. On the contrary, they are quietly proud of their fine points and look for opportunities to utilize them for their own benefit and for the benefit of others.

Competence and worthiness. Suppose a person has a feeling of competence but lacks a feeling of worthiness. Can this person have high self-esteem? No. The feeling of worthiness is critical; without it, self-esteem will be low.

One case in point is the wealthy businessman who was constantly on the go and in the forefront of community activities. He had a wall full of plaques and accolades, yet he would confide privately to others that they meant nothing to him. He knew he was competent, but because he was missing a feeling of worthiness he had low self-esteem.[1]

There are highly successful physicians, admired by patients and colleagues, who also have negative feelings about themselves. And there are venerable Torah scholars who, despite their mastery of Torah, do not respect themselves.

These people are aware of their competence but do not feel fundamentally worthwhile. Maybe they grew up with overly critical parents who constantly reminded them of their faults. Maybe they have an overly critical inner voice which always reminds them how "inept" they are. Whatever the cause, they do not like or respect themselves. Indeed, these people know they are competent, but it is not enough. As long as they have the gnawing feeling of worthlessness, their self-esteem will remain low.

Does this mean that one can have high self-esteem with the feeling of worthiness alone? No. There must be an accompanying feeling of competence. One who feels so incompetent or hopelessly inept cannot possibly have a high level of self-esteem.

High self-esteem and humility. Can a person with high self-esteem be humble? Are humility and self-esteem mutually exclusive or can they work hand in hand?

---

1. Rabbi Abraham Twerski, *Life's Too Short*, St. Martin's Press, 1995, p. 136.

Let us look at Moshe Rabbeinu for an answer. Moshe was the most humble person who ever lived.[1] Does this mean that Moshe Rabbeinu had low self-esteem? Absolutely not. He knew that he was the specially chosen leader of the entire Jewish nation. He knew that he had the singular opportunity to talk with Hashem face-to-face. He knew that if he were not a worthy and competent individual, Hashem would not have chosen him for his mission. He certainly had high self-esteem, and at the same time he was extraordinarily humble.[2]

It is commonly assumed that humble people feel lowly about themselves, assuming that everybody else is better than they, and that they lack the assertiveness to speak up when they have to. This is a mistake. Moshe Rabbeinu, the prototype of humility, did not hesitate to confront Pharaoh or chastise the Jewish nation when necessary. His humility did not deter him from getting involved with unpopular activities or waging war with enemy nations. He was assertive and self-confident, and he was humble too.

The Chofetz Chaim is another example of the synthesis of humility and high self-esteem. The Chofetz Chaim was also a paradigm of humility. Yet he was an outstanding *talmid chochom* who had no reservations about making halachic decisions and formulating ethical principles. He even said that he felt personally responsible for the welfare of his entire generation.[3]

The Chofetz Chaim was certainly aware of his competence and his value; otherwise, he would not have assumed such leadership. Yet he was extraordinarily humble.

So what is humility? Humility is the recognition that you were born with certain strengths which must be used to meet your potential, and that when you do meet your potential, it is only because you were born with it in the first place.[4]

> If you have learned a great deal of Torah, do not take the credit for yourself, because you were created for this (*Avos* 2:9).

---

1. *Bamidbar* 12:3.

2. See Rabbi Eliyahu Lopian, *Lev Eliyahu*, Jerusalem, 1961, p. 294.

3. *Ohr Elchonon*, Vol. 1, p. 64.

4. Rabbi Eliyahu Lopian, *Lev Eliyahu*, Jerusalem, 1961, p. 294; Rabbi Leib Chasman, *Ohr Yahel, Shemini*, Vol. 2, p. 93.

While *Chazal* here discussed humility in regard to Torah mastery, the idea is the same with any project. No matter what you do or who you are, you can take pride in a job well done, but do not take credit for having extraordinary talents or for being "G-d's gift to mankind," because all you did was use the talents that Hashem gave you at birth. Whenever you succeed, you are merely doing what you were created to do.

Humility is the recognition that you are valuable and have made valuable contributions to the world, along with the awareness that your innate worth is no better than anyone else's and that you are simply doing the job that you were assigned to do. The person who realizes this has no reason to become conceited or to be a braggart. Unlike a braggart, he knows his true worth and has no need to prove it to anyone. Unlike a conceited person, he does not need the acclaim of anyone else to validate his worth.

Benefits of being aware of one's talents. As we saw earlier, the Torah requires us to be aware of our strengths. This awareness holds several benefits.

First of all, we will know what we are capable of accomplishing. We will then be able to achieve all that is within our power. Rabbi Yeruchom Levovitz said:

> Woe to the person who does not recognize his deficiencies, because he does not know what to correct. But even more woeful is the person who does not recognize his attributes, because this person is not even aware of his own tools (quoted in *Alei Shur*, p. 169).

Rabbi Aharon Kotler also discussed the result of low self-esteem:

> Generally, a person does not recognize his great worth; rather, he only recognizes himself by his deficient side, because he is close to it due to his materialistic nature and his habit from a young age — for the inclination of man is evil from his youth[1] — so he becomes lowly and ignoble in his own eyes, with the result of actually becoming small. For example, the wealthy person who does

1. *Bereishis* 8:21.

not recognize his wealth and therefore does not use any of his riches — this person is really like a poor person (*Mishnas Rabbi Aharon,* Vol. 1, p. 157).

Rabbi Kotler went on to explain why high self-esteem is critical to a person's growth, whether it concerns *middos,* attitudes, or *mitzvah* performance:

A person is obligated to contemplate and recognize the great importance that lies within himself. With the strength generated by this recognition, and as he continues to recognize it, his importance will grow and increase. This is a great and essential force that brings about self-perfection, greater than any other force, because when he recognizes his importance he will always consider whether his actions are befitting him, and he will refrain from any action that does not meet his standard of honor and importance (ibid.).

Similarly, we are told that Hashem cherishes us and that He has shown us a particularly special love by *letting us know* that He cherishes us.[1]

Why was it necessary for Hashem to inform us that He cherishes us? Because when we realize how much Hashem loves us, we will feel elevated and important. We will then act in an elevated way, avoiding sins and pursuing *mitzvos.*[2]

When we realize that we are special, we will not only feel important, but we will feel *dignified.* We will strive to retain a high level of dignity and will refrain from committing sins.[3] Even more, when we realize that an inappropriate deed, whether minor or major, causes damage in the Upper Worlds, we will be too frightened to commit any sort of sin.[4]

Another benefit in recognizing our worth is that it gives us the strength to climb higher and higher. Our self-image sets the boundaries of our accomplishments; it defines what we can or cannot do. If we expand our self-image, we expand the area of the possible.

---

1. *Avos* 3:14.
2. Rabbi Chaim Mordechai Katz, *Be'er Mechokek,* p. 1.
3. Rabbi Chaim Shmulevitz, *Sichos Mussar,* 5732:15.
4. Rabbi Chaim Volozhin, *Nefesh HaChaim* 1:4.

We learn this from the artisans who constructed the *Mishkan* after the Exodus from Egypt. They were not trained or skilled in architecture, masonry, embroidery, weaving, diamond-cutting, or gold and silversmithing. We might expect such unskilled people to throw their hands up in the air and say, "There is no way I can do this." Instead, they volunteered their services, saying, "We will do whatever we are asked." They felt capable and valuable, and this led them to find the aptitude within themselves to succeed. They discovered that "there is no limit and no end to what a person who holds himself valuable and important can do."[1]

Finally, when we recognize our worth, we accept ourselves for who we are, with all our weaknesses. We all have shortcomings, but we often lack the security to look at those faults and accept their existence. With high self-esteem, though, we can comfortably acknowledge those misgivings because we also acknowledge our strengths. We can then accept ourselves for exactly who we are.

The Self-Esteem/Self-Confidence Connection

As we saw earlier, people with high self-esteem feel that they are worthy and competent. Not only do they feel fundamentally good about themselves, they also feel capable of utilizing their talents effectively. So when they have a skill, whatever it may be, they have confidence in themselves and believe that they have a very good chance of succeeding. Their high self-esteem translates into high self-confidence.

This is important, because the degree of a person's self-confidence often determines the degree of his success in life. Let us explain.

Self-confidence empowers. A person with high self-confidence has an "I-can" attitude, believing that he can succeed at his tasks. He performs enthusiastically and accepts full responsibility for completing a job. Mistakes or obstacles do not weaken his drive; rather, his faith in himself motivates him to persevere. Just as the wings of a bird enable it to stay airborne and fly, high self-confidence enables such a person to soar and reach his goals.

Self-confidence is the engine that powers the machine of achievement. A self-confident person is more creative, more imagi-

---

1. Rabbi Chaim Shmulevitz, loc. cit.

native and more solution-oriented. He speaks more effectively and has less fear and self-doubt. He has a positive attitude toward himself and others. A self-confident person can define his life more clearly and has greater control in choosing its direction. He has a sense of inner security and is less resistant to the suggestions of others. With his strong engine of self-confidence, he is empowered to achieve.

On the other extreme, the individual with low self-confidence believes he cannot succeed. He performs unenthusiastically and below his real level of capability. When confronted with a challenge, he is more concerned with the problem and the fear of failure than with the solution and the rewards of success. Instead of *making* things happen, he *lets* things happen. Feeling inadequate and vulnerable, he often resists the suggestions of others. His weak engine of self-confidence does not deliver much fuel for achievement.

Rabbi Moshe Feinstein described the outcome of low self-confidence. We once quoted his words in Chapter Two, and they deserve repetition here:

> Many people do not reach their potential and also become sinners because they degrade themselves or the matter at hand. For example, a person thinks he cannot do great things such as learn Talmud with all its commentaries. He therefore does not learn because, according to his opinion, it will not help to know anything anyway. The result is that he is unable to learn and he becomes an ignoramus (*Darash Moshe*, p. 111).

Low self-confidence does not express itself only in relation to Talmud study. It influences many other areas of life as well. We can observe its effects in a person who feels he is incapable of making friends and therefore does not exert himself to do those things that will attract people to him. He says to himself, "Nobody will like me, so why bother trying to *make* them like me?" Another example is the person who thinks he is not athletic. Because of his conviction, he will not put out much effort in sports activities.

Additionally, when faced with a decision to do something that requires courage and commitment — and we all have to make these kinds of decisions — the person with low self-confidence will back off and take the path of least resistance, even if it is not the most beneficial path for him. He has the capability to succeed, but his feelings of inadequacy hold him back.

A person with low self-confidence performs at a level below his true capability because his negative attitude is projected into his performance. Since he believes he is not capable of succeeding, he performs unenthusiastically and without conviction. After all, in his mind he will not succeed anyway. His chances of success are therefore reduced, even if he has the skills. This is the self-fulfilling prophecy at work.

But if he thinks he can succeed, and he has the skills to succeed, chances are that he will. His positive attitude is projected into his performance. He performs enthusiastically, with conviction, and to his true level of capability. Because he expects to succeed, he makes the appropriate effort. His prophecy for success becomes self-fulfilled because of his positive attitude.

The artisans who built the *Mishkan* teach us that a person performs better when he expects to succeed. As we mentioned earlier, these artisans were not trained in the crafts needed to build the *Mishkan,* but they did have untapped talents. They recognized these talents and came forth to volunteer their services.[1] They also had a feeling that they were fitting for the work, and they were secure in their abilities.[2] They had a drive to undertake the project and therefore completed it successfully.[3]

It is fair to assume that after the artisans recognized their untapped talents, they received training. Otherwise, they could not have performed so well. But what trait motivated them to make the commitment and get the training in the first place? Their strong drive and high self-confidence. They did not say, "Who, me? I can't do those things. I have no training. Let someone else do it," as other people in their situation might have done. Instead they expected the best, and they succeeded.

To a large degree, your *attitude* determines your *altitude.* Whether you are a craftsman, a Torah student, a homemaker or an athlete — if you think you can succeed, you increase your chances of

---

1. Ramban, *Shemos* 35:21.
2. Rabbi Chaim Shmulevitz, *Sichos Mussar,* 5732:26.
3. Rabbi Yeruchom Levovitz, *Daas Torah, Shemos,* p. 348.

success. You become enthusiastic, goal-driven, and solution-oriented, and you do everything in your power to perform excellently.[1]

This is not to say that high self-confidence will enable you to do anything you want. If you are not trained in surgery, you will never be a successful surgeon. If you do not know how to measure and cut wood, you will never be a successful carpenter. Without proper qualifications, you *cannot* be successful. But if you are properly qualified and you also have high self-confidence, you will be empowered to perform better.

Note the choice of words: You will be *empowered.* There is no guarantee. King Shlomo said, "Trust in Hashem with all your heart and do not rely on your understanding."[2] No matter what you do or how hard you try, in the final analysis you need the help of Hashem to succeed in any endeavor. Be confident and say, "I think I will succeed" or "I think I have the ability to succeed," but do not be overconfident, saying, "I know I will succeed." Even if you recognize your skills and the probability of success, there is no guarantee that you will succeed, unless Hashem wills it that way.

Indicators of Low Self-Esteem

"I can't."
"I'm afraid to try."
"I'm no good."
"I'm a loser."

These statements indicate low self-esteem and low self-confidence. This is not to say that a person who says such things from time to time should become alarmed and run for professional help; people with high self-esteem can also have periodic moods of low self-confidence. However, when a person expresses these ideas frequently, it is an indication of a problem.

Another indication of low self-esteem is sensitivity to criticism. A person with low self-esteem already feels inferior. He does not want to be told about mistakes, preferring to conceal them. Instead of becoming open and receptive, he becomes hurt and defensive.

---

1. Rabbi Chaim Shmulevitz, loc. cit.
2. *Mishlei* 3:5.

However, a person with high self-esteem is secure with himself. His feelings of self-worth are not dependent on other people or external situations.[1] He is not concerned with hiding his shortcomings; in fact, he may even want to work on them.

A person with low self-esteem may overreact to compliments and flattery. Since he does not value himself, he needs the approval of others to validate his worth.[2] Thus, he is extremely grateful to anyone who praises him. An insincere flatterer can easily take advantage of such a person. However, a person with high self-esteem takes compliments in stride. He has no reason to overreact because he already feels good about himself.

Another indication of low self-esteem is the tendency to criticize others. The person with low self-esteem values himself so little that he looks for artificial ways to build himself up. By putting others down, he creates the illusion that he is superior. Although he considers himself noble and sincere, the more faults he finds in others, the better he feels about himself. The person with high self-esteem, though, has no need to build himself up. He is comfortable with himself and does not feel the urge to put others down.

Yet another indication of low self-esteem is the tendency to blame others for one's own mistakes and shortcomings. By shifting the blame, one avoids feeling inferior. The person with high self-esteem, though, is secure with himself and has no need to divert blame to anyone else.

A person with low self-esteem may also have a tendency to avoid other people. In its simplest form, he behaves shyly; in its extreme form, he becomes reclusive. Either way, avoiding others alleviates the feeling of inferiority that assails him every time he is around people. The person with high self-esteem, though, is not afraid of other people and feels worthy even in the presence of people who are perceived as more successful than he.

Also, a person with low self-esteem tends to assume that others see him in the same way that he sees himself. Even though others may see him in a much better light,[3] such a person might further

---

1. Rabbi Nosson Tzvi Finkel, cited in *Tenuas HaMussar*, Vol. 3, p. 273.
2. Rabbi Eliyahu Dessler, *Michtav M'Eliyahu*, Vol. 1, p. 99.
3. *HaChofetz Chaim*, Vol. 3, p. 1060, cited by Rabbi Z. Pliskin, *Growth Through Torah*, p. 331.

complicate the matter by behaving according to his notion of others' perception. What will others think of him then? Exactly what he thinks of himself.

A person with high self-esteem does not run into this problem. On the contrary, he sees himself favorably and thinks that others see him this way, too. He behaves according to his expectation, with the result that others continue seeing him in a positive light.

Interestingly, researchers have found that people who join gangs often have a negative self-image. It doesn't matter that gangs are corrupt, dangerous and detrimental to society; their affiliation gives them the sense of importance that they derive from no other source.

People with negative self-images are also more prone to substance abuse. They feel so inferior that they turn to drugs to provide them with a sense of fulfillment. And it doesn't even matter that they are harming themselves; after all, they see no value in their minds and bodies anyway.

People with positive self-images do not need gangs or drugs to give them value or fulfillment, because they already value themselves and derive a sense of fulfillment from other activities. Besides, they want to protect themselves from the harmful effects of drugs and gangs.

Another indication of low self-esteem is the inability to compliment others. "My praise isn't worth anything," they think, "so why bother? Besides, I may make a fool of myself."

A mother of four children once told me that this was the reason she could never praise her children. She always thought, "What does my praise mean to my children anyway? I am not worth much, and neither is my praise." But with more self-esteem, she would feel that her praise has value.

The overuse of titles is another indication of low self-esteem. Since a person with low self-esteem does not take pride in who he is, he looks for something else to take pride in. A title is a convenient substitute. "I am a *talmid chochom*"; "I am a doctor"; "I am an attorney"; "I am an entrepreneur"; "I am the owner of a Mercedes Benz." This person answers the question, "Who am I?" by telling what he *does* or what he *has*.

People with high self-esteem, though, do not need titles to feel better about themselves. Their lives are more than their jobs and possessions. First of all, they are Jews, with souls sparked by G-d. They are also sons and daughters to adoring parents, husbands and wives to loving spouses, and fathers and mothers to children who depend on their guidance and wisdom. They have their own unique talents, which cannot be duplicated by anyone else. Such a person answers the question, "Who am I?" by telling *who* he is.

> One of the misfortunes of our generation is that we confuse titles with greatness . . . But greatness — true greatness — is not to be measured by the position one occupies, or the title one bears (Rabbi Chaim Dov Keller, "Of Identity and Success," *The Jewish Observer,* May 1982, p. 7).

A yeshivah student may aspire to the title of *talmid chochom, Rosh Yeshivah* or *maggid shiur.* To him, this is a symbol of greatness. But he is making a mistake. In truth, he achieves greatness only if he achieves his full potential. And once he appreciates his achievement, he will not need a title to give him a boost.[1]

This principle is not limited to yeshivah students; no matter what profession a person holds or what possessions he has, his greatness is best defined by the extent to which he fulfills his potential.

Masks of low self-esteem. Sometimes, people behave as if they have high self-esteem, but in truth have very little.

The obstinate individual is an example. In his eyes, he is always right, so he disagrees with everyone about everything, giving the appearance of being extremely confident. But is he?

Probably not. In all likelihood, he suffers from *low* self-esteem. And it is exactly this feeling that causes him to hold onto his opinions with such tenacity; it gives him a sense of value that is otherwise lacking. His obstinacy really says, "Look at me. I am important. My opinions count."

A person with high self-esteem does not need this attention. He listens courteously to others and is always prepared to change his mind if necessary. He is secure with himself. He knows that he is capable of making mistakes, and that when he does make one, it does not reflect his basic worthiness. He has no need to proclaim his value, because he knows he is valuable.

---

1. Rabbi Chaim Dov Keller, "Of Identity and Success," *The Jewish Observer,* May 1982, p. 7.

The put-down artist is another example of a person who may be hiding low self-esteem. He is quick to criticize others and sure of his opinion. He gives the appearance of having a great deal of self-confidence. But is it really so? Probably not. His practice of putting others down may be nothing more than a clever way of building himself up. If he had high self-esteem, he would have no need to build himself up. He would understand that putting others down only serves to hurt their feelings.

The class clown is yet another example. We are all familiar with the student who constantly disturbs the lesson with jokes and wise-cracks. He becomes the center of attention and loves every minute of it. Although this child appears to have high self-esteem, he is probably suffering from a negative self-image, feeling so awful about himself that he has a need to build himself up. So he makes himself the center of attention. When this child makes jokes, he is really saying, "Look at me. Give me attention. I need to feel important."

Loud and arrogant people are two more examples. Is their display of confidence a reflection of *true* self-confidence? Probably not. They too feel inferior and have a need to build themselves up. The way they do it is by advertising themselves. Their obnoxious behavior is nothing more than a bluff to cover up their feelings of inferiority and a way to draw attention to themselves.[1]

"Why," you may ask, "do all these people behave in such a repulsive manner? Don't they know that they are pushing others away from them? If they want recognition, they should behave in ways that attract people."

They do not see it this way. Their logic may go like this: "I do not deserve a lasting relationship with anybody. And even if I would begin to develop one, the other person will sooner or later realize how inferior I am, and will then leave me. Therefore, why make the effort of trying to attract others to me by befriending them?" So they behave in negative, shocking ways; they learned a long time ago that this always attracts the attention they so desperately need. The *Midrash* sums up this logic with a metaphor:

> They asked the Euphrates River, "Why do you flow so quietly?" It answered, "I do not have to make noise. My

---

1. See *Alei Shur*, p. 182.

deeds announce my presence. A person plants a tree near me, and it grows in just thirty days. If he plants a vegetable near me, it grows in just three days."

They asked the Tigris River, "Why are you so noisy?" It answered, "Hopefully, my sounds will be heard and I will be noticed."

They asked the fruit trees, "Why are you so quiet?" They answered, "We do not have to make noise. Our fruits affirm our presence."

They asked the barren trees, "Why do you make noise?" They answered, "Hopefully, our sounds will be heard and we will be noticed" (*Bereishis Rabbah* 16:3).

The one who is aware of his value and productiveness has no need to call attention to himself. But the one who sees himself as unproductive and unworthy has a need for recognition. So he behaves in ways that draw attention to himself.

The Detractors of Self-Esteem

Self-esteem is not constant. As a person's mood swings upward and downward, his self-concept often goes along for the ride. This means that everybody has times when he thinks highly of himself and times when he does not think so well of himself. What, then, is the difference between a healthy person and an unhealthy person? The healthy person's self-concept is predominantly high, while the unhealthy person's self-concept is predominantly low.

It is most healthy to maintain the high mode as frequently as possible. To do this, it is important to be aware of the forces that repress self-esteem. You can then protect yourself against their negative effects.

Fear. One of the most powerful detractors of self-esteem is fear. On the way to an important meeting you may freeze up with fear, thinking, "Maybe I will not present myself well. Maybe I will not succeed." Or you may be about to take an important exam, and just as you lift the pencil the thought comes: "Maybe I didn't study enough. Maybe I will fail." Fear of failure sets in, and your self-confidence drops.

Fear of failure can express itself in other ways, too. Procrastination is one way. "There is no rush," you say. "I can do it tomorrow or the next day." On the conscious level, the intent is simply to postpone the job. But it is often the fear of failure that is holding you back.

Sometimes, fear of failure can cause you to become complacent. "Oh, what's the difference anyway?" you say. "Who says I have to do it altogether?" Or you may say, "If I don't try, I won't fail." Once again, on the conscious level, you are simply downsizing the importance of the task, but fear of failure may be the real problem.

Why do we mention the ways that fear holds you back? Because if you are aware of the presence of fear in your behaviors, you can be on the lookout for it and stop it from sabotaging your success.

Discouraging opinions. Another detractor of self-esteem is the discouraging opinions of others. Suppose you want to run for a political office and your friends say, "Are you sure you will win? Who is going to vote for you anyway?" This is very discouraging, especially since it comes from friends. It can throw your self-confidence down the same drain as the position you so much want to attain.

No matter what your goal is, the discouraging comments of others can deflate your self-confidence to a point where you lose all interest in the project. Without realizing it, you allow yourself to become a victim of someone else's opinion.

But if you realize that these people are draining you of your enthusiasm, you would be in a position to hold onto it. First, you would "name the game" by identifying what these people are doing — discouraging you from your plan. You would then gather your convictions and take this attitude: "That's what you think. I disagree. I think I can do it, and I am going to try."

This does not imply that one should always ignore the opinions of others. On the contrary, it's important to analyze the validity of the comment. If it is valid, there may be merit in considering it. But if it is nothing more than a useless, negative remark, ignore it. Act confidently. Don't allow someone else to spoil your dream.

Create a Positive Self-Image

As we mentioned earlier, if you don't like yourself, you can change. You can learn to view yourself positively, to respect yourself, and to become more self-confident.

Changing your self-image does not mean changing yourself; it means changing your *perception* of yourself. You will always be who you are, with the character and potential that you were born with. But with a positive self-image you can release the full power of your character and potential, and become everything you are capable of becoming. As we saw in the story of Reb Zushe, this is as much as anyone is expected to do.

There are people who think they are not capable of improving their self-image. Some say they do not have the ability; others are just not willing to try. This is a mistake, because every human being has the capacity to expand himself.

> Some people think that since one's self-image is largely based on his early upbringing (how his parents, teachers, and friends treated him when he was young), they therefore can do little to change their self-image. But this is wrong. It is true that our self-image is based largely on our past. But what counts is how we judge ourselves in the present. Regardless of how we were considered by others, we have the ability to change our own attitude towards ourselves.
>
> Imagine a monarch's young son who was captured by bandits and raised by them. They treated him as a lowly servant and that is how he viewed himself. At the age of twenty-five he was returned to his father the king. His attitude towards himself will be transformed almost immediately. The prince now realizes that his original view of himself was based on a mistaken notion, and he will now view himself as a member of royalty.
>
> That is the Torah evaluation of man. Every person is created in the image of his Creator. We are all noblemen and should view ourselves accordingly. Lowly self-images are based on mistaken notions and we all have the ability to change those notions if we choose (Rabbi Zelig Pliskin, *Gateway To Happiness*, p. 119).

Suppose someone pushed you down and your arm broke. Who would go to the doctor to have the arm set — you or the person who pushed you? Of course, you would go. You are the one who is in need of help, not the other person. Although that person caused the problem and should be censured for it, it is nevertheless your problem now.

Improving your self-image is a similar problem. Suppose you have a negative self-image as a result of critical parents. Who has to get the help — you or your parents? You may want to send your parents to a therapist to learn how to raise children more positively, but does this really solve the problem?

While it may be convenient to expect the one who caused the problem to get help, it will always remain your problem and therefore your responsibility. Blaming the problem on someone else and neglecting to take action is unproductive, and if the problem is neglected for an extended period of time, it can even become destructive.

How does one improve his self-image? By recreating and reshaping that image. You can reshape your image of yourself by acting in ways that suggest a more positive persona. We will now outline several activities that can be used to build a healthy self-image.

Self-Image Builders

The upcoming image-building activities will probably go against your natural tendencies. As you begin to do the activities, you may find that your mind and body resist. Don't stop. Instead, think of yourself as a professional weight lifter.

How does the weight lifter learn to heave a three-hundred-pound barbell over his shoulders? In the beginning, he lifts fifty pounds. This is challenging, yet attainable. As his muscles strengthen, he adds more weight. He continues this program until he reaches his final goal.

As he forces his body to withstand more and more weight, it resists. If it could talk, it would probably say, "No. Please do not add more weight. I have just become comfortable with the last increase, and now you want to try to break me with another!"

Although the weight lifter's body has a natural resistance to each weight increase, he acts against it and forces his body to yield. It is exactly this fight — his action against his own natural resistance — which builds his muscles and enables him to reach his final goal.

Indeed, he does not *feel* like going above his comfort level, but he knows that this is the only way to reach his goal. So he makes the commitment and follows through.

People with low self-esteem have a natural tendency to wallow in their negativity and to perform with little self-confidence. But just as a weight lifter disregards his comfort for the sake of his goal, the person who wants to improve his self-esteem must defy his comfort for the sake of his goal. As he continues doing image-building activities, his mind and body tend to resist, but the more he forces himself to yield, the more he will see himself as the person he wants to be.

Before choosing any of the upcoming activities, please keep in mind that each one has a different level of difficulty and a different outcome. Therefore, experiment first with the ones that fit your needs and that you are most comfortable doing. Don't try too many at once. Take on more only after you have become comfortable with the first ones.

If you do an activity and find that it is not bringing about dramatic improvement, don't become discouraged. Even if it brings about a twenty-percent improvement, your situation will be twenty-percent better than it was before. Relatively speaking, this is significant progress.

Challenge your inner voice. In Chapter One, we explained that the inner voice is the voice of your self-image.

Parents, teachers, siblings, friends and you have all planted ideas about yourself in your mind. If those ideas were positive, your self-image probably emerged healthy. But if the ideas were negative, your self-image probably emerged negative.

For this reason, the way you picture yourself may not be the real you. You may really have greater potential than you think you have. You may really be capable of greater achievement than you have been displaying. The problem is that negative ideas are so imbued in your psyche that you are operating as if they were all true.

It does not have to be this way. Just as your thoughts control the way you see yourself now, your thoughts have the power to change that around. This means that you can think yourself into the image you would like to have. You can take control of your conscious mind and reshape your self-image by thinking the thoughts that you would *expect* to think if your personality were recreated.

As we mentioned in Chapter One, when you make a mistake and your inner voice criticizes you, or when you are about to begin a project and you hear your inner voice expressing doubts about your ability, tell it that it is irrational and that you will not rely on it. By standing up to your inner voice and setting it straight, you will feel better about yourself and your self-confidence will remain intact.

Sometimes it helps to identify the origins of your inner voice. One example was a little girl whose brothers nicknamed her "Ug." When a friend phoned her, her brothers would announce, "Ug, you have a phone call." Whenever her name had to be used, her siblings replaced it with "Ug." Is it any wonder that as an adult she thought she was ugly? Her inner voice kept repeating the message that her siblings had sent as she was growing up. As a result, her self-esteem suffered.

This woman could have maintained a higher level of self-esteem had she identified the origin of her inner voice. In this case, she might have found it easier to disconnect from it and maybe even silence it altogether.

Sometimes the inner voice is your own, carried over from childhood. For example, as a child you may have had difficulty getting along with others. Since then, your social skills have improved, but your inner voice still discourages you from making new relationships. "Why bother?" it says. "You will eventually get into a fight, and the relationship will fall apart anyway." But if you would identify the inner voice as that of an unskilled child, it would be easier to disconnect from it. Your self-confidence would improve and you would be able to create lasting relationships.

Act the new image. In the first chapter we described one of life's rules: Attitudes follow actions. This means that if a person lacks a certain attitude and acts as though he has it, he will develop that attitude. Using this principle, if you perform actions which express a high self-image, you can actually enhance your self-image. This does not mean that you must act haughtily or arrogantly, but rather, with ordinary self-confidence. Here are some examples.

Greet others enthusiastically. When meeting a friend or being introduced to a stranger, give a firm handshake, a friendly smile, and a cheerful "Hello! How are you?" Stand upright with your head and shoulders high, and speak with poise and clarity.

Initiate conversation. If you meet an acquaintance or someone with whom you would like to become acquainted, take the initiative and approach him with an enthusiastic greeting. Then begin a conversation. Express your opinions with confidence, and at the same time give value to those of the other person. Even if he does not see you, approach him first. Don't let the opportunity for an image-building activity go by. If you make it a point to greet several people and to initiate conversations every day, you will feel more confident about yourself, and when they respond agreeably, you will feel even better.

Smile. When you turn up the corners of your mouth, even if you do not feel like smiling, another strange thing happens; you begin to feel happy and better about yourself. But a smile does more. It tells others that you like them.[1] When they see this, they feel appreciated and respond in kind.[2] When you see that they like you, you will reciprocate. As the relationship develops, so does your self-esteem.

Walk tall and dress nicely. When you walk with a bounce and an upright posture, radiating joy and confidence, you begin to feel that way too. And when you dress nicely, you feel even better. It is hard to feel inferior when you act with confidence.

When you act out the new image with any of these image-building activities, you may find that other people take more of an interest in you. Your self-confidence will then receive a real boost. And unless you sabotage the good intentions of these people by doing something that will drive them away, you may be on your way to an enriched life.

What if you are quiet and non-talkative? What if you are not interested in initiating conversations, greeting other people or smiling? Perhaps you would rather read, study or take quiet walks. How can you be motivated to do something of little interest?

Consider the fact that after doing these activities, you will feel better about yourself and your life will be enriched. The benefit of these activities is not so much what they do for others as what they do for you. Even if your preference is to be quiet and reserved, it is worth the effort to be friendly and outgoing.

---

1. See *Torah Temimah, Bereishis* 49:12.
2. See *Tiferes Yisrael* and Rabbeinu Yonah, *Avos* 1:15.

Visualize a new self-image. Visualization is a mental rehearsal of an upcoming event. As we explained in Chapter Two, the more you are able to visualize future success, the greater your chances of succeeding. By the time you actually perform, you will already have been there in your mind many times.[1]

For example, a person may be timid and shy because she thinks that she cannot relate well to others. Before going to work or meeting acquaintances, she should create mental pictures of greeting everyone with a cheerful "Good morning" and entering into conversation with them. She should picture herself talking with poise and confidence, while the other people reciprocate positively. By visualizing her own confidence, she will act with greater confidence when it really counts.

Affirm a new self-image. Affirming is another method of internalizing positive images of yourself. As we mentioned in Chapter Two, affirming is the process of repeating inspirational slogans about yourself. Over and over, affirm your worthiness and competence. The messages you repeat will leave you with positive images of yourself.[2]

Here are some examples: "I am a worthy and valuable individual"; "There was never anybody like me and there never will be"; "I am special"; "I have the seeds of greatness within me"; "I have the skills to succeed." As you repeat these slogans, you will begin to internalize the ideas.

Take an inventory of your personal assets. Some people have a tendency to dwell on their shortcomings while overlooking their strengths. This is self-defeating because dwelling on flaws reduces self-esteem and inhibits good performance.

If you are like this, you can get in touch with your strengths by taking an inventory of all your personal assets. Make a list of all your mental and physical attributes, such as looks, talents, memory, creativity, intelligence and physical strength. From time to time, review the list and allow it to make an impression on you.

Make a victory list. Similar to the inventory of assets, the victory list is a recollection of good performances and personal success

---

1. Rabbi Eliyahu Dessler, *Michtav M'Eliyahu*, Vol. 4, pp. 252-254.

2. Rabbi Yisrael Salanter, cited in *Tenuas HaMussar*, Vol. 1, p. 253; Rabbi Yeruchom Levovitz, *Daas Chochmah U'Mussar*, Vol. 1, p. 114; *Cheshbon HaNefesh*, Ch. 1.

stories. While the inventory of assets is concerned with one's *potential*, the victory list is concerned with one's *achievements.*

Perhaps somebody offended you, and instead of hurting his feelings or becoming angry, you remained calm and quiet. This experience elevated you as a person and is something to be proud of.[1] Add it to your victory list.

Perhaps you received a job promotion or a special community tribute. Maybe you made a sale that you thought could never be made, or you healed a relationship you thought impossible to heal. These victories are significant and are certainly eligible for the list.

However, a victory does not have to be so impressive. It can also be something less visible. Take, for example, a homemaker. Many homemakers without a professional career do not recognize their own importance. They put themselves down by saying, "I am just a plain housewife." This is an unwarranted put-down, because a housewife has countless victories every day of her life.

There is a wall poster that hangs on the walls and refrigerators of many homes. Its message casts a homemaker in the proper light. The poster reads: "The most creative job in the world: It involves taste, fashion, decorating, recreation, education, transportation, psychology, cuisine, designing, literature, medicine, handicraft, art, horticulture, economics, government, community relations, pediatrics, geriatrics, entertainment, maintenance, purchasing, direct mail, law, accounting, religion, energy and management. Anyone who can handle all those has to be somebody special. She is. She is a homemaker."[2]

Whether you are a homemaker, shoemaker, salesman, computer programmer or Torah scholar, don't sell yourself short. If you take a look, you will find many everyday successes, minor and major, which can be included on your victory list.

If you cannot think of anything outstanding, include successes that are commonly taken for granted, such as learning the three R's, making friends and being able to hold a conversation with others. This is what one woman with a severe self-image problem did. This woman was a practical nurse, yet she weighed over two hundred

---

1. *Alei Shur,* p. 95.
2. Cited in *Gateway to Happiness,* p. 23.

pounds, had an alcohol problem and suffered from depression. She knew she was in trouble, so she sought help. A counselor suggested that she begin a victory list. At first, she could not think of any outstanding achievements, so she wrote that she had learned how to read and how to attend school.

But as she continued to do the right things, her self-image improved and she was able to add more victories to her list. In the end, she lost her excess weight and almost totally stopped drinking. She even went back to school and became a physician.

Was it her victory list that brought about such remarkable results? No, not alone — but it helped. It helped her see progress every step of the way. Keeping her in touch with her achievements, it served as a platform on which she continued building her self-image.

Associate with positive people. Your associates have a strong influence on your attitudes.[1] If they are critical, sarcastic, non-supportive, demoralizing or otherwise negative, they will have a detrimental effect on your self-image. On the other hand, if they are supportive, encouraging and optimistic, they will have a healing effect on your self-image.

Adopt positive role models. Find a person who has high self-confidence. See how effectively he deals with other people and with life's challenges. Make him your secret "mentor" and emulate him.[2]

Read about people who have grown up with limited opportunities and have overcome their difficulties. Defying the odds, they emerged as winners. What were they thinking during those trying times? Did high self-confidence play a role in their success? Find out. Adopt them as role models. Let them be a source of encouragement. Say, "If they can do it, so can I."

Without them even knowing about it, you can use your role models whenever you are in a difficult situation. Imagine the confidence they would feel, then do the same.

Avoid the negative media. When you listen to a charismatic, inspiring speaker, don't you walk away with corresponding feelings?

---

1. See Rambam, *De'os* 6:1: "Man's nature is to be drawn after his friends, in both attitude and action ..."

2. See Vilna Gaon, *Mishlei* 12:26: A person who wants to become righteous should explore the ways of a *tzaddik*.

For example, you hear an inspiring speech on Yom Kippur about *teshuvah*. Doesn't it put you in the mood to do *teshuvah*? Maybe you have read impressive stories about people who do *chessed* or who have made sacrifices for their children, friends, nation or religion. In some mysterious way, you are transported to the world of the speaker, leaving you with a desire to follow suit.

For this reason, television has been coming under more and more scrutiny because of the deleterious effects it has on the minds of viewers. It has been a topic of discussion among ethicists and educators for many years, and now the scientific community is beginning to take seriously the growing evidence that it does indeed have a negative effect.

The things you see and hear affect the way you view the world. If your mind is filled with pictures of corruption and impurity, your view of the world will be negatively tainted. But if your mind is filled with images of virtue and morality, your view of the world will be an uplifting one.

It doesn't stop there. The images that fill your mind also affect the way you see *yourself*. If you read literature or view videos which portray the base side of humanity, such as murder, theft, dishonesty, violence and other types of corruption, you begin to lose respect for mankind — of which you yourself are a part. And if you read about people who lose faith in themselves or who behave inappropriately to boost their sense of worthiness, it draws you into the same depressed mood and affects your own feeling of worthiness. However, if you pursue media that depict man as kind, gentle, worthy and loved by G-d, your mind will be transported to that world.

Do something nice for others. Service is the key to enhancing one's feeling for others.[1] When you help others satisfy their needs, they appreciate what you have done and develop good feelings for you. When you see that others think so highly of you, your self-respect in turn will improve.

Another benefit of doing something nice for others is the feeling that you have helped other people improve their lives. This makes you feel important and productive.

---

1. *Derech Eretz Zuta*, Ch. 2.

Finish the job. When you finish a job — whether it is reading a book, mowing the lawn, painting the house or helping someone in need — you typically feel good about yourself. The completed job affirms your sense of competence. Also, the praise you receive for doing such fine work builds your sense of worthiness. With a heightened sense of competence and worthiness, your self-esteem grows.

Finishing the job does even more than that. It motivates you to take on more projects, because after succeeding once, you will want to enjoy the feeling of success again. There is nothing that breeds success more than success itself.

Winners don't quit, and quitters don't win. To be a winner, you cannot quit. Finishing every job you undertake, and doing it successfully, makes you a winner and enhances your self-esteem.

Consider your worth. As we mentioned earlier, you were created in the image of Hashem. You have His spirit in you. You are cherished by Him. You have a body that is priceless. You have the potential to make a unique contribution to the world, one which nobody else can offer. You have the seeds of greatness within you. Thinking about these points can enhance your self-esteem.

Don't allow others to put you down. Suppose you are a salesperson. You approach five prospects, but not one buys your product. Would you feel rejected or less worthy? Many people do. They internalize their failed attempt as a reflection on themselves, and their self-confidence suffers.

This is a mistake, because when people turn you down they are not rejecting *you*, they are rejecting your *product.* They hold nothing against you personally; they simply have no need for what you are offering.

The same holds true for people who insult you and are nasty to you. They are most likely not acting this way to hurt you, but rather, they themselves are probably hurting.

A wise school principal, Mrs. Buna Shulman of Monsey, New York, once used this concept to pacify a teacher who was hurt by a parent's criticism. At a P.T.A. conference, the teacher was meeting with the father of one of her students. This man was quite upset, and in a rough way proceeded to tell the teacher about her mistakes and give suggestions for how she should teach.

Understandably, the teacher's self-esteem took a blow. The next day she met with Mrs. Shulman and told her what happened and how she felt about it. Mrs. Shulman said, "If that man could be so belligerent with you, think about how he talks to his children. Your job now is to be especially nice to that child."[1]

The reason this story is so touching is that Mrs. Shulman did the opposite of what many others would do. Instead of calling the father to discuss his behavior or advising the teacher to ignore the insult, she realized that this man's attack was most likely a reflection of his own problems, and that his children were probably receiving the brunt of his hostility. She told the teacher not to allow this man to put her down, but rather, to use the incident to help the child and to make herself a more sensitive professional.

You cannot be put down by other people unless you allow it. Of course, there is no way to stop others from being nasty, but you don't have to let them hurt your feelings. For the sake of your self-image, never give anyone permission to put you down.

Avoid comparisons. Many people lose faith in themselves when they see others perform more competently than they. This is not a fair reaction, because every person is different, each with his own set of talents. Therefore, what one person accomplishes has no bearing on the next. As long as each person makes the effort to do his best, he can take pride in his performance.

If you did your best, consider yourself a success, even if your performance did not match the performance of someone else. Take pride in your effort. Hold your head up high, because you did the best you could with the abilities that you have.

Allow for failure. A failure can cause dejection, depression and a general loss of faith in one's competence and sense of worthiness. So when you fail, what can you do to maintain a positive self-image?

As we mentioned in Chapter Three, failure is a temporary inconvenience. It is a normal part of life for everyone. It is an opportunity to learn to do better the next time. Failure is a powerful medium of growth.

With this attitude, it is possible to put failure into a positive light. Even when you fail, if you learn a lesson from the experience

---

1. Heard from a member of the Shulman family.

and are able to perform better next time, there is no reason to let it hurt your self-esteem. On the contrary, be thankful and optimistic. Yes, you made a mistake. As a human being, you are fallible. But you also have the capability to repair errors and to improve.

By transforming failure into opportunity, you can make sure never to let a mistake reduce your self-worth to the point where you do not want to try again. You may not want to take the risk of another failure. But with a positive attitude, you will understand that by not trying again, you are taking an even greater risk — the risk that you will remain as you are and not grow.

Avoid negative memories. When you recall your mistakes and failures, how do you feel? Do the memories lift your spirits or depress them? Depressing memories probably upset you. This is normal.

So why bring up these memories? If you made mistakes in the past, let them stay in the past. Don't be like a broken record, playing the past over and over again. This only serves to demoralize you. Instead, learn from the past, and look to the future with confidence and optimism.

The past is gone, the present lasts for a moment; only the future is a wide, open expanse of unexplored territory.

Seek professional help. Some people find that these image-builders are not effective in improving their self-images. These include people with deep-seated clinical problems, or those whose depression is not amenable to self-help. Assuming these people want to improve, they will need professional help.

Even so, many avoid seeking therapy. This is a mistake; one should do everything in his power to seek to better his life, and if no other methods have helped, he should seriously consider getting the help of a trained professional, just as he would if his ailment were physical. Otherwise, the problem will linger, disrupting a life that could be happier and more productive.

Helping Children Develop Self-Esteem

Parents and teachers possess the power to make a child's life miserable or joyous. They can be instruments of torture or inspiration, humiliation or encouragement, degradation or support. They are the decisive elements in the home and in the classroom, because their behavior impacts on the emotional health of their children.

The most important people in the life of a child are his parents and teachers. A child's developing self-image depends on the messages he receives from these adults. If the messages are positive, the child will believe them and feel positive about himself, and will very likely lead a happy, productive life. But if the messages are negative, the opposite may occur. And it makes no difference if the messages are conveyed explicitly or implicitly — children can read between the lines quite well.

For this reason, parents and teachers must behave in a way that says, "My children are important. They are valuable individuals." One expert even recommends that parents and teachers imagine a sign on the forehead of every child that reads, "Make me feel important."

But the message of importance is powerful only when adults both *say* it and *act* it, because one without the other is futile. As we said, children can read non-verbal messages. They know when adults are sincere.

We will now list several ways that parents and teachers can help children develop self-esteem and imbue them with the notion that they are important and valuable.

Treat the child with respect. The most significant message a child can hear is "I respect you." And when this message is unconditional, it impacts positively on the child's sense of worthiness. This does not mean that all behaviors are excusable whether they are appropriate or not; rather, the love, respect and concern that a parent or teacher has for the child is independent of his actions. Therefore, avoid statements such as the following:

"Good children always do their work."

"I like you when you behave properly."

"In my class, the students who work hard are valued."

These statements say that affection and respect are contingent on performance. This leaves the child with the notion that his very worth as a person depends on his actions and behavior. He concludes that as the quality of his performance goes up, his fundamental worth also goes up; and as the quality of his performance goes down, so does his worth.

However, when the message conveys unconditional respect and affection, the child is left with a different impression. When he hears things such as, "I love you," "I respect you," and "You have special talents that nobody else has," he gets the sense that he is fundamentally worthy even if his performance is lacking and he is not as productive as he could be. This should help him improve his overall behavior.

Words alone cannot convey this message. Even if we tell the child that we respect him, the message is not complete until we actually treat him that way. When we *do* treat him with respect, another thing happens: Channels of communication open. Feeling respected, the child becomes receptive to our suggestions. The Sh'lah explained a point in *Mishlei* with this concept:

> "Do not rebuke a scorner lest he hate you; rebuke a wise person and he will love you" (*Mishlei* 9:8). When you rebuke another person, do not degrade or insult him by saying, "You are a scorner," because he will hate you and will not listen to you. But "rebuke a wise person" and say to him, "You are so wise. Why are you doing this?" and he will love you and listen to you (cited in *Chovas HaTalmidim*, Ch. 1).

The Sh'lah said that even if you think a particular child does not deserve respect — he is a scorner, a "difficult" child — respect him anyway. Relate to him as a wise person, as if he is already on the level you want him to reach. He will like you and will cooperate with you. But if you treat him disrespectfully, he will hate you and reject everything you say.

Two components of a healthy relationship are mutual respect and open lines of communication. Treating a child with respect produces both. This is important, because when we have a healthy relationship with the child, we lay the groundwork for the ongoing development of his self-esteem.

Acknowledge the child's concerns. When a child cries over something that seems trivial, such as a lost toy or a sibling's insult, we sometimes dismiss the problem, saying, "Oh, stop worrying about such a silly thing." What goes on in the child's mind when he hears this? In his mind, the toy or insult is important, and when we so easily dismiss it, he gets the message that his feelings are not important. This invalidates the child and reduces his self-esteem.

However, if we acknowledge the child's concern and treat it as a real problem, as it truly is to the child, he gets the message that his feelings are valid and important. This enhances his self-esteem.

When a child is sulking over a mistake or a shortcoming and says, "I'm stupid," don't invalidate him by saying, "You don't really mean that." This leaves him with the impression that his feelings are not valuable. Instead, sympathize and show that you understand how he feels. Take him seriously. Say, "It must feel bad to think you are stupid." Afterwards, if his mood allows, you can add, "That is your opinion. And you are entitled to your opinion. As for me, I think you are smart."

This acknowledges his feelings, validates his opinion, and shows that you understand. Your response may not impress the child at the time, but once the mood passes he is left with the impression that you respect him and consider him important. Knowing this, he learns to respect himself, too.

In Chapter Seven, we will discuss in depth a method of communication, called *EAR*. EAR is an acronym for *Explore, Acknowledge, Respond*. It is a three-part technique for listening in a way that validates a child's importance.

First, explore what the child is thinking. What is the reason for his opinion? Why does he think he is right? Second, acknowledge the child. Prove that you understand him by paraphrasing what he said. Third, respond to him. Without creating a debate or being disagreeable, tell him what you think.

The EAR method is beneficial whether you totally disagree with the child or you are simply having an ordinary conversation. By exploring and acknowledging the child's position before telling him what you think, you are showing that he is important.

Let children make their own decisions. When a child lacks the maturity or wisdom to make a decision on his own, parents must make it for him. However, if the child is capable of making his own decision, encourage him to do so. This gives him the feeling that his opinion is important.

There is a story of a little girl who went with her parents to a restaurant. After taking the parents' order, the waitress asked the child what she wanted. The little girl said, "I'd like a Coke and two hot dogs." The mother then smiled at the waitress and said, "She will take roast beef along with potatoes and vegetables." Shortly afterwards, the waitress came back with their orders. To the little girl's delight, she brought her two hot dogs and a Coke. The mother was quite surprised. But the child was excited, and with the biggest smile she announced, "Look, Ma! The waitress thinks I'm real!"

While the mother had the right idea of proper nutrition, she disregarded the child's "self." This is how loving, devoted parents sometimes unintentionally undermine a child's tender self-esteem.[1] This does not mean that parents ought to let their children make all decisions for themselves, especially where such basic things as diet and safety are concerned. Obviously, this is not a good policy. However, if parents are aware of the impact a child's decision-making has on the development of self-esteem, they will use their better judgment before cutting the child out of the process altogether.

Let children find solutions to their own problems. If children have a disagreement with a teacher or an argument with a friend or sibling, if they have trouble with an unclear homework assignment or cannot find a lost article, encourage them to find a solution. With a little effort, they will solve the problem efficiently and independently.

For example, Chezky came crying to a teacher, saying, "Daniel won't let me use the ball. It's the school's ball and he has no right to keep it." The teacher might have used the quick and easy approach, ordering Daniel to share the ball. But would this really have helped Chezky? True, he would have had the ball, but he would also get the feeling that he is unable to solve his own problems. However, if the teacher would have urged Chezky to find a solution, and he found one, he would have learned that he can solve his own problems.

Urging children to find their own solutions sends this message: "You are responsible for your life, and you must seek solutions to your own problems." As children take more responsibility for their own decisions, their self-confidence improves.

---

1. Rabbi Abraham Twerski, *Life's Too Short*, pp. 156-7.

Don't do children's work for them. When children fail to hang up their coats or put their rooms in order, even after several reminders, how might you react? Many parents do it themselves, sermonizing all along about the importance of responsibility and how awful it is that they have to pick up after their children.

True, the bedrooms are now orderly and the coats are hung in their proper places, but something even more important is missing — responsible, independent children. By doing the children's work for them, the children learn that whenever a task is unappealing, they can count on their parents to come to the rescue. And although the sermon tells them that they still have to do their job, the parents' behavior — which leaves the strongest impression — tells them otherwise.

The problem doesn't stop there. As children continue to depend on their parents, they may begin to feel that they are incapable of other difficult tasks. They may even develop unwarranted feelings of helplessness and inferiority. These feelings may persist throughout life, making it difficult to cope with the challenges of adulthood. But if, while they are growing up, their parents hold them accountable for their work, demanding that they do it themselves, they will learn that they are capable of difficult tasks.

Instead of handicapping children and undermining their self-confidence by letting them off the hook, parents can help their children become responsible and independent by demanding that they fulfill their duties. And when children do not want to live up to their responsibilities, parents can view it as an *opportunity,* not as a challenge, to teach the children that they are capable of fulfilling their duties independently. This enhances self-esteem.

Chazal said, "If I am not for myself, who will be for me?"[1] This means that people should assume the responsibility to do a job independently. In terms of developing good character traits, finishing the job is important. But in terms of developing self-esteem, finishing the job is crucial.

Avoid criticism. Parents often unknowingly destroy their children with critical remarks. Although they do not say so explicitly, their criticism often implies, "You are lacking. Your performance is

---

1. *Avos* 1:14.

not good. You are not a good person." The child hears this message between the lines and believes it. With enough repetition, the child will begin to believe that he is unloved, unworthy and incompetent.

What else *should* he think? "If they really think I am a good person," he reasons, "why are they always attacking me?" He has no idea that his parents really love him but simply do not know how to criticize constructively, or that their approach springs from their own maladjustments. All he knows is what he hears and perceives.

Miriam Adahan calls non-constructive criticism a "death wish." It is another way of saying, "You are not the kind of person I want in this family. I wish you were not alive and could be replaced by somebody who meets my standards."[1]

Children are very susceptible to the destructive effects of criticism because they are young and impressionable, and because their self-images are still undeveloped. Attacks on their efficacy deeply influence their developing self-concepts and lead them to make damaging conclusions about themselves.

Thus, they become negatively programmed as children, and these feelings carry over into their adult lives, preventing them from reaching their potential in life. Their intellectual, emotional and social development is stunted by haunting feelings of inferiority.

Some parents and teachers think that too much success overinflates the ego and spoils, so they take children who are high, even if they do not display any sort of conceit, and knock them down a few pegs. These people are making a big mistake. Success energizes, propels and encourages growth. Failure, on the other hand, results in bitterness and low self-esteem.

Periodic criticism has its negative effects, but continual criticism chips away at the self-concept of the child and constitutes bona fide *child abuse*. The spilled milk, the unfinished dinner and the awkwardly rolled toothpaste tube pale in significance to the damage wrought by criticism for such minor episodes.

One of the major causes of emotional maladjustment and misbehavior in children is chronic criticism. Children who are criticized improperly feel rejected. They either respond with active hostility, such as more disobedience, anger or disrespect, or with

---

1. Miriam Adahan, *Living With Difficult People*, Feldheim Publishers, 1991, p. 143.

passive aggression, such as carelessness, slow movement or withdrawal. They may also develop other stress-related symptoms such as bed-wetting, psychosomatic illness or sleep and eating disorders.[1]

This does not mean that children should never hear a negative word. Quite the contrary. At times they must be criticized, albeit in a constructive way. Like scraped knees, these are the unavoidable bumps of childhood. But it is the number of negative messages and the way they are delivered that make the difference between a subsequent negative or positive self-image.

A young man recently told me that he had grown up with a critical father. Because of the constant criticism, he never felt loved or cared for. Now, as an adult, he is very insecure and has low self-esteem. He also has strong feelings of hostility toward his father; he sees him as a monster. This young man feels that he was ruined by criticism.

The father, not understanding his son's pain, would like to rebuild the relationship. "Okay," the father says, "maybe I was a little critical. Maybe I hit when it wasn't necessary. But let's start again. Let bygones be bygones." But the son remains hostile and unforgiving.

Inappropriate criticism is the single most powerful killer of self-esteem. It chips away at the self-image and attacks the very soul of a human being.[2]

Avoid sarcasm and abusive language. Sarcasm and abusive language are the opposite of saying, "You are important." However, they are two different forms of negativism. Whereas abusive language is a direct put-down, sarcasm is more subtle. Here are three examples of sarcasm:

"Were you brought up in a jungle?"

"Did you leave your brains at home today?"

"Are you a space cadet? Earth calling . . ."

Asking a child if he left his brains at home is another way of saying that he is not thinking, but it is worse than that; it is making a joke of the fact that he is not using all his mental faculties. Similarly, implying that he grew up in a jungle is another way of deriding him for being sloppy. And calling a child a space cadet is just another

1. Miriam Adahan, *Raising Children to Care*, Feldheim Publishers, 1988, p. 219.

2. See *Make Me, Don't Break Me*, Mesorah Publications, 1994, Ch. 7, on the topic of criticism.

insulting way of saying that he is not attuned to the circumstances around him.

When a person makes a sarcastic comment, he assumes that the child is smart enough to understand the implication and realize his error on his own. Still, it is a put-down. Straightforward criticism, with the bite that it carries, is bad enough, but making light of the child can carry a double bite. Even if the child responds with a laugh and says that the sarcasm does not bother him, don't believe him. His nonchalant reaction may be nothing more than a cover-up.

Praise liberally. When a person is praised, he feels good about himself. His spirits are lifted and he becomes motivated to succeed.

Why does praise make such an impact? Because people consider themselves important and have a need to be recognized as important. In fact, it is the strongest force within a person's psyche.[1] Praise satisfies this need to be recognized and affirms a person's sense of importance. Praise is to the soul what air is to the lungs and blood is to the heart.

Praise brings out the best in children. With praise, children realize their own worth and strengths, and become encouraged to continue growing and building on those strengths.[2] Therefore, use praise liberally. You don't need an excuse to do it. Catch children doing things right. Be on the lookout for the times they do something praiseworthy and call attention to it. Be like a gold miner who finds gold by digging through the dirt, all the time focusing on the gold. Look past the children's "dirt"; focus on their good points and bring out the best in them.

When a child does well on a test, praise him for it. Display the paper on the refrigerator door. Drink a *l'chaim* over a glass of orange juice. Look for all the good things the child does throughout the day and call attention to each and every one. The child will feel good about himself and will be motivated to repeat his good performance.

Some people say that praise is nothing more than hot air. Even if it is, both praise and air are very important. Air helps an airplane take off. Air inside an automobile tire gives the vehicle a smooth

---

1. *Mesilas Yesharim*, Ch. 19.

2. Rabbi Chaim Mordechai Katz, cited by Rabbi Z. Pliskin in *Love Your Neighbor*, p. 374.

ride. Praise, when appropriate, also develops a child's self-esteem, giving him a smooth ride through life.[1]

Expect the best. Gold miners focus on the gold, not the dirt which surrounds it; nurturing parents focus on their children's strong points, not their weak points, and then formulate correspondingly high expectations for their children. When the children hear positive things about themselves and know that their parents have high expectations of them, they learn to believe in themselves and they develop positive self-images.

On the other extreme, there are parents who focus on their children's weak points and do not expect the best from them. They magnify the negative through criticism and frequently overlook the positive. These children may begin to see themselves as incompetent and unworthy.

When a child receives a failing grade in school, don't say, "You are not living up to your potential." Say instead, "You have great potential, and I know you can do well. These grades do not reflect your true ability."

If a child steals, don't say, "You are a thief" or "You are not worthy of anything good." The child may continue to steal and become exactly what you don't want him to be. Say instead, "You just stole something" or "You just behaved poorly." Then say, "You are better than that, and you know better." This generates a positive attitude. The child will probably discontinue the undesired behavior and become the refined person you want him to be.[2]

Rabbi Abraham Twerski wrote that as a youngster his wise father would rebuke him with the words *"Es past nisht."* It means, "This is not for you. You are better than that. You are expected to live up to the high standards which you already have." He emphasized how the behavior was incompatible with a child of such high caliber.[3]

Search for your children's good traits and articulate your high expectations for them. Share your belief in them, saying, "You are so capable of greatness. If only you would work, you would reach

---

1. See *Make Me, Don't Break Me*, Ch. 2, on the topic of praise.
2. Rabbi S. R. Hirsch, *Yesodos HaChinuch*, p. 64, and Rabbi Klonimus Kalmish Shapira, *Chovas HaTalmidim*, Ch. 1.
3. Rabbi Abraham Twerski, *Generation to Generation*, CIS Publishers, Vol. 1, p. 15.

the goal."[1] Keep reminding them that they are competent and worthy. Trust them to do the job right. Give them the benefit of the doubt. Call them "winners." Tell them how successful they are and how successful they *can* be.

Rabbi Nosson Tzvi Finkel always instilled in his students a strong awareness of their potential. He would bestow great honor on his students, telling some that they were destined for greatness, and complimenting others in public for their brilliance or their righteousness. He would even stand up in honor of some students or ask them for a blessing.[2]

The saying goes: "Treat a person as he is, and he will remain as he is; treat a person as if he were what he *could* be and *should* be, and he will become what he could be and should be." This is not to say that parents and teachers can control the level of success a child has. Rather, the saying expresses the idea that parents and teachers have a strong influence on their children. Through their expectations, they influence a child's attitude and behavior, either in a positive or negative way.

How high should you go with your expectations of the child? Does the principle mean that the higher you set your expectation, the greater the effect? There is no rule and no easy answer. On one hand, you should believe that the child has greater potential than he or she displays. On the other hand, you cannot expect more than the child can achieve. It isn't easy to determine the right approach.

But one thing is certain — if the child is capable of reaching certain goals, you should expect him to reach them. If the child is not capable, do not expect it.[3] Expecting a child to reach an unattainable goal will result in failure. The child will most likely not conclude that the adults' unrealistic expectation led to the failure, but rather that his own deficiency caused it. With every failure, he will see himself more and more as an inferior individual, further depressing his self-esteem and jeopardizing future achievements.[4]

Call attention to strengths and achievements. People with low self-esteem typically overlook their talents and achievements.

---

1. Rabbi Klonimus Kalmish Shapira, *Chovas HaTalmidim*, Ch. 1.
2. *HaMeoros HaGedolim*, p. 256.
3. Heard from Rabbi Shimon Schwab.
4. See *Make Me, Don't Break Me*, Ch. 6, on the topic of expectations.

But if they were to break the cycle and recognize their good points, their self-esteem might improve. This is where parents and teachers come in. They can help children recognize their good points by pointing out their strengths and achievements.

Every child does something right at some time. Maybe he scores high on a test, does someone a favor, or acts with courage, responsibility or maturity. By pointing this out to him, adults can help him develop a better view of himself. He will feel elevated and will be inspired to reach even higher levels of success.[1] Also, as the child sees that others recognize him for who he is and what he has accomplished, rather than comparing him to others, he will feel more comfortable with himself and will respect himself more.

Offer a truthful appraisal. Parents and teachers often praise children for a job well done, when in fact the performance is quite the opposite. You have seen it before. A student does poorly on a test but the teacher gives him a good grade and praises him for studying so hard. A child finishes only part of his dinner but the parent praises him anyway.

While the intention of these adults is to motivate the children to perform better the next time, it usually does not work. As far as the children are concerned, they have already performed well and there is no need for improvement.

Does this distortion of the truth enhance self-esteem? If the child believes it, his self-esteem will improve temporarily. But the feeling will be short-lived, until the day he realizes that all along he has not been performing well.

Applaud effort. *Chazal* said, "Your duty is not to complete the task, but you do not have the freedom not to try."[2] Although they said this regarding Torah study, it can be extended to all matters consistent with Torah ideals.

In these matters, effort is a goal in itself.[3] Praising effort transmits this ideal to the child. It tells the child, "Whether you perform excellently or not, it is just as important to make a genuine effort to do your best."

---

1. Rabbi Yechezkel Levenstein, *Ohr Yechezkel, michtavim* 240.
2. *Avos* 2:16.
3. Rabbi Moshe Feinstein, *Darash Moshe*, p. 111.

If the child studies for a test and does poorly, recognize the effort and emphasize its importance. Say, "I saw you studying and I am very proud of your effort. This indicates that you are a serious student. I know you will score better next time."

Even if the child does well, you can still reinforce the significance of effort. Say, "I see you scored a 95. Because you studied, you did well."

When we applaud a child's efforts, he feels good about himself. He is then motivated to put effort into all his other endeavors. But there is another payoff. When we applaud a child's effort even before he reaches the goal, we validate his sense of competence at an early stage, enhancing his motivation to reach the final goal.

Allow for mistakes and failure. Suppose a child fails a test or handles a household chore poorly. Parents often react in one of two ways, by scolding the child or by simply allowing him to cry over the mishap. The problem is that neither accomplishes anything, except to reduce the child's self-confidence.

Parents, however, can do something else. They can make the event into an *opportunity* by helping the child discover why he made the mistake and find ways to do better next time. When the child realizes that he is a "mistake-breaker" as well as a mistake-maker, he views himself in a positive light and his self-concept remains intact.

Parents and teachers can help instill this attitude by creating a laboratory environment in their homes and classrooms, where children can try to reach their goals without receiving a penalty for occasional blunders. They would make a rule that whenever a child makes a mistake, nobody is allowed to make fun of him. In this environment, children would feel comfortable making mistakes, and they would understand that mistakes do not reduce their importance in any way.

Help children be comfortable with themselves. Children often feel inferior to those who are stronger, faster, smarter, taller or richer than they. They put themselves down for their inborn physical and mental characteristics, which do not appear to measure up to those of others. The effect on their self-images is obvious.

Here is an activity that can help children become comfortable with their own set of endowments. Gather a group of children together and ask the tallest one to stand up and take a bow.

Compliment him or her for being so tall and ask all the other children to clap. Then ask the one with the blackest hair to stand up and take a bow. After complimenting him or her for having such black hair, ask the other children to clap. Do the same for the one with the bluest eyes, the darkest skin, the loudest voice, etc.

How will the children react? After a while, they will probably say, "This is silly. So what if he/she has the blackest hair or the loudest voice! It doesn't make him/her special or better than anyone else. Why should you give a compliment, and why should we clap?" And of course, they are right.

Now you can explain: "Of course, you are right. They deserve no credit for having these qualities because they did not work for them. They were born with them. It is the same with any inborn characteristic. If a child is born to rich parents, he will be rich. If a child is born with good looks, physical strength or a brilliant mind, he does not deserve credit for it. Therefore, unless he worked for his strength, riches, looks or intelligence, he is no more special than anyone else, and you should not feel inferior to him."

You can then add, "And if you worked hard to improve your strength or increase your knowledge, even if you still do not match up to the other person, you can take comfort in knowing that you are special, because you made the effort to use the abilities that you were born with. This is all one can be expected to do."

Set up a consequential environment. There is a law of nature that says, "For every action there is a reaction." The same law applies to our behaviors. If we behave in an acceptable way, we will be rewarded; if we behave in an inappropriate way, there will be a penalty. For everything we do there is a consequence, good or bad.

For example, if we come to work on time and do our job diligently, we will continue getting paid and maybe even receive a raise. But if we act irresponsibly, we may lose those benefits. Is the consequence a result of our action or the employer's? It is our action that brought about the reward or penalty, and we alone are responsible for the outcome.

Let us look at the way consequences work with children. When children act according to our expectations, we are happy with them, and they continue to receive their privileges. When they do not meet our expectations, though, the opposite may occur. Is the consequence a result of the children's actions or ours? It is the children alone who are responsible for the outcome.

We can set up a consequential environment by letting children know that we do not reward or punish them. Rather, we are facilitators who enforce the reward or punishment that they choose to take as a result of their behavior. When children realize that their behaviors bring about corresponding rewards and penalties, they begin to feel that they have control over their lives. This gives them a sense of importance.[1]

Create opportunities for small achievements. Self-confidence comes from the knowledge that one is competent. Doesn't it make sense, then, that the way to develop a child's self-confidence is to create opportunities for success? The more he succeeds, the more convinced he will be of his competence.

Adults can provide these opportunities for children by setting small but challenging goals for them. As the children reach those goals, they become more convinced of their ability and begin to see themselves as competent individuals. This enhances their self-confidence and motivates them to accept even bigger challenges. In other words, competence leads to confidence.

If a child cannot sit still to do his homework for more than ten minutes at a time, set the timer for twelve minutes and ask him to stay seated until the buzzer goes off. If the child constantly puts others down, ask him to compliment three people every day. If the child does not share his toys with friends or siblings, have him share his toys two times every day. Every time the child reaches the goal, offer praise and maybe even a small reward. As he becomes accustomed to the goals, increase the challenge by expanding them.

These opportunities force the child to go beyond the boundaries of his usual behavior. However, there is another kind of opportunity: the type that expands the skills that the child already has. For example, if the child can draw nicely, ask her to draw a picture for a school play or an upcoming birthday party. If the child can write poetry, ask her to write a poem for a sick friend or relative. If the child is a responsible baby-sitter, find baby-sitting opportunities for

---

1. See *Make Me, Don't Break Me,* Ch. 5, on the topic of consequences.

her. Whatever the child's ability, target it and create opportunities for small achievements.

The key here is success. Don't wait for a time when the child's talents are needed; create the need now. And as the child succeeds, he will begin to believe in himself.

Protect children from negative influences. Children are fragile, inexperienced and undeveloped in their sense of right and wrong. They are therefore very susceptible to the influences of negative people, more so than adults. For this reason, children should not associate with people who can have a negative influence on their budding self-images.

How can children with undeveloped judgment know whom to avoid? Parents and teachers can tell them. They can even go out and find appropriate friends for their children.

Adults can also protect children from the negative media, i.e., radio, videos, television and literature, by making rules about what is allowed and what is not allowed. But parents and teachers can go one step further; they can go out and find kosher alternatives. In the marketplace, there is a wealth of books, videos and computer software that can focus the minds of children on productive, self-expanding thoughts instead of the destructive, self-limiting kind.

In a nationwide survey of ten- to sixteen-year-old children, one-third of the respondents said that they often wanted to try things they saw on television. Two-thirds of the respondents said that their friends were influenced by what they saw on television. The moral of the story: Even youngsters recognize the influence of television.[1]

Some adults from the liberal camp object to these suggestions. "If children are sheltered from the negative influences of the street," they protest, "how will they ever be prepared to live in the real world?"

The answer is that they will be even more prepared for the real world. Having avoided the street's negative influences, they will emerge with a clear set of values and a strong sense of right and wrong. Their minds will not be cluttered with the nonsense considered important by the world; rather, they will be imbued with

---

1. Washington Post, cited by *Reader's Digest*, August 1995, p. 178.

attitudes that will help them succeed and overcome life's challenges. What better preparation for the real world can one have?

Be a role model. Parents with high self-esteem help their children develop self-esteem by example. When children observe their parents exhibiting a sense of worthiness and confidence, they adopt those attitudes and develop a healthy self-image. But if they observe their parents wallowing in feelings of inferiority, their own sense of low self-esteem is not far behind.

> Self-concepts are contagious. Parents who have feelings of security and self-confidence are likely to pass these on to their children. Parents who have negative self-concepts pass those on to their children. The most effective way to instill self-esteem in one's children is for the parents to develop it themselves (Rabbi Abraham Twerski, *Life's Too Short*, p.153).

Parents unknowingly help their children develop high or low self-esteem by modeling that attitude. No matter how much they say, if their actions are not aligned with their words, all the sermons in the world will not help. The message parents send their children is conveyed by their actions as well as their words. Even the most thought-out, constructive statement loses its full impact if the parents' actions do not support it.[1] As the saying goes, "Actions speak louder than words."

Let your children know that you feel good about yourself. When a problem arises, think of a solution and let your children know what you have done. When challenged, proceed with confidence and an "I-can" attitude, and make sure your children see it. When you are complimented, accept it gracefully instead of saying, "Oh, that's not true." When you make a mistake, let your children see that you have grown from it and that your self-esteem remains intact.

Admit to your mistakes. When a child makes a mistake, parents usually expect him to admit to it and to apologize for it. But what happens when parents make mistakes and do *not* admit to them? The child may conclude that he is the only one in the family who makes mistakes. He then surmises that there must be something fundamentally wrong with him.

---

1. Chazon Ish, *Emunah U'Bitachon* 4:16.

However, when parents admit to their errors, the child sees that others make mistakes too. He will then be less likely to condemn himself for his own.

Parents can even share with their children the mistakes they made when they were young and explain how they grew from those mistakes. For example, say a child gets in trouble for cheating in school. He feels bad about it and his self-esteem takes a blow. The parent can tell the child about a time that she got in trouble for cheating and how she decided never to do it again. "If my mother did it and learned a lesson from it," the child reasons, "I too should learn a lesson. And if my mother became a better person as a result of her mistake, I should also become a better person and not walk away feeling inferior."

This does not mean that parents should tell their children about all of their mistakes. On the contrary, parents should use good judgment in deciding what to share. Otherwise, the result may be counterproductive.

Spend time together. Adults convey the message "You are important" by making it clear that their children's activities are important to them. They talk with them about their projects, interests, hopes and dreams. They go to their sporting events, drama presentations, award ceremonies, science fairs and parents' day at school. This gives children the feeling that they truly are important.

Never embarrass a child. Public embarrassment is a profound violation of a person's pride. It is the most insensitive thing one can do to another human being. Public embarrassment is so severe that *Chazal* compared it to murder.[1]

While the Torah requires us to rebuke others, it categorically forbids public rebuke.[2] This means that parents should not hit, yell, admonish or criticize their children in any form when they are outside the house or in view of other people. If you are on the street, in a store, or in the house when guests are present, use gestures to convey disapproval, but save the reproof for a private setting. Some experts even recommend removing a child from his siblings' presence before admonishing him.

---

1. Talmud *Bava Metzia* 58b.
2. Talmud *Arachin* 16b and Rashi there.

Never threaten to leave a child. Picture this scene: A mother is shopping in a supermarket, accompanied by her six-year-old son. As they enter the candy aisle, the little boy demands a certain candy. The mother tells him, "No." But he is not satisfied with that. He plants his feet on the floor and refuses to budge until the mother gives in. Then he begins to scream. Giving in to his demand at a time like this sets a bad precedent, so the mother, in exasperation, turns her back and tells him, "If you do not come with me now, I will leave you here."

Different versions of this scenario occur all the time. The parent may threaten to lock the child in his room, call the police, put him in jail, or send him to an orphanage. Can you imagine how a child feels when he is confronted with the possibility that his parent will leave him? He feels devastated. He is fragile and totally dependent on his parents. He respects them and is desperate for their love. "Does she really love me? Does she really care about me?" he thinks. Once the doubt enters his head, he may conclude that the parent really does not care about him and that he must not be worth much.

Why do parents threaten their children in this way? Because they are at wit's end and do not know what else to do. But this is not a reason to take out hostile feelings on a child. The price the child pays is too high.

Teach children to engage in image-building activities. Children can build their self-images with the same activities that you use to build yours. With your guidance, they can make a victory list and an inventory of assets. They can learn to challenge their inner voices, and to act, visualize and affirm a new self-image. They can adopt role models, consider their worth, finish a job, and avoid comparisons and negative memories. Whatever you do to build your own self-esteem, children can do as well.

Each child is different. Each has his own disposition, personality and set of strengths and weaknesses. Therefore, when guiding a child in any image-building activity, first consider his level of self-confidence, along with his talents, temperament and needs. Then match the activity to the child.

Also, before recommending any of the activities, the child should *want* to build his self-image. Otherwise, it is unlikely that he will perform optimally. How can you know if he wants to improve? Ask him. Assuming you have a healthy relationship, he will probably tell you the truth. And if he tells you that he is not interested, it will not be beneficial to force him.

What can you do then? Does this mean that he will never improve? No, not at all. You can still relate to him in all the ways that say, "You are important. You have value." With your help, he can develop his self-image and live a richer, more productive life. You will help him achieve *success*!

Chapter Seven

Create Positive Relationships

A good friend is hard to find. Once you find one, you do whatever you can to maintain the relationship. Why is it so important to have friends? Because they are the ones with whom you share your pains and joys. Being able to share your experiences with others helps make life more fulfilling.

King Shlomo said, "A friend loves at all times, and becomes a brother in adversity."[1] Rabbi Eliyahu Dessler said, "A happy, successful life depends on the number of friends one has."[2] The Chofetz Chaim wrote, "A reclusive person cannot be happy."[3] The Vilna Gaon wrote that a friend "gives good advice, sweet to the soul."[4] The Talmudic sage, Rabbi Chanina, said, "I learned a great deal from my

---

1. *Mishlei* 17:17, following Rabbi S. R. Hirsch, *From the Wisdom of Mishlei*, Feldheim Publishers, p. 185.
2. *Michtav M'Eliyahu*, Vol. 4, p. 243.
3. *Ahavas Chessed* 2:2.
4. *Mishlei* 27:9.

teachers, but I learned even more from my friends."[1] Along these lines, Rabbi Shamshon Raphael Hirsch said that if you depend entirely upon yourself, your intellect will stagnate, but when you share your thoughts with someone else, you become sharpened. Furthermore, the other person can help you strengthen your weak character traits.[2]

Rabbi Avraham Grodzinsky wrote that we need good relationships so we can develop social skills and learn about the needs and sensitivities of others. With such an understanding, we will not insult others, and we will be quick to say the positive things they need to hear.[3]

When Choni HaMa'agal awoke after seventy years of sleep, people neither recognized him nor offered him the same companionship as before. Heartbroken, Choni prayed that his life be ended. His outlook was, "Either companionship or death."[4] He knew that an insular life would stunt his intellectual, emotional and social growth.[5] The Me'iri wrote, "A person without a friend is like a left hand without a right hand."[6] The Rosh said, "Do not waver in seeking friends, and do not have even one enemy."[7] *Tiferes Yisrael* wrote that a person has "no greater success than to have many friends and people who respect him, because without friends — whether he is rich or poor — he is like a lonely person in the desert."[8]

Chazal also told us, "Acquire for yourself a friend."[9] You may have to spend a great deal of time with that person or conduct yourself in an especially congenial way; you may have to avoid disagreeing with him; you may have to tolerate his undesirable behaviors; you may even have to give him money or gifts — but all of these things are worthwhile for the sake of having a friend.[10]

---

1. Talmud *Taanis* 7a.
2. *From the Wisdom of Mishlei*, pp. 183-184.
3. *Toras Avraham*, p. 372.
4. Talmud *Taanis* 23a.
5. See Rambam, *Avos* 1:6: A friend "helps a person improve his actions and all his affairs. As *Chazal* said, 'Either companionship or death.' "
6. *Mishlei* 17:17.
7. *Orchos Chaim LeHaRosh* 90.
8. *Avos* 1:15.
9. *Avos* 1:6.
10. Rabbeinu Yonah, *Avos* 1:6.

Positive relationships on the job. Good relationships are so important that, according to a recent statistic, well over half the people fired from their jobs meet their fate as a result of not getting along well with their bosses. Although they have the technical expertise for the job, the lack of a healthy employer-employee relationship gets them into trouble.

> Hatred arouses quarrels; love covers up all transgressions (*Mishlei* 10:12).

If one person dislikes another, he will be provoked by even the most trivial gesture of the other person. But if he likes him, he will disregard his faults.[1]

Every employee knows that if the boss likes you, you can get away with a lot — even if you lack technical expertise. But if the boss does not like you, he will find problems that don't even exist.

Job security is not the only benefit of a healthy employer-employee relationship. When the employee gets along with his boss, there is an atmosphere of trust and respect. The employee will try to satisfy his boss by working to the best of his ability, and he will also be open to guidance and suggestions. When they do not get along, though, the employee will be closed to his boss's suggestions and will not be motivated to satisfy him.

Human-relations skills are so important that John D. Rockefeller, a past owner of Bethlehem Steel Company, said that he would pay more for the ability to deal with people than for anything else. For this reason, he hired Andrew Carnegie to manage his company. Mr. Carnegie openly admitted that there were many other people in the company who knew more about the steel industry than he. However, he had something that they did not have — the ability to deal effectively with people. And with this ability, he was able to motivate his employees and bring about change for the benefit of the company, the employees and himself.

People often think that successful workers — whether they are teachers, mechanics, secretaries, salespeople or computer program-

---

1. Vilna Gaon, *Mishlei* 10:12.

mers — will naturally become successful managers. This is not true. People who are promoted to a management level because of their proven technical skills do not always succeed. As managers, they need a different set of skills.

When these people were workers, they had to be skilled at the task for which they were hired. Whether their job was to type, write, cut, hammer or talk on the phone, their primary focus was their task. However, as managers their primary focus shifts from the task to the people whom they supervise. Now their job is to motivate the workers, build relations with them, and constantly be on the lookout for their well-being. As workers they had to be task-oriented, but as managers they have to be people-oriented. These orientations require different sets of skills.

Parents and children, teachers and students. Some parents and teachers say, "I don't care about the relationship I have with the child. I am not competing in a popularity contest; I am preparing this child for adulthood."

This attitude is a mistake, because the extent of success parents and teachers have in raising and teaching a child is largely dependent on the relationship. If the child sees these adults as people whom he can trust, respect and look up to for guidance, he will accept their motivational attempts, whether the attempts are positive, such as praise, rewards and persuasion, or negative, such as criticism or the threat of a penalty. King Shlomo made this point thousands of years ago:

> The wounds of a loving person are faithful, and the kisses of a hater are a burden (*Mishlei* 27:6).

If the child sees his parents and teachers as people who are concerned with his welfare, he will accept the "wounds" — the restrictions or rebuke — to which they periodically subject him. Within this positive relationship, the child will also accept their motivational attempts and will likely become the kind of person they expect him to be.

But if the child sees his parents and teachers as people who do not have his best interests at heart, he will want no part of them, not even their kisses and favors. With this negative attitude, the child will reject their motivational attempts and may turn out to be a very different person from what they expected.[1]

≈)≈

Everybody wants to be recognized and appreciated. Friends and spouses expect recognition and appreciation from each other. Children hunger for their parents and teachers to recognize and appreciate them. Employees need the same treatment from their bosses. But it goes in both directions; teachers also want recognition and appreciation from their students, parents want it from their children, and bosses want it from their employees.[2]

Positive relationships are important because everybody wants them, and as we said earlier, such relationships can determine one's happiness and success in life. How can we create positive relationships? What is the secret?

Giving Value Helps Create a Positive Relationship

> If you want to become attached to the love of your friend, do something for his benefit (*Derech Eretz Zuta,* Ch. 2).

Chazal told us that thinking about the other person is not enough to create positive feelings; you have to do something for him. If you notice that an acquaintance is overwhelmed with responsibilities, alleviate the load by offering to perform a service for him. If you are driving your car and see an acquaintance walking on the street, give him a ride, even if it means going out of your way.

Any time you help another person, you are not only fulfilling the *mitzvah* of *chessed,* you are also creating positive feelings. Obviously, these feelings alone will not create an enduring relationship; a relationship is the result of much more than doing nice things for others. However, it does contribute by bringing about positive feelings, the foundation of a healthy relationship.

Why does helping others have this effect? Simply speaking, when the other person sees that you care about him, he responds with affection for you. But Rabbi Eliyahu Dessler and Rabbi Chaim

---

1. See Rabbi S. R. Hirsch, *Horeb,* Soncino Press, 1981, p. 414, for the long-term impact of a positive relationship.
2. See Rabbi Shlomo Wolbe, *Alei Shur,* p. 191.

Shmulevitz offered another explanation. They said that when one person helps another, it does not cause the receiver to love the giver; rather, it causes the giver to love the receiver. They explained that when one person helps another, the helper actually gives the other person a piece of himself. Since a person loves himself, the helper therefore loves the person to whom he has given a piece of himself. According to this, love is the product of doing for others; as the giver does more and more, his love for the receiver grows and a relationship develops.[1]

However we look at it, the positive feeling is a result of "doing something for the other person's benefit." It is the outcome of helping to satisfy another person's needs. It follows, then, that the more people one helps, the more friends he will have.[2]

And when the other person does the same, no matter how different his personality may be, they complement each other and the relationship blossoms. They are always asking, "What does the other person want? How can I help him get it?"[3] It also means that they focus on common goals instead of personal interests.[4] But if each one worries only about himself, always looking to see what he can *take* from the relationship and constantly trying to pull the other in his direction, they end up disliking each other.[5]

The boomerang effect. There is an added bonus to helping other people:

> When someone chases after opportunities to do good deeds and initiates kind activity for other people, it is as if he makes an appeal to have his own desires fulfilled, because through his actions the blessing of goodness will come on him. But when someone looks to do bad to others, the same bad thing will happen to him (Vilna Gaon, *Mishlei* 11:27).

If you help enough people get what they want, you eventually will get what *you* want. Work for the benefit of others, and you will

---

1. *Michtav M'Eliyahu*, Vol. 1, pp. 35-38, and Vol. 3, pp. 89-90; *Sichos Mussar*, 5732:4, 22.
2. *Michtav M'Eliyahu*, Vol. 1, p. 37.
3. Rambam, *Avos* 1:6; *Michtav M'Eliyahu*, Vol. 3, pp. 33-34.
4. *Michtav M'Eliyahu*, Vol. 4, p. 16.
5. *Michtav M'Eliyahu*, Vol. 3, pp. 33-34.

be rewarded; work for the detriment of others, and you will be penalized. Like a boomerang, the effort you put forth will come back to you as a corresponding gain or loss. As the saying goes: What goes around comes around.

People have many needs. People have needs that pertain to themselves, their property and their emotions. We can help them satisfy their physical and material needs by assuming some of their chores and protecting them and their belongings from danger. We can help them satisfy their emotional needs by being kind to them, protecting them from emotional pain, helping them live a peaceful life, and making them feel happy, valuable and comfortable.[1]

When we begin to consider a person's emotional needs, the first thing that comes to mind is: "There are so many. If we are not trained in psychology, how can we possibly pinpoint even a portion of a person's emotional needs? How can we help a person satisfy his emotional needs if we don't even know what they are?"

It is not as difficult as it sounds. The reason is that most emotional needs revolve around a single theme — the need to feel valued. Every person wants to feel important and valued. Whether the relationship is between employers and employees, parents and children, teachers and students, husbands and wives, friends, neighbors or siblings, each party has a need to feel valued. If, in all their interactions, they answer the question "What can I do to give him or her value?" they will be working for "the other person's benefit" and will probably be doing the right thing. We will now discuss ways of showing others that we value them.

Make the Other Person Feel Important

Five friends once went to a restaurant. After placing their orders, they began chatting among themselves. The waiter came out with the first course, and as he was serving it, all but one disregarded him. This one looked up and pleasantly said, "Thank you." When the waiter brought out the next course, the same person told the waiter, "That is very kind of you."

After the main course, they all decided to order a scoop of ice cream for dessert. As the waiter was bringing out the desserts, they

---

1. *Mesilas Yesharim,* Ch. 19.

noticed an interesting thing. Each portion was no larger than the size of a golf ball — except for one, which was the size of a baseball. Can you guess who received that portion? Of course, it was the one who had thanked the waiter throughout the meal.

The other four, somewhat amazed, asked the lucky one, "Are you acquainted with that waiter?" He answered, "No, I am not acquainted with him personally, but I know a lot about him. He is a human being, and like all human beings, he wants to feel important."

The waiter was made to feel important. He appreciated the recognition that he had received, and he then proceeded to do the only thing he could do to reciprocate the feeling — he gave a larger portion of ice cream to the person who had valued him. A relationship — of sorts — was created.

The story illustrates a powerful aspect of human nature: People consider themselves important and have a need to be recognized as important. As mentioned in earlier chapters, this need is the strongest force within a person's psyche.

> The desire for honor is greater than the desire for wealth . . . Honor is the driving force because one cannot endure being and seeing oneself lower than another . . . Honor drives the heart of a person more than all the yearnings and desires in the world (*Mesilas Yesharim*, Ch. 19).

The honor discussed by the *Mesilas Yesharim* is on different levels. On the highest level, it is status and glory; on a lower level, it is simple recognition and appreciation. But no matter what level of honor is meant, it is a driving force within one's personality.

Throughout history, famous leaders have illustrated this basic drive of human nature — sometimes with fatal consequences.

> Many stumbled and were destroyed in their pursuit of honor. Yeravam ben Nevat lost his share in the next world because of his pursuit of honor . . . Honor caused Korach and his group to be destroyed . . . The spies spoke negatively about the land of Israel and brought death to themselves and their entire generation because they feared that their honor would be reduced after entering the land and that others would replace them. Shaul began to chase Dovid because of honor . . . (Ibid.).

All these leaders were driven by a need to feel important. King Shaul launched a campaign to kill Dovid because Dovid was given more honor after they both returned from war. The spies tried to prevent the Jewish people from entering Israel because they did not want to lose their distinguished status. Korach and his band of rebels sought Moshe Rabbeinu's position; they were warned of the danger but persisted anyway. Hashem offered the wicked Yeravam ben Nevat a spectacular reward if he would repent — a walk in *Gan Eden* together with King Dovid and Hashem. When he learned that he would walk behind King Dovid, he rejected the offer and continued in his evil ways.

Rabbi Yeruchom Levovitz said that every person wants recognition; it is as if every person "stands and yells loudly, in all forms of announcement, 'Consider me and make me important; don't embarrass me or degrade me; recognize my words.' "[1]

Because people need to feel important, they have difficulty seeing their own faults. They even justify their mistakes.[2] King Shaul illustrated this tendency when he allowed Agag, the king of Amalek, to live. He acted in direct violation of Hashem's mandate, yet he did not accept full responsibility for his action afterward. He blamed the people for encouraging him to spare Agag's life.[3]

The need to feel important causes jealousy and hatred. We see this from the fact that skilled craftsmen dislike the other members of their trade. Each craftsman wants to be recognized as the most skilled in his trade, but the existence of competitors reduces that possibility.[4]

When people see group photographs, whose face do they look for first? That's right — their own! Each one feels he is the most interesting and most important member of the group.

Rabbi Eliyahu Dessler said, "To most people, there is no word more beloved than 'I' and there is nothing more beautiful than their own name."[5]

---

1. *Daas Chochmah U'Mussar*, Vol. 3, p. 68.

2. Talmud *Kesubos* 105b, explained by Rabbi Yoel Schwartz, *The Eternal Jewish Home*, Jerusalem Academy Publications, 1982, p. 43.

3. *I Shmuel* 15:9, explained by Rabbi Yoel Schwartz, ibid.

4. *Bereishis Rabbah*, Ch. 19, explained by Rabbi Yoel Schwartz, ibid., p. 42.

5. *Michtav M'Eliyahu*, Vol. 4, p. 244.

Many years ago, the New York Telephone Company conducted a study to discover which words people use most frequently. They found that people use the word "I" most frequently. Is it any wonder? As one expert put it — people think about themselves before breakfast, during lunch and after dinner.

A former president of the United States, Theodore Roosevelt, used to make people feel important, and they loved it. After his term of office was over, he once visited the White House on a day that President and Mrs. Taft were away. As he walked the halls, he greeted all the servants by name. When he saw the kitchen maid, he asked if she still made the corn bread she used to make for him. She replied, "Sometimes, for the workers. But nobody else eats it." Roosevelt answered, "They don't appreciate good things. When I see the President, I shall tell him." The maid quickly brought him a piece and he proceeded to eat it as he continued his visit, greeting the gardeners and other workers just as he had done in the days when he was in office.

A long-time White House worker later said that this day was their happiest day in two years, and that none of them would trade it for a hundred dollars.

What did Roosevelt do? He made people feel important by showing appreciation and recognition. They appreciated it and even attached a price tag to it.

Here is another story that illustrates the power of making people feel important. A man whom we will call David once traveled with his wife to visit her elderly Aunt Miriam in another town. After visiting for a short while, David's wife left him with her aunt as she went off to visit some cousins.

While David was sitting with Aunt Miriam, he began admiring the beauty and careful detail of her home. Aunt Miriam told him that she and her husband had planned the house themselves and added many personal touches to make it more comfortable and appealing. As she showed him around the house, he continued praising what he saw: the silk draperies, Wedgewood china, French furniture, silver tea set and fine woodwork.

At the end of the tour, the aunt took him to the garage where an antique Packard in mint condition was standing on four blocks. She explained that her husband had given it to her as a gift just before he died and that she had never ridden in it. She then told David that she wanted to give it to him as a gift. David refused, saying that she had blood relatives who really deserved it. She answered, "Yes, I have blood relatives who would love to have the car; in fact, they have been waiting for me to die so that they can finally get it! I don't want them to have it. I insist that you accept it." He tried to get out of taking the gift, but she persisted, and he eventually did accept it.

Aunt Miriam was an old widow with much to be grateful for. She lived in a comfortable home and had raised a large family. She had fond memories of a loving husband and years of happiness. But she needed more. She needed sincere recognition and appreciation, something that she had not received for some time. When she finally got it, she responded by offering David her cherished Packard as a gift.

Did David have an ulterior motive? Was he manipulating Aunt Miriam with the intent of getting something from her? Not at all. The only thing he wanted was the feeling that he was able to do something for her. He wanted to walk away feeling good about making her feel important. He not only did that; he also walked away with a new relationship and the unexpected gift of a valuable antique automobile.

David knew that though there are four billion people in the world who go to sleep every night starving for a decent meal, there are five billion people who go to sleep every night starving for a few words of sincere praise and appreciation.

Rabbi Eliyahu Dessler said, "Every person thinks that he excels in something more than you, and he is probably correct. Agree with him, and he will love you for it."[1] Complimenting, praising, and giving credit and recognition are all ways of affirming a person's sense of importance. They all satisfy the most compelling emotional need in human nature. By satisfying that need, you are doing something for the benefit of the other person.[2]

Making people feel important is a *mitzvah*. Since man was created in the image of Hashem, all people deserve honor and respect,

---

1. *Michtav M'Eliyahu*, Vol. 4, p. 244.

2. See Chapter Six on how to help children develop self-esteem. Using any of these ideas will make both children and adults feel important.

whether they appear higher or lower than us.[1] And when we do give people honor and respect, we are doing more than being polite; we are expressing honor and respect for the image of Hashem.[2] Making others feel important is therefore a *mitzvah.*

Chazal told us more about the *mitzvah* of honoring others:

> Honor others the way you honor yourself (*Avos* 2:10).
>
> Having a "good eye" [means] that one is not jealous of his friend, and that his friend's honor is as dear to him as his own (Rashi, *Avos* 5:19).
>
> Righteous people praise and honor other people for every attribute they have. Evil people look for the faults and mistakes of other people, to put them down (Rabbeinu Yonah, *Sha'arei Teshuvah* 1:18).

Rabbi Yeruchom Levovitz was once sitting with a group of students, among them Rabbi Chaim Shmulevitz. Rabbi Levovitz showed them a letter he had just received from a student who traveled to America. In the letter, the student reported that he had delivered a lecture he once heard from Reb Chaim and that the audience had enjoyed it. As Rabbi Levovitz mentioned Reb Chaim's name, he pointed to Rabbi Chaim Shmulevitz.

Rabbi Shmulevitz later recounted that he felt honored by the credit given to him — even though he was sure that the student who wrote the letter was not referring to him, but rather to Reb Chaim of Brisk! He realized that the honor he felt was imaginary and invented, and he even criticized himself for appreciating the commendation. Regarding this experience, he said:

> Although one must distance himself from honor as much as possible, for it is forbidden to accept honor, this is only in relation to oneself. However, in relation to other people, one is obligated to give other people honor in every way and in every situation, without boundaries or limits. One is even obligated to give illusory honor. [For this reason,] Rabbi Levovitz pointed to me, to honor me,

---

1. Rabbi Chaim of Volozhin, *Ruach Chaim* 4:1; Rabbi Yeruchom Levovitz, *Daas Chochmah U'Mussar,* Vol. 2, pp. 38-39.
2. Rabbi Shlomo Wolbe, *Alei Shur,* p. 118.

although he probably also knew that the letter was referring to Rabbi Chaim of Brisk (*Sichos Mussar*, 5732:29).

Indeed, the *middah* of humility makes it necessary for us to come down off our pedestals when we feel too high. However, we are required to do the opposite for others. We must delve into the areas in which each person needs honor and use that understanding to build him up. We must view each person as having a craving for honor, as Haman had, and then give him that honor.[1]

See Things from the Other Person's Point of View

Rabbi Eliyahu Dessler said that a powerful way to create positive relations is "to view the other person as he views himself."

> All anger, hate, fights and arguments are the result of each person seeing himself from a different perspective, refusing to see himself from the perspective of his counterpart. For example, a poor man asks a rich man for a large donation of money. The rich man sees this as *chutzpah* and becomes angry. In the meantime, the poor man becomes upset, thinking, "Hashem gave the rich man so much. Why can't he just give me what I need?" So the two separate with an argument and hurt feelings. If only each party would try to understand the view of his counterpart — even if he were not to validate it — they would be able to bypass almost every debate and hard feeling between them.
>
> This is not so difficult; it just requires a change in the way one thinks. But it is a profound piece of advice for improving all of one's *middos*, because this concept applies to almost all *middos* that concern human relations.
>
> There is another consideration that can motivate a person to adopt this approach easily: A happy, successful life depends on the number of friends one has, and a person who is in the habit of always seeing others as they see themselves will have many friends (*Michtav M'Eliyahu*, Vol. 4, p. 243).

---

1. Rabbi Yisrael Salanter, cited in *Toras Avraham*, p. 400.

Come over to the other person's side. Put yourself in his shoes. See life as he sees it. See him as he sees himself. You don't have to agree, but at least understand his point of view. This puts you on a totally different level of understanding and communication, a level that can bring both of you together in a way that might otherwise never occur.

For many people, this way of thinking does not come naturally. Therefore, psychologists suggest that one *permit* himself to understand the other person. We use the term "permit" because attaining a deep understanding of other people goes against one's natural tendency. Let us explain.

When another person expresses a thought or opinion, the listener's first reaction may be judgmental. He thinks, "That's right," "That's wrong," "That's ridiculous," "That makes sense," or "That's unreasonable." If the listener is ever going to really understand the rationale of the other person, he will have to go against his natural tendency and make the effort — and it may take real effort — to understand precisely what the other person is saying before coming to any judgment or conclusion. He will have to *permit* himself to understand the other person.

Understand the other person's troubles. The Steipler Rav was known to have said that every person has problems, that underneath any facade of security and stability, there are troubles.

In fact, if we were to approach a person about whom we know very little and quietly say, "I heard about your problem," he would probably take a step backward and ask in surprise, "Who told you?" For this reason, if we would just treat every person as if he has some sort of problem, even if we do not know what it is, we would be treating him properly.

Suppose a person offends you or does not give you the respect you believe you deserve. You can try to understand why he is behaving this way. The odds are that he is not trying to hurt you, but rather, he himself is hurting. You can then sympathize with him. This will raise you to a level of communication where you do not feel compelled to return hostility for hostility. Instead, you will be able to respond with compassion. You may even turn him into a friend.

This technique can be used to deal with another common occurrence. Suppose your boss or your spouse screams at you for making a minor error. You know that your oversight did not deserve such an emphatic reaction, so you take offense. How can you deal with it in a way that will keep the relationship growing?

First, understand that there is probably an underlying problem that brought on the offensive behavior. Something is bothering that person. Maybe a friend or a family member offended him that morning. Maybe he is ill. Maybe he needs attention or sympathy, and the only way he knows how to receive it is through negative behavior. Although you do not know the answer to this question, you can still assume that a problem is causing his unreasonable behavior. Knowing this, you will be able to think more clearly and tone down your own reaction. Instead of screaming back and jeopardizing the relationship, you will be able to respond to the slight with sympathy and respect.

The same approach works with children. Take the "difficult" child as an example. He appears bullheaded, bent on doing exactly as he pleases, even if he hurts his parents on the way. There is no talking to him because he is argumentative and spiteful. How can we come over to his side? We can consider the possibility that he may have poor self-esteem and behaves this way to build himself up. Maybe his parents are also difficult to get along with and, as role models, have taught him to do the same. Whatever the cause, if we put ourselves in his shoes and give him the benefit of the doubt, we will move the relationship forward.

The goal is to understand the other person. You can come to a deep understanding of another person by opening your mind to him and listening carefully to what he has to say; by asking questions and considering the validity of his words; by closing your eyes and putting yourself in his shoes, considering his disposition and the rationale and motives that cause his behavior.

Once you see the other person's point of view and you agree with it, tell him so. He will respect you for your honesty, and new channels of communication will be opened.[1] But even if you disagree, you can still show him that you understand him and value him as a person.

Know your counterpart. Rabbi Eliyahu Dessler said that when you deal with other people, you should not relate to them with cold

---

1. *Michtav M'Eliyahu*, Vol. 4, p. 245.

logic; rather, consider their character traits and individual personalities.[1] Discover what makes them tick — their tastes, desires, emotional strengths and weaknesses, and the things they perceive as necessities of life. Then you will be in a position to give them the kind of value that is meaningful to them; you will be able to relate to them according to the things that *they* consider important, not that *you* consider important.[2]

Be like the fisherman who is fond of chocolate cake. When he goes fishing, he does not think, "I always enjoy a good piece of chocolate cake, so I am going to bait my hook with a piece and then watch all the fish come after it." He knows that fish like worms, not chocolate cake, and that the only way to lure them is with something that *they* want. So he dangles a worm from his rod and tempts the fish with something that they appreciate.

This concept is especially important when trying to motivate other people to do something that they do not yet consider important. Whether they are people with whom you work, live or play, they all look out for their own best interests. They want what *they* want, not what *you* want; therefore, if you expect to sell them on an idea, show them how it meets *their* standards of importance and satisfies *their* needs. And if they really buy into the plan, they will *want* to do it.[3]

Successful salespeople use this approach to sell their products. They do not tell the customer why *they* think it is important to own a product, but why the *customer* would think it is important. They do not discuss how the item satisfies their own needs, but rather how it satisfies the customer's needs. Once the customer recognizes his own need for the product, a strange thing happens: He buys it without any further convincing.

Take an interest in the other person. To connect with other people, it makes sense to become sincerely interested in them. And when you talk with people, talk about the topic that interests them more than anything else — themselves.[4]

---

1. *Michtav M'Eliyahu*, Vol. 4, p. 244.
2. *Rambam, Avos* 1:6; *Toras Avraham*, p. 400; *Michtav M'Eliyahu*, Vol. 1, p. 99.
3. *Michtav M'Eliyahu*, Vol. 4, p. 244; also see Rambam, *Pirush HaMishnayos, Sanhedrin*, Ch. 10. Also see *Make Me, Don't Break Me*, Ch. 4, on the topic of persuasion.
4. *Michtav M'Eliyahu*, Vol. 4, p. 244.

Rabbi Yeruchom Levovitz takes this idea one step further, saying that we can become close to others by being concerned with them and thinking about them perpetually, just as a father constantly thinks about his son.[1]

If you doubt the truth of this, think about this point: When a person's arthritis acts up or he gets a painful headache or his best friend insults him, there are few problems in the world that are of greater importance. These issues take precedence over all the wars and epidemics in the world. Indeed, the Torah requires us not to be this way, but one's natural inclination is still to consider himself more significant than anything else in the world. Doesn't it make sense, then, that the way to make people feel valuable is to take a sincere interest in them and to talk to them in terms of themselves?[2]

Did you ever meet someone who seemingly took an interest in you, but after a very short time turned the topic of conversation toward him/herself? The conversation may have gone like this:

Other: "Tell me, have you ever traveled?"

You: "Yes, I recently returned from Italy."

Other: "Oh, that sounds so interesting. You'll have to tell me all about it . . . you know, I just returned from France and it was fascinating."

And the conversation takes a detour to France. After an hour the conversation comes to an end, and you never even had a chance to discuss your trip to Italy. Why? Because the other person is naturally more interested in himself than in you.

A shrewd diplomat once said, "Talk to people about themselves and they will listen for hours." The way to get people interested in you is not by talking about yourself, but by expressing an interest in *them.*

This may be the reason that the dog has earned the distinguished title of "man's best friend." When a dog spots its master walking down the street, what happens? It takes a flying leap in the air and runs at top speed to meet him. With its tail wagging, it

---

1. *Daas Chochmah U'Mussar,* Vol. 2, pp. 8-9.

2. See *Toras Avraham,* p. 400: Discover all the physical and emotional needs of other people and try your utmost to satisfy every one.

jumps up to meet its master with excitement. What does the dog want from the master? What is its ulterior motive?

The dog wants nothing; it is simply showing affection for its master, unconditionally and without motive. The master loves the attention. The result is that he becomes emotionally attached to the dog, and a relationship develops.

If a human being appreciates the interest and affection of a dog, how much more so does he appreciate the interest and affection of another person! You can offer this by taking a sincere interest in the other person — unconditionally and without motive — and allowing him to talk about himself.

Here is a story that illustrates the effect of taking a sincere interest in another person.

The owner of a bakery had been trying to sell a line of cakes to a certain restaurant. For four years, he pursued the manager by calling him every week, attending the same social affairs, and even eating in his restaurant several times a month. After all this, he still did not get the account.

He decided to use a different approach. Instead of trying to get the manager interested in his product, he decided to become interested in the manager. He discovered that the manager was a member of a club of restauranteurs and that he attended all their meetings. He had even been appointed president of the organization because of his enthusiasm.

One day the baker approached the manager and engaged him in a conversation about the club. The manager's eyes lit up. He kept the baker for half an hour, telling him all about his favorite club. After the conversation, they shook hands and the baker walked away without even mentioning a word about his products.

Two days later, the baker received a call asking him to deliver samples to the restaurant. The manager was very impressed with the baker and wanted to explore the possibility of doing business with him.

In thirty minutes, the baker had accomplished more than he had in four years. The cakes were the same; the people were the same. The only difference was the way he related to the manager. Instead of getting the manager interested in him, he became interested in the manager.

Avoid arguments, disagreements and criticism. Suppose a person voices an opinion with which you disagree. Should you offer your opposing view? It depends on the nature of the remark. If it warrants correction, as mandated by the *mitzvah* of *tochachah*, say something.

But don't say, "You are wrong." This is an unnecessary put-down and arouses resentment. Instead, state your position in a way that still shows respect for the other person. You can disagree, but you don't have to be disagreeable. Here are some examples of how you can disagree while still showing that you value the other person:

> "Maybe we can look at it this way . . ."
> "What do you think about this idea . . .?"
> "I would tend to think that . . ."
> "Is it possible that . . .?"

These simple statements are effective because they get the point across without arousing hostile feelings. They send the message that you still care about the other person's opinion, reducing the sting of a straightforward disagreement.

You can even say, "I think otherwise, but I may be wrong. If I'm making a mistake, please let me know. Let's examine this a little closer." Yes, you are disagreeing. But the bite is reduced by your admission to the possibility of being wrong. After all, who can fault you for admitting that you make mistakes?

What if you sense that your objection is either unnecessary or will not have an impact on the other person? Should you say something? No. It may harm the relationship.

> Tolerate his words. Even if he states an opinion that contradicts yours, do not respond to him; otherwise, his love for you may cease, because people's minds work differently (Rabbeinu Yonah, *Avos* 1:6).

You can never know in advance if your disagreement will reduce the other person's affinity for you, so why take a chance? You will be more productive by tolerating the other person's opinion, as unreasonable as it may sound, than by debating the issue. Say instead,

"I understand what you are saying. That's interesting." This is an honest response and still shows value for the other person.[1]

Are people really so stubborn and closed-minded that they will dislike anyone who disagrees with them? Let's see.

A person's ego is tied to his opinion. The idea is his — he created it — and he is convinced that it is right. Your disagreement is a blow to his sense of good judgment and intelligence, and is therefore a challenge to his pride and ego.

Furthermore, a person's opinion is the product of his disposition, experiences and conditioning. If you would have the same disposition and experiential background as he, you would probably have an identical set of opinions. But since no two people are alike, no two people will ever have identical opinions. For this reason, opinions are frequently neither right nor wrong; they just *are*. It stands to reason, then, that at times, disagreeing with another's opinion will not generate any sort of agreement, and if the other person feels challenged, he may even begin to dislike you.

Because we are human, we often form opinions without much attention or thought, yet when others attempt to change our minds we become intractably attached to our ideas. If nobody would attempt to change our minds, we might even do so ourselves without much emotion or resistance. But once we are challenged, we become defensive and hold onto our positions with undue rigidity.

Obviously, the reason we so passionately cling to our ideas is not necessarily because of their intrinsic value, but because our sense of pride is threatened every time the validity of our ideas is challenged. We hunger for a sense of importance, and if someone threatens to reduce it by disagreeing with us, we hold tightly to our opinion just to maintain the sense of importance that is attached to it.[2]

This defensive aspect of human nature can be illustrated with a story. A woman whom we shall call Dalia once purchased new furniture for her home. At the time, she did not realize how expensive

---

1. See *Michtav M'Eliyahu*, Vol. 4, p. 244: "Do not enter into sharp debates with your friends, because it will cause a breach in the relationships." Whereas *Michtav M'Eliyahu* warns against sharp debates, it appears that Rabbeinu Yonah warns against even moderate disagreements.

2. Harvey Robinson, *The Mind in the Making*, cited by Dale Carnegie in *How to Make Friends and Influence People*, Pocket Books, 1981, p. 126.

it would be, so when she received the bill she was taken aback by the high cost.

The next day, a friend came by to see the new pieces of furniture. She admired them, but when she was told how much they cost, she said, "I think you paid too much." Dalia had the same feeling, but instead of agreeing, she defended her purchase, saying, "You know, you get what you pay for. This is the best quality, and that's the price you have to expect."

The following day, another friend visited. She also admired the furniture. But instead of remarking on the high cost, she announced that she wished she could one day afford to have such beautiful furniture in her own home. Dalia's reaction this time was, "I really couldn't afford it, you know. In fact, I think I paid too much. If I had to do it again, I would choose something different."

There you have it. Tell a person he made a mistake, and he will defend his action. Tell him he did the right thing, and he will admit to the possibility that he made a mistake. It's human nature — without logic, full of bias, with opinions that are tightly tied to one's sense of pride.

This is why, when it is not mandated by the Torah, it is so often useless to debate or argue with other people. As the popular adage goes, "A man convinced against his will is of the same opinion still."

You can rarely win an argument, because whether you win or lose, you lose. Even if you disprove the other person's position with logic and fact, you have made him feel inferior. While this victory may give you a sense of triumph, your opponent may be feeling hurt and probably resents you for it. Yes, you had a theoretical victory over the other person, but it was at the cost of his good will. Which would you rather have?

Criticism has an even worse effect. Criticism attacks a person's pride, reduces his sense of importance and arouses even more resentment than disagreement does. Criticism is often useless because when the recipient feels attacked, he instinctively tries to justify his position. Even the most vicious murderer will try to justify his act.[1]

Charles Schwab, a master motivator and the first president of the United States Steel Company, once said that there is nothing

---

1. *Michtav M'Eliyahu,* Vol. 4, p. 244.

that destroys a person's ambitions more than a manager's criticism. He therefore tried not to find fault in anyone, but brought out each one's best by showing appreciation and encouragement.

Arguing and criticizing usually do not change people because people are not logical beings; they are creatures of emotion, full of pride, prejudice and vanity. When confronted with a piece of logic that opposes their actions or opinions, their emotions usually take over and prevent them from making any sort of change. A popular ditty illustrates the futility of unnecessary arguments and criticism:

> Here lies the body of William Jay,
> Who died maintaining his right of way.
> He was right, dead right, as he sped along,
> But he is just as dead as if he were wrong.

Yes, you may be right and the other person may be wrong. You know it and can unequivocally prove it. So you speed along, maybe even showing a little anger just to strengthen your position. Where does all this leave you? With a bad relationship. Instead of changing the other person's mind, you have lost his good will and maybe even turned him into an enemy. You may be right, but when your assertion accomplishes nothing — and maybe even makes things worse — it is the same as if you were wrong all along.

But what if the other person offends you or does not give you the respect you believe you deserve? How should you react then? The rule is the same — tolerate it; don't offer correction. No person is able to weigh every word that leaves his mouth. If you were to notice each and every inappropriate remark and bring it to the other person's attention, you would quickly lose his affection. Instead, give the other person value by ignoring his comment and letting it slide off your back.[1]

Does this mean that you should never criticize? Absolutely not. There are times when you are required to criticize, as mandated by the *mitzvah* of *tochachah*. But even then, make your point indirectly, in a way that shows the other person respect and supports his dignity.[2] In

---

1. Rabbeinu Yonah, *Mishlei* 17:9.
2. *Michtav M'Eliyahu*, Vol. 4, p. 244. Also see *Make Me, Don't Break Me*, Ch. 7, on how to criticize properly.

the same way that you can disagree without being disagreeable, you can criticize without being critical.

Until now, we have been talking about correcting other people. The assumption is that you are right and they are wrong. But how do you know that your judgment is accurate in the first place? Is it possible that *you* are making a mistake and that *you* are the cause of the problem?

Whenever people quarrel — whether it is parents and children, teachers and students, spouses, siblings or friends — each party points the finger of blame at the other, saying, "Look at the awful thing he/she did. It is his/her fault that we are quarreling. How can I get him/her to see the light and change?"

Did you ever notice that every time a person points the finger of blame at someone else, he simultaneously folds the other three fingers in his own direction? There is a message in this gesture: Instead of looking at the person to whom the *one* finger points, look at the person to whom the *three* fingers point.

Examine your own actions first.[1] Ask, "What might I be doing wrong? Did I cause the problem? Am I not seeing the light?" Maybe you provoked the other person to act as he did. Maybe you were oversensitive and made a mountain out of a molehill. Be open to the possibility that you are in error and that if you would adjust *your* behavior, the relationship might continue to develop.

Creating positive relationships is not easy, especially when the other person's behavior alienates you. When this happens, remember this idea: "Instead of telling the other person where to get off, help him get on." Instead of arguing or criticizing, show the other person that you value him and try to figure out why he behaves as he does. This attitude breeds kindness, tolerance and sympathy, three building blocks of a good relationship.

Any fool can turn a friend into an enemy, but it is only the astute person who can turn an enemy into a friend.

Sympathize with the other person. Suppose a child, spouse or friend experiences a failure and tells you, "I am a loser. I always was and I always will be. I will never succeed." How can you relate to a person who has just poured out such heart-wrenching words?

---

1. Talmud *Bava Metzia* 107b. Also see Me'iri, *Avos* 4:14: When disagreeing with another person, the goal should be to discover the truth, not to prove oneself right.

You can connect by showing sympathy; by listening to his concerns and showing that you understand; by letting him know that you consider his feelings important and that you also feel his pain;[1] by giving value to his feelings.

This suggestion is quite basic. However, when it comes time to put it into practice, people frequently fall into other patterns. Here are eight responses that people typically use to sympathize with someone.

1) *The brush-off*:

> "How can you say that?"
> "Don't say that."
> "I don't want to hear you say that again."

The *brush-off* response invalidates the other person's feelings. It shows no understanding or sympathy, implying that you are not interested in hearing about the problem altogether. The other person will sense the lack of interest and will probably not bring up the subject again.

2) *The sermon:*

> "You have to learn the right attitude toward failure and then you won't feel that way. Let me tell you what your attitude is supposed to be . . ."

The *sermonizing* response implies that you know more than the other person and that you would like to share some of your wisdom with him. If he is in the mood to hear a sermon, this approach might be appropriate. But the odds are that he is not. He is down and out, and is probably not interested in a speech that may make him feel more inadequate than he already feels.

3) *The denial:*

> "You don't really feel that way."

The *denial* response is a total invalidation of the other person. It disputes the existence of his feelings altogether. How will the recipient react? He will not stop feeling like a loser just because you told him that he doesn't really feel that way. Even worse, he may deduce

---

1. See *Avos* 1:6: "Carry the yoke with your friend."

that you do not respect him. "After all," he thinks, "if you respect-ed me, you would not doubt my word."

4) *The advice:*

"Just ignore it."

The *advice* response also minimizes the other person's feelings. Although it does not deny the existence of the problem, it does deny its impact. And after everything is said and done, the recipient will probably not listen to your "sage" advice. He is in pain and cannot simply ignore it.

5) *The blame.*

"Maybe it is your fault."

The *blaming* response really strikes a raw nerve. The other per-son is already upset and his self-esteem is low. In his condition, he does not need someone accusing him of being the source of the problem. Not only does this response minimize his feelings, it is an insult to whatever pride he has left.

6) *The put-down:*

"You are acting like a baby."

The *put-down* response makes a person feel worse than he al-ready does. "But," you may protest, "he really is acting like a baby. He ought to know it; then he will stop." This is a mistake. He feels bad, even if you think he has no right to feel that way, and he will not stop just because you try putting him in his place. Instead, he will feel invalidated and will probably not share his feelings with you again.

7) *Talk him out of it:*

"You received a 90 on the last test. You are obviously not a failure."

"You were congratulated by the president last week. Only a winner gets something like that."

The *talk-him-out-of-it* response attempts to change the other person's mind by proving that he is successful. Will he be receptive? If he is, keep talking. But this may not be the case. He is feeling up-set, and he may need someone just to understand his feelings. He may not be looking for someone to agree or disagree; he may just want some sympathy and understanding.

8) *Impose your opinion.*

> "In my opinion you are a very capable person with all the potential in the world."

The *impose-your-opinion* response attempts to lift the other person's spirits by declaring your confidence in him. The question is, will it change his mind? If he is in the mood for encouragement, it may make him feel better. But he may be so convinced of his inadequacy that he will not be open to your support. Even worse, he may become frustrated because he feels you do not understand what he is going through. He may even feel that you are negating his feelings.

These eight approaches are all missing one basic ingredient: a sense that you understand what the other person is going through and that you care about his feelings. They lack a show of true sympathy. This is not a problem if the other person is not looking for sympathy, but the odds are that a person who makes such an emotional statement *is* looking for sympathy. He is not interested in his great potential or past achievements; he is depressed and just wants some understanding.

If this is the case, give it to him. Tell him, "If I were in your shoes, I would certainly feel the same way." This is the absolute truth; if you had his disposition, his conditioning and his set of experiences, you could not help but feel as he does. How will this response make him feel? He will know that you understand what he is going through and that you care about his feelings. He will feel valued.

An inexperienced school principal once took a position in a school where many teachers were unhappy about a schedule that they found difficult to keep. The schedule had already been instituted before his arrival, and he did not have the authority to adjust it. One teacher approached the principal, telling him that the schedule was unfair and that she deserved a higher salary if she was to be expected to keep it. She was distraught and angry.

First, the principal defended himself, saying, "I had nothing to do with it, you know." When she continued grumbling, he tried talking sense into her, saying, "We can work at adjusting the schedule for next year, but for now it cannot be changed. There are many programs and personnel affected by the schedule, and if we were to adjust it now, we would have to make too many major changes."

The teacher became even more angry at this, and even turned disrespectful. At that point, the principal scolded her for her attitude and concluded, "There is nothing that can be done." The teacher walked out in disgust and never brought the subject up again, nor did she pursue her demand for a higher salary. Instead, she became an avowed enemy of the principal and made sure to share her opinion with other teachers on the staff.

Let us analyze this incident. The teacher had a legitimate complaint. She came to the principal to air her feelings and seek a solution. So what did the principal do? He gave his honest opinion. As valid as it was, though, he offered no sympathy and assigned no value to her point of view. The results were devastating for everyone.

Had the principal asked the big question — "How can I give value to this teacher?" — he might have said, "I can see how you feel. If I were in your shoes, I would feel exactly the same. It's not easy to keep an unfair schedule, especially when you feel you are being underpaid. Let me see what I can do about it, and I will get back to you."

How might the teacher have reacted? She would probably have said "Thank you," and walked out holding her head high, confident that her boss cared about her. What would the principal have done then? The next day, he would have approached the teacher and told her, "I understand how you feel, and you have good reason to feel that way. I would like to help you, but I am sorry to say that it is out of my hands. Please let me know if things get too difficult, and I will see how I can help you."

Would the teacher have been angry at the principal? Maybe, at first. But after a short while, she would have realized that although she had the support of her boss, he was really not able to help her. The problem would have been diffused, and the teacher would have learned to make the best of the situation.

Did this principal learn his lesson? Yes, he did. Several months later, the financial director of the school was facing a problem issuing payroll on time. Teachers were quite perturbed about being paid late. When they came to the principal to complain about it, he could have said, "You have to understand that it's not easy to raise so much money. The economy is tight, tuitions are not coming in, and our major supporters are not contributing as in the past. Besides, look at other schools that also pay late. We are not the only one. Have patience. You will eventually get paid."

He knew that this would not be productive and that his people might even be more upset after hearing such rhetoric. So he sympathized with them, saying, "I know how you feel. A late payroll means that you are not able to pay your bills on time. I really feel for you. I wish I could wave a magic wand and solve the problem. If there is anything I can do to make your situation easier, please let me know." He listened, he cared, he sympathized, and he let his teachers know that they deserved better. And he became their friend.

There is another way to sympathize. It is called *mirroring*. Here are some ways of mirroring to the person who thought he was a failure:

> "So you feel you have not been very successful."
> "It must feel bad to think you are a failure."
> "I see that something did not work out."

When mirroring, you do not offer your opinion or attempt to change the other person's mind. You do not agree or disagree, and you do not sermonize or offer words of encouragement. You simply repeat what he said and feed his emotions back to him. This shows that you value him and understand what he is going through.

Although the response is short and to the point, it is not a signal that you want to end the dialogue. Much to the contrary, it should signal that you are interested in hearing all about the problem. How can you convey this message? By stopping whatever you are doing, making eye contact, giving the other person your undivided attention and showing that you really care. He will sense your support and will continue sharing his feelings. As this happens, you once again mirror those feelings back.

Here is an example of mirroring with children.

> Student: "My art work is ugly. I can't even paint a simple picture!"

Teacher:	"You don't think it's good, do you?"
OR:	"You must feel bad thinking you can't draw."
Child:	"I am never picked for a team. Everyone hates me."
Parent:	"You feel disliked, don't you."
OR:	"It must feel bad not to be picked."

When mirroring, the adult does not agree or disagree with the child. Why should he? The child is not asking for an opinion; in fact, she may prefer not to hear it altogether. She may only be interested in having the adult listen, understand and sympathize. Parents or teachers certainly have the capacity to do that, whether they agree or disagree.

Does all this mean that whenever another person voices a gripe, we should never share our opinion or give words of encouragement? No. There are times when such a response is in order, and the alert individual will have to determine when to sympathize and when to offer something more. He can make this decision by asking the question, "How can I show value for the other person?" If the situation calls for an opinion, he will give it. But if it calls only for sympathy, he will withhold the opinion for another time.

Show People that You Like Them

There was once a little girl who transferred to a new school. After several days, she came running home with exciting news: She had made a new friend. Her parents were equally ecstatic and asked, "What does your friend like about you?"

"Oh," the little girl replied, "she likes the way I draw and the way I play. She also likes my sense of humor, and she agrees with me on a lot of things."

"That's interesting," her parents continued. "And what do you like about her?"

The little girl responded, "I like the fact that she likes the way I draw and play. I also like the fact that she likes my sense of humor and agrees with me so often."

This story illustrates an important aspect of human nature: We like people who like us. If they like us, we feel valued. We appreciate the value and reciprocate in kind. King Shlomo, the wisest of men, said it this way:

> As with water, the face that you show it, it shows to you, so too the heart of a person is to a person (*Mishlei* 27:19, following Rashi).

When a person looks into a clear pool of water, the water mirrors his face back to him. If he smiles at the water, the face in the water will also smile at him; if he frowns at the water, the face in the water will also frown at him.

Human relations work the same way. If one person has good feelings for another, the other will have the same good feelings for him, and the converse is also true. And even if the second is not consciously aware of what the first is feeling, he will still reflect the feelings that the first has toward him. Like water reflecting the face that is looking into it, the second person reflects the feelings that the first person has for him.[1] This is the reason the little girl liked her new friend — because her new friend liked her.

There was once a wise man who used this idea to save his own life. He was a rabbi who rendered the decision that the meat of a certain butcher was non-kosher. The butcher was so angry at this decision that he devised a scheme to murder the rabbi. One day, he asked the rabbi to go with him to a certain destination. While traveling on a lonely road, the butcher took out a knife and announced his intention to kill the rabbi.

The rabbi pleaded for mercy, but the butcher was not deterred. When the rabbi saw that his pleas were of no avail, he decided to focus on all the attributes of the butcher. Suddenly, the butcher changed his mind. He kissed the rabbi, and with tears in his eyes, asked for forgiveness.[2]

Rabbi Shlomo Wolbe wrote that whenever we come into contact with another person, we should try to find his virtues and his good points.[3] While Rabbi Wolbe's suggestion is in the context of honor-

---

1. Vilna Gaon, *Mishlei* 27:19. Also see Vilna Gaon, *Mishlei* 14:17: People hate a person who has evil thoughts even if he does not reveal them. This is because the people reflect those same negative thoughts back to the first person.
2. Told by Rabbi Chaim Zeichik, *Mayanei HaChaim*, Vol. 3, p. 191, cited by Rabbi Z. Pliskin in *Consulting the Wise*, pp. 261-262.
3. *Alei Shur*, p. 119.

ing people, it holds an added bonus; when we discover the virtues of those we meet, we will feel love toward them. The result will be that they will feel love toward us, and a relationship will develop.

How does this work? We can easily understand that if one is aware of another's feelings toward him, he will feel the same, because it is only natural that we like the people who like us, and vice versa. But if the second is not aware of how the first feels, why should he feel the same way? Is it an intuition, some sort of mysterious power imbued in the human race?

There is nothing supernatural about it. The way you feel about another person shows. Your gestures, facial features and body movements all come together in a manner that sends the message. It is a non-verbal message, and even if the other person does not know what you are thinking, it still comes through. As the other person detects your feeling, even if it is on an intuitive level, he will naturally feel the same about you.

> A happy heart brightens the face, but with sadness of the heart there is a broken spirit (*Mishlei* 15:13).

People think that they can hide their feelings of joy and sadness. But King Shlomo instructs us that it is not so. We cannot hide those feelings; they are likely to show on the outside. So too, we usually cannot hide the feelings we have for other people. And once the other party senses it, although he may not realize it at the time, he will reflect that same feeling back to us.

Obviously, the secret of a good relationship is not simply to like the other person. There is more to a relationship than just liking the other person. However, liking is critical because it is the foundation of a good relationship. After laying the foundation, we have to take the appropriate actions to continue building the relationship.

There are many blocks in the structure of a healthy relationship. We already mentioned some: making the other person feel important, seeing things from his point of view, taking an interest in him, and talking to him about himself. We will now discuss more. Like the others, these also revolve around the theme of giving value.

Greet people with a smile. Why do people appreciate a smile? Because it says that you like them and are happy to see them.[1] But

---

1. *See Torah Temimah, Bereishis* 49:12.

it does more than just *say* that you are happy with other people; it *shows* them. As a result, they will conclude that you appreciate them, and a relationship will develop.[1]

A typical scene that illustrates the power of a smile is the waiting room of a busy doctor's office. Six people are scheduled for a one-o'clock appointment, and the doctor is late. They would all prefer to be somewhere else and are unhappy with the long wait, but they have no choice. So they make the best of things by sitting quietly, reading, knitting, dozing or writing letters.

A young mother enters the office, holding a small baby in her arms. She finds a seat next to a rather distraught old man. Just as she sits down, her baby does what babies so often do; she looks at the man and gives a broad, pleasant smile. What happens then? The old man smiles back. He then asks the mother how old the baby is, and a conversation begins. He talks about his grandchildren, may even show pictures of them, and soon everyone in the room joins in the conversation. What had been a boring and tense occasion turns into a pleasant and enjoyable event — all because of a single sincere smile.

You have experienced it. A passerby gives you a warm smile, and your spirits are lifted. The boss gives you a smile and a cheerful "Good morning," the kind that shows that you are appreciated, and you feel lighter on your feet. Especially if you are going through some sort of pressure in your personal or professional life, that smile has a most gratifying effect.

> The one who shows the white of his teeth to his friend does more good than the one who offers him milk to drink (Talmud *Kesubos* 111b).

We are not talking about an insincere grin; this is shallow and mechanical, and does not fool too many people. Rather, we are talking about a sincere show of warmth and friendship that comes directly from the heart. It becomes your carrier of good will and has the power to cheer up the ones who see it.

Speak pleasantly. A person's choice of words can be sensitive or offensive, and his manner of delivery can go either way as well. The

---

1. Rabbeinu Yonah and *Tiferes Yisrael, Avos* 1:15.

result is that the second person will either like the first or dislike him. Therefore, he should speak softly, without screaming or becoming angry, in a way that makes others happy to talk with him.[1]

The way we speak has such an impact on others that we can placate angry people by speaking to them in a soft, friendly tone of voice, or we can create new hostility with those we do not even know by speaking in a harsh tone.[2] For this reason, our tone of voice and choice of words should be warm, sweet and positive.

> Pleasant words are like a honeycomb, sweet to the soul and healing to the bones (*Mishlei* 16:24).
>
> Points presented in a very pleasant way are sweet as honeycombs to the listener, and they help the soul and body. This is the way to draw the hearts of people to one's opinion, whether it is related to an ethical matter or a physical necessity (*Metzudas Dovid*, ad loc.).

This rule is especially critical when we try to motivate workers or children to do the things they are supposed to do. If we speak angrily or impatiently, they will sense an attack and will be unreceptive to what we say. But if we use soft words and a gentle approach, they will be more receptive and will probably do what we ask.[3]

Make sure other people know you are doing something for them. Sometimes people help others out but do not tell them about it. "I am doing it out of the goodness of my heart," they say, "so it makes no difference if the other person knows about it. Besides, I am fulfilling the *mitzvah* of *chessed*, and it would be boastful to publicize it."

While these people are sincere, they are also making a mistake. *Chazal* told us that when a person gives a gift to someone else, he must notify him, so that the recipient will appreciate it and an affinity will emerge between the two.[4] Whether the gift is a tangible

---

1. Rabbi Eliyahu Lopian, *Lev Eliyahu*, p. 66. Also see *Peleh Yoetz, Mesikus*, and Rabbeinu Yonah, *Avos* 1:15.

2. *Mishlei* 15:1, following Vilna Gaon and Rabbeinu Yonah.

3. Talmud *Shabbos* 34a: "One must say it gently so that they will accept it." See also Rabbi Shlomo Wolbe, *Alei Shur*, p. 261 and Vilna Gaon, *Even Sh'leimah* 6:5.

4. Talmud *Shabbos* 10b. See *Tosafos* there: This rule applies only when the recipient will not be embarrassed.

item, a verbal message or a service, there is no room for secrecy. A bond will grow after the other person knows what was done for him.

Listen attentively. Did you ever talk with someone and get the feeling that he was not listening carefully? Instead, he was thinking about his upcoming response or something totally unrelated. Many people do this. An effective listener, however, pays careful attention to the other person. He connects by opening his mind to the other person's ideas and detaching himself from all unrelated thoughts.

Giving the other person exclusive attention, without distraction or interruption, and allowing him to finish what he wants to say, gives him the sense that you really care about him and consider his thoughts important. There is nothing more flattering.

One mother discovered this when, after having a discussion with her son, he sat pensively at the table and said, "Mom, I know that you love me." The mother was touched by this remark, and she answered, "Of course, I love you. Was there ever a time when you thought I did not love you?"

The little boy answered, "No. But I know that you love me because every time I want to talk with you, you stop whatever you're doing and listen."

There you have it. The power of undivided attention sends a strong message: "I value you. You are important." Even if you assure the other person that he is important, it means little unless you prove it by giving him undivided attention.

Receiving attention is so important that people often behave inappropriately just to make others focus on them. The opinionated loud-mouth and the obnoxious critic are two examples. They are so starved for attention that they try drawing it to themselves through antisocial behavior. However, once the listener makes them feel important by giving them the attention they hunger for, they often tone down and may even listen to what he has to say.

Substance messages and ego messages. Suppose an employee approaches his manager to ask for a raise in salary. After he explains why he deserves the raise, the manager can either grant the request or deny it. The manager's answer is called a "substance message."

Although the substance message is all the manager articulates, he communicates more information with his gestures and choice of words. These messages are called "ego messages" because they tell the employee what the manager really thinks of him. The ego message is so important that it alone often determines how the manager's response affects the relationship. Here are four examples of substance messages and ego messages.

Negative substance message/negative ego message:

> "You will not get a raise. I cannot believe you are even asking for one. You know that money is tight now and that we cannot afford to give raises."

The raise is denied — a negative substance message. However, the boss didn't stop there; he criticized the employee for making the request. This is an attack on the employee's pride — a negative ego message.

How does the employee feel? After being denied a raise for a reason which he may be able to understand, he is needlessly put down. He will walk away from this conversation feeling bad about the boss because his sense of importance has been invalidated.

Negative substance message/positive ego message:

> "I know you work hard and deserve a raise, but we just don't have the money now."

The raise is denied — a negative substance message. However, the boss expresses his appreciation for the employee — a positive ego message.

How does the employee feel now? Although the request is denied, the ego message is very supportive. It validates the employee's sense of importance, allowing him to walk away feeling good about himself *and* the boss.

Positive substance message/ positive ego message:

> "You will get a raise. You have worked hard, and you deserve it."

The raise is granted — a positive substance message. And the manager expresses his appreciation for the employee's hard work — a positive ego message.

How does the employee feel now? His request is granted and he is made to feel important. This clearly enhances the relationship.

Positive substance message/ negative ego message:

> "You will get a raise. But I think it is selfish of you to ask for one now. Money is tight, and when the others hear about it, they will also want a raise. I will have to turn them down, and then they will accuse me of preferential treatment."

The raise is granted — a positive substance message. However, the boss insults the employee for making the request — a negative ego message.

How does the employee feel about the raise? Although he is getting exactly what he wants, he resents his boss's biting criticism. Even though he is satisfied in substance, he is dissatisfied in ego. This will have a negative effect on the relationship.

The point is obvious: The ego message is the one that counts. You can say "No" and leave the other person feeling satisfied; you can say "Yes" and leave the other party feeling dissatisfied. The tone of the relationship is not necessarily set by what you say about the issue at hand, but by what you imply about the person.

Expect others to want your friendship. There is a parable about a man who was thinking of moving to a certain city. He visited that city and met a wise man. He asked, "Are the people here nice?" The wise man responded, "What are the people like in the city where you currently live?" He answered, "Very nice." The wise man then said, "I think you will find that the people here are very nice, too."

Several days later, the wise man was approached by another person who wanted to relocate. He also asked, "Are the people here nice?" The wise man responded, "What are the people like in the city where you currently live?" He answered, "They are a bit nasty." The wise man said, "I think you will find the people here are also nasty."

A bystander heard both conversations and was baffled by the two opposing answers, so he asked the wise man why he had responded differently to the two travelers. The wise man explained, "The attitude you have toward other people sets the path for the way they behave toward you. If you think people are nice, you are probably expecting the best from them, and are behaving in a way that draws their friendship. If you think people are nasty, you are probably expecting the least from them, and are behaving in a way that evokes their disfavor.

"The person who said that the people in his city are nice has always expected them to be nice, and he has been sending them this positive message without even realizing it. His neighbors have been responding in kind. So no matter where he lives, he will always expect the best from people and they will always respond in kind.

"But the person who said that the people in his city are nasty, without even realizing it, has been sending them a negative message. He has been expecting the worst, and they have been responding in kind. So no matter where he lives, he will continue expecting people to be nasty, and they will also respond in kind."

Can our expectation of others actually control the kind of relationship we have with them? Is the power of expectations rooted in magic or the supernatural? No, it isn't. It is rooted in a fact of life called the "self-fulfilling prophecy." As we explained in previous chapters, a prophecy is self-fulfilling when the expectation of an event induces behavior that increases the likelihood of that event. Once a person has an expectation, he tends to act in accordance with it, thus setting the stage for the expected outcome.

Suppose someone waves at you from across the street. Before you wave back, you remember that he owes you five hundred dollars. You begin to wonder, "Why is he waving at me? If he had the money, he would just come here and give it to me. He probably has decided not to pay and is now being friendly to cover up for it." So you ignore his display of friendship and go on your way. How will the other person react the next time he sees you? He will probably avoid you.

His intentions today were genuine, but you expected the worst of him. Without realizing it, you displayed that expectation by ignoring him. So what did he do? He later treated you with the unfriendliness that you expected of him.

An elderly couple once moved from Minnesota to Florida. After several months, though, they decided to move back to Minnesota. One of their new Florida neighbors noticed the moving truck and asked why they were leaving so soon. "We moved here because we had grown tired of the cold Minnesota winters," the man told him.

"We were looking forward to warm weather and the friendship of people our age. The problem is that my wife feels that nobody in this community has reached out to befriend us. She has old friends back in Minnesota, so we are returning."

The neighbor asked, "What did your wife do to let the community know that she was interested in their friendship?"

The man paused for a few moments of thought. He understood the point. His wife had stood by waiting for others to befriend her, but she never showed them that she was interested.

At first, this man's wife had expected the residents to welcome her to their community. That is the way it should be. So when they did not extend themselves, she assumed the worst, thinking, "These people don't want to be my friends." She remained reclusive, waiting for them to approach her first. Her reclusiveness, though, sent this message to the others: "I am not interested in you." She set the stage for her own expectations to come about.

Instead, she should have expected the best of her new neighbors, saying, "They are busy with their own families. They really want to be my friends but are just not getting around to it." With this attitude, she would have gone out to make friends, sending the message that she expected the best from them. She would have set the stage for her positive expectations to come about, and the outcome would have been pleasant.

Our behavior — our choice of words, tone of voice, facial expressions, body language — reflects our attitude toward people. We may want to hide our feelings, but more often than not they come out anyway. And once they come out, others detect it and respond in kind. Through our behavior, our prophecy becomes self-fulfilling.

Expecting the best from others is another way of saying, "I think you are nice. I would like to be your friend." This attitude becomes a building block in a positive relationship because what you give out tends to come back to you.

Develop A Value-Driven Attitude

We have been talking about assigning value to others. The value that is most meaningful is the kind that comes from the heart and finds its way out through words and actions; it is the kind that reflects a corresponding *attitude of value* from deep within. Attitude: that is the key. Attitude is the spirit behind your words and actions. It sets the tone for how you relate to others. Attitude is the driving force behind any value-giving act.

But suppose for a moment that you are selfish or self-centered, or you simply do not consider people valuable. If this is your attitude, your words and actions will most likely take on the same tone. How can you behave with an attitude of value if you do not have one?

One approach is to play the role even if you do not feel it. Eventually, your actions will result in a corresponding attitude.[1]

While this approach is valid, the attitude will not become part of your character immediately. It will take time. So the question is, how can you infuse a spirit of value into your words and actions now, without waiting for it to become ingrained in you later?

You can do this by entering into a value-giving frame of mind. In this mind-set, you will be able to show value for others through your words and actions, and to do so authentically. Here are six ways to put yourself into this frame of mind.

1) Man is the image of Hashem. Using this idea, imagine that you are dealing directly with Hashem every time you interact with another human being.[2]

2) Before any interaction, close your eyes and ask yourself, "How will this act show value for the other person?" Transfer yourself from the world of "you" to the world of "him" or "her."

3) Imagine that you will be living with the other person in a small room for the rest of your life. You'd better make him or her feel appreciated or you may be in for a lifetime of distress.

4) Imagine that the other person is a barber giving you a haircut, or a surgeon standing over you in surgery. You'd better make him feel valuable or he may not go the extra mile to do a perfect job.

---

1. Vilna Gaon, *Mishlei* 4:26; *Sefer HaChinuch, mitzvah* 16; also see Chapter One for a discussion on this topic.

2. Rabbi Yeruchom Levovitz, *Daas Chochmah U'Mussar* 1:260.

5) Picture the other person wearing a sign that reads, "Make me feel important." Then respond to the request.

6) Decide to become generous. Give the other person the "gift" of importance by talking in a way that will help him like himself and feel important.

While these strategies put you into a value-driven frame of mind, it is still not enough. There is a higher goal — to internalize a deeply felt value-driven attitude. And for this to happen, you need time and practice. After days, weeks and months of following these strategies and acting the role of a value-giver, you will feel the impact on your personality.

Valuing others is a life-style, not a plan of action. It is not a thing you pull from a bag of tricks or a calculated act of manipulation for the purpose of getting something from others; rather, it is a consistent attitude toward people and life. It is a mind-set which acknowledges the human need for appreciation and a commitment to provide it. This is why a deeply internalized value-driven attitude is so important.

Communicating Effectively

Communication is a major component of any relationship. It can move a relationship forward or take it backward.

If, after each communication, all parties feel good about themselves and about each other, their dialogue was probably effective. But if either party has a negative feeling about himself or the other, their interchange may not have been effective. This is important, because the effectiveness of a dialogue is one of the keys to a good relationship.

The purpose of communication. Some people think that dialogue is nothing more than an opportunity to release what is in their minds. So instead of listening to the other party and trying to understand him, they plan what they will say next and grab the first opportunity to express themselves. To them, dialogue is nothing more than two monologues.

This is a mistake. Communication is more than two or more people taking turns talking. It is a give-and-take process, with each party striving to understand the other and to be understood. It leads to a meeting of the minds and enhances the relationship.

Like everything else in a positive relationship, good communication is founded on giving value. Listening carefully to the other person, understanding what he says, acknowledging him, and responding to his point — the four steps of the communication process — are all value-giving activities. They all send the message, "You are important. Your ideas are important. Because you are so valuable, I am making the effort to understand you, and I will respond to what you are saying."

First, listen to the other person. Then give him or her an EAR, an acronym for Explore, Acknowledge, Respond. We will now discuss these four steps.

Listen

Did you ever converse with a person who was not really listening to you? Perhaps, as you began to talk, he interrupted. When you asked one question, he answered another. As you were talking about one idea, he took a detour onto another. When you voiced an opinion, he passed it by, as if you had never said anything at all.

How did you feel? You probably felt snubbed, ignored and devalued.

Good communicators listen. But they do more than listen; they listen *effectively*. They listen carefully to everything the other person says, and they detach themselves from all unrelated thoughts while the other person is talking.

> "A wise person . . . does not interrupt the words of his friend, and he is not quick to respond" (*Avos* 5:7). The wise person allows the other person to speak until he finishes all his words; then he gives an answer (Rabbeinu Yonah, ad loc.).
>
> "The one who answers a word before he understands, it is foolishness to him and an embarrassment" (*Mishlei* 18:13). It is necessary to listen to the points of the questioner and all his doubts, and afterward to come to a clear decision. He earns the questioner's respect by doing this (Malbim, ad loc.).

After listening effectively, you are ready for the first step of the EAR protocol — Explore.

Explore

Suppose you listen to the other person but do not fully understand him. This problem must be solved; otherwise, you will not be able to respond to him according to his needs. *You* will then be guilty of taking the detour.

The solution is simple: explore. Make an effort to understand the other person's opinions and emotions. Find out why he feels as he does. Ask him to explain himself. Ask him to support his position.

People frequently say things that we do not fully understand. If we would reach out to understand them, we would be doing much to enhance the relationship. For this reason, we should be aware of the types of messages that are most frequently misunderstood.

Hidden and garbled messages. A hidden message is an idea or opinion that the speaker does not clearly articulate, but that the listener is expected to understand anyway. For example, an ill wife tells her husband, "You may go out this evening. I'll be all right." While it appears that she is amenable to his plan, she may be hiding her real feelings. Her hidden massage may be, "I am ill and I would really like you to stay home. But if you insist on going out, I will not stop you."

Another example is a student telling his teacher, "I don't care if I pass the test." While it appears that the child has a bad attitude, he may be hiding his real feelings. His hidden message may be, "I do not understand the subject matter. If I would understand, I would make an effort to pass the test. But under the circumstances, I do not care."

How can the husband know what his wife really wants? How can the teacher know how the child really feels? If they are astute, in touch with the feelings of the other person, they would figure it out. But if they are not so clever, they will have to discover how the other person feels. They can explore by asking questions and using the answers to uncover the true feelings.

Another illustration of a hidden message is the four-year-old boy who accompanied his mother on a visit to a kindergarten. As the mother sat with the teacher, the little boy went to play with the toys. But before he went off, he looked at the teacher straight in the eye and said, "I am going to break all the toys." The mother was floored, thinking, "What an obnoxious thing to say! How could my son embarrass me this way?"

The teacher was not taken aback, though. She understood the boy's hidden message to be a question: "If I break a toy, will I be in trouble? How understanding are you?" So she calmly replied, "We want you to play with the toys. That is why they are here. But sometimes they break when children use them." With a look of satisfaction, the little boy went off to play.

This teacher heard the child's threat and explored it for meaning. She detected a hidden message and responded to it. The little boy now knew that he would not be punished for unintentionally breaking a toy. This small interchange set the stage for a successful relationship.

A garbled message is different; it is much more unclear. If the listener is perceptive, he may be able to figure out what the other person is trying to say. But if he is not so discerning, he can explore, asking, "What do you mean? Would you repeat it?"

It is said that a careful listener uses two ears. With one he listens to what is said. With the other he listens to what is not said. There are times, however, when he needs a third ear: to listen to what the other person *wants* to say but doesn't know *how* to say.

When we realize that hidden and garbled messages are common forms of everyday communication, we will be on the lookout for them. When we are faced with these messages, we will try to understand the other person before making judgments or coming to conclusions. Having the capacity to understand hidden and garbled messages will also help us deal with offensive people; before coming to conclusions about their inappropriate remarks, we will first look for underlying messages. All this will enhance communication and help our relationships grow.

Irrelevant messages. Did you ever speak with someone about an important matter and find his response irrelevant to your point? You wondered, "Why is he saying that? Did he hear what I said?"

He may disagree with your point, not understand it, or perhaps consider it unimportant. But most likely, he is using this conversation to satisfy his need to discharge his own feelings about the irrelevant issue. While you have one purpose in the conversation, he has another.

People often become preoccupied with other concerns and have a need to talk about them. And it makes no difference to them if their remarks are irrelevant to the issue at hand.[1]

As long as the other person is preoccupied with his own feelings, he will not give you much attention. What can you do? Let him express himself first. Having satisfied his need to share, his preoccupation with his point will be dissolved to some extent, and he will begin to direct his attention toward you.

But you can do more than just listen. You can show value for the other person and make him feel important by exploring his feelings and demonstrating that you understand. If appropriate, you can even sympathize with him. His issues are important to him, and when you assign value to those concerns, you enhance communication.

Here is an illustration of how *not* to deal with a listener's irrelevant comments. While the scenario concerns an adult and a child, the same idea holds true for two adults.

> **Teacher:** "It is hard to read your paper when the handwriting is sloppy."
>
> **Student:** "You ought to see the work I do in art. I got an A in art."
>
> **Teacher:** "That is very nice. But we are talking about handwriting now. What can you do to improve your handwriting?"
>
> **Student:** "Maybe I can get a different pencil. When it gets too short, I can't hold it properly. Sometimes I have trouble throwing a small ball. But I'm still a very good pitcher. In fact, I was just awarded a trophy for winning my last game."
>
> **Teacher:** (frustrated) "Let's get back to your handwriting. I notice that even when your pencil is long, it is difficult to read your papers."

---

1. See Talmud *Yoma* 75a on *Mishlei* 12:25: A person wants to talk to others about his concerns.

Student: "You're right. Sometimes I have difficulty throwing a larger ball, too."

Teacher: (perturbed) "Can we stick to the subject? We don't have time to talk about your art and your pitching."

Student: "Sorry."

Teacher: "Can't you see your handwriting needs improvement? Now, what are you going to do about it?"

Student: (silence)

The teacher wants to talk about sloppy handwriting, but the student wants to talk about art and baseball. The teacher sees no relevance in the child's response, so she becomes frustrated. Sensing this, the child shuts down. The result? A breakdown in communication.

When the child introduced a point that was not relevant to the conversation, did his thinking process go haywire, or did he misunderstand the teacher's logic? Most likely, neither happened. Rather, the child was probably thinking about something more important than his handwriting: his pride. He had just been criticized by the teacher for his sloppy handwriting, and his ego was hurt. His concern then was to build it back up. This became his primary purpose in the conversation. To him, the only relevant issue was his sense of pride, not his handwriting. This is the reason he did not respond to the teacher's agenda.

How could the teacher have known what the child was thinking? By paying attention to what he said, then using it as a link to his thoughts. The teacher should have seen the very incongruity of the child's words as a signal that he had another need which was pressing for expression.

The teacher could have drawn the child back to her agenda by answering the question, "What can I do to show him that I value him?" Then, she would not have dismissed the child's "irrelevancy" so quickly. Instead, she would have paid attention to his incongruity, using it to discover what his underlying need was. She would then have been able to respond in a way that would have maneuvered the conversation back to her agenda. With this attitude, the dialogue might have gone like this:

Teacher:	"It is hard to read your paper when the hand-writing is not neat."
Student:	"You ought to see the work I do in art. I got an A in art."

[The teacher links his irrelevant remark to his thoughts, and focuses on validating his feelings and making him feel important:]

Teacher:	"You are obviously a very neat person. Otherwise, you would not do well in art."
Student:	"That's right."
Teacher:	"Now, do you think your handwriting is as neat as your artwork?"
Student:	"No, I guess it isn't."

[The teacher now maneuvers the discussion back to her agenda, asking the child if he recognizes the problem:]

Teacher:	"What do you think is the solution?"
Student:	"Maybe I can get a longer pencil. When it gets too short, I can't hold it well. Sometimes I have trouble throwing a small ball. But I'm still a very good pitcher. In fact, I was just awarded a trophy for winning the last game."

[The teacher links this new irrelevancy to the child's thoughts, and once again makes him feel important:]

Teacher:	"I want to see that trophy one day. Can you bring it to school to show the class?"
Student:	"Yes, I will."

[Now the child is ready to discuss the handwriting issue:]

Teacher:	"Now (displaying another sloppy paper), look at this paper, please. You completed this yesterday. Which pencil did you use?"
Student:	"I used a long pencil."
Teacher:	"Is it neat?"
Student:	"No, I guess not."
Teacher:	"So, even with a long pencil, your work is still

sloppy. Is it possible that the size of the pencil is not the problem?"

Student: "I guess I have to try to be neater."

Each time the student took the discussion off course, he was really asking for validation. The teacher was clever enough to discover it and do as she was "requested." This brought the child into a receptive frame of mind, permitting the teacher to direct the discussion to her purpose. She brought about a meeting of the minds by exploring the child's "irrelevancy" and responding to it.

In the first instance, the teacher was not as perceptive. Instead of drawing out the child's feelings, she persisted with her objective. But as long as the child felt inferior, he persisted with his own objective. This resulted in a standstill. By dismissing the child's remarks, the teacher inhibited communication.

Pride is not the only feeling that needs expression. People may want to share feelings of sadness, gladness or worry. They may even have a need to share an exciting personal experience.

When people are happy, they look for someone to share the good news. When they are down, they look for sympathy. Like steam inside a pressure cooker, their emotions need to be released. Until they are, the pressure continues to build.

A person can release the pressure in one of two ways: 1) Approach a friend and talk about the event; 2) blurt it out at the first available opportunity, even in the middle of a conversation on a totally different topic. If he chooses the second way, the listener will probably view the comment as irrelevant. But if he understands that it has relevance to the *other person,* he can use it as a link to his thoughts. He will then be able to respond in a way that will satisfy the other person's need, and bring the focus back to the discussion at hand.

Let's see how the teacher maneuvers the dialogue in the following illustration.

Teacher: "Look at this spelling test. You are such a smart boy, but it looks like you failed this test."

Student: "Yes, I did fail."

Teacher: "Don't you think you can do better in spelling?"

Student: (bubbling with excitement) "I went to Disney World during vacation."

What is happening in the child's mind? Does he not value his grades? How could he respond with a report about a vacation? The answer is simple. The child is obviously excited about the trip. He has a need to talk about it. Like pressure that needs a release, he is full of excitement that needs a release. The teacher could dig her heels in and refuse to veer off the topic. But this will not achieve anything, because the child will not be receptive until he releases his excitement and talks about his trip. Instead, the teacher helps the student out:

Teacher: "And I bet you had a good time."

Student: "I had a great time."

Teacher: "Sometime soon you will have to tell me all about it."

Student: "Okay."

Teacher: "Now, let's talk a little about your spelling?"

The child will now become receptive, clearing the way for a meeting of the minds. The teacher will then be able to bring the conversation back to her objective.

Acknowledge

The second step of the EAR protocol is to acknowledge the other person. Show that you understand by paraphrasing what he says. This assures him that you have connected with him. He will feel valued and will be more receptive to you.

Respond

After having explored, you understand what the other person said and why he said it. After having acknowledged, you have shown value for the other person by making it clear that you understand. You are now in a position to tell him what you think. If you agree, tell him so. He will appreciate it. If you disagree, there are times when you should voice your opinion and times you should say nothing, as discussed earlier in the chapter.

One more component of effective communication is establishing rapport. Rapport is the climate in which the communication takes place. That climate can bring about healthy communication or stifle it. How can we enhance rapport?

Enhancing Rapport

The climate that brings about a meeting of the minds is a result of the feeling that each party has toward the other. If either side dislikes the other or is not interested in the dialogue, and shows it, rapport is reduced and channels of communication become blocked. The opposite is also true.

We can enhance rapport by doing things that convey our positive feelings. And, as with everything else in a positive relationship, if we consider the value of the other person in everything we say, we will most likely enhance rapport.

Explicit and implicit messages. Explicit messages are substance messages. They are the words themselves. They can be harsh and accusatory or gentle and conciliatory. Obviously, explicit messages have a powerful impact on the climate.

Then there are implicit messages. These are the unspoken messages found between the lines. They are the signals that you send though body language.

A smile, frown, look, touch, handshake, nod of the head or a sincere "please" and "thank you" — or lack of any one — tells a person what you really think of him, no matter what else you say. These are implicit messages, which confirm or disconfirm the sincerity of your words. As the saying goes, "I can't hear *what* you are saying because *how* you are saying it is so loud."

Suppose you told a person how special he is, but when he talks to you, you frown or show little interest. What does he think then? He probably thinks that you are really dissatisfied with him. This is the implicit message. But if your face lights up with genuine interest, he thinks you are sincerely satisfied with him. Obviously, this has a significant impact on the rapport.

In any dialogue, the important thing is not necessarily *what* you say, but *how* you say it. You may be saying the right words but your style, demeanor, facial expressions and listening habits may detract from the narrow meaning of those words. We saw it before with the power of ego messages, and we see it now with the power of other implicit messages. Because implicit messages qualify the sincerity of your words, what you don't say is often more important than what you do say.

Use a friendly approach. There was once a man whose rent was increased by his landlord. He could not afford the increase so he decided to vacate his apartment at the end of his lease. Although he wanted to stay, he did not say anything, because he had heard that the landlord was a stubborn person and would never agree to decrease the rent. So he wrote the landlord a letter, stating that he would vacate at the end of his lease.

After receiving the letter, the landlord came to visit his tenant. When he came to the door, the tenant greeted him with a smile. Instead of complaining about the increase, he complimented the landlord on the fine management of the apartment complex. While he was talking, he maintained a pleasant and cordial demeanor. He then mentioned that he would like to remain but could not afford the increase.

The landlord was not accustomed to such a warm reception from a tenant. So he began talking about his troubles; one tenant had become abusive in his interactions with the landlord; another had threatened to vacate before the end of his lease. "But you are satisfied," he said. "It is nice to have such a tenant."

Then the landlord, on his own, offered to reduce the increase in the rent. The tenant said it was still too high and told the landlord what he could afford. The landlord accepted it without any further discussion. But it didn't stop there. As the landlord was about to leave, he turned around and asked, "Is there any improvement you would like to have done?"

If this tenant had used the tough approach that all the other tenants had used, he would not have gotten what he wanted. Instead, he used the friendly approach and enhanced rapport by sympathizing and showing appreciation.

Being friendly means smiling, listening attentively, making eye contact, and being kind, patient and cordial toward the other person. All these gestures send the message: "I like you. I am glad you are here. You are important." They give value to the other person and enhance rapport.

> "A gentle reply turns away wrath, a harsh word creates anger" (*Mishlei* 15:1).

Being harsh and unfriendly can generate new feelings of anger. However, a gentle tone of voice and friendly words have the power to placate a person's anger.[1] This approach reduces friction and creates good feelings.

There is a fable about the sun and the wind. They had a disagreement, each claiming to be stronger than the other. One day, the wind saw a man wearing a coat and said, "I can take that man's coat off quicker than you. This will prove that I am stronger."

So the sun hid behind the clouds, and the wind began to blow. But the harder it blew, the tighter the man held onto his coat. Then the sun came out and shined on the man. Several minutes later, the man wiped his face and removed his coat.

The moral is obvious: We can accomplish more with kindness and gentleness than with force. Why? Because nobody appreciates force, and it only serves to weaken rapport. But everyone appreciates a friendly approach.

Allow for the release of strong emotions. Did you ever try to reason with an angry person? Did you succeed in getting your point across? It is difficult, if not impossible, to communicate with a person who is full of anger. He is not open to other opinions, so you cannot talk him out of his position. He is not prepared to adjust his emotional state, so you cannot talk him out of his anger. Anger simply does not respond to reason.[2] What should you do? Let him scream and yell. Allow him to finish releasing his emotion. He will then be in a more reasonable frame of mind.

Every good manager knows this. When a customer or employee comes to him with an angry complaint, a good manager remains calm and quiet and listens carefully to everything the complainer says. He does not interrupt or try to interject his opinion, and he does not respond until the complainer has released all his emotion. This gesture gives value to the complainer, opening channels of communication and enhancing rapport between the two.

To some degree, this is the way it works with any strong emotion. You cannot talk the other person out of his feeling, and as long as he is in an emotional state of mind, dialogue will be blocked.

---

1. Vilna Gaon and Rabbeinu Yonah, *Mishlei* 15:1.
2. Maharal, *Derech Chaim, Avos* 4:19.

Therefore, take a detour from the focus of the conversation and encourage the other person to talk about his feelings. Sympathize with him. Mirror his feelings. Make it clear that you understand him and that you value his thoughts.

Developing a Positive Relationship with Children

Parents and teachers have the responsibility of motivating children to succeed in life. This task demands more than just using a few motivational techniques; it requires an environment in which children want the guidance of their parents and teachers, and are receptive to their influence. With some know-how, adults can create such an environment. But they first have to do one thing — they have to create a positive relationship with the children. Then they will be in a position to exercise their influence.

When constructing a building, a foundation must first be laid. Without it, the building cannot stand. In addition, the deeper and sturdier the foundation, the stronger and more functional the building will be. Raising children and teaching them works the same way. Parents and teachers must first lay a foundation before beginning the task of preparing their children for success. That foundation is a positive relationship. It is the basis for the influence they will have over the child. Just like a building, the deeper and stronger the relationship, the deeper and stronger the influence they will have.

A veteran high-school teacher once told me the secret of his success: He works to develop a positive relationship with his students. Once they learn to love and respect him, they want to please him. They do not want to let him down, so they produce good grades to satisfy his expectations. They want him to be proud of them.

This approach is not new. Thousands of years ago, Aharon HaKohen, the brother of Moshe Rabbeinu, used the same technique to motivate people.

> When Aharon walked on the street and met an evildoer, he would say, "Hello." The next day, when that man considered committing a sin, he said to himself, "Woe is me. How will I look at Aharon? He greeted me, and I will be ashamed." That person would reconsider and would not commit the sin (*Avos d'Rav Nosson* 12:3).

What was the key to Aharon's influence? A simple "hello" could not possibly have had such a powerful effect. Rather, his influence resulted from the overall relationship he had with people. People loved and respected him, and they wanted to please him. They knew what he expected, and he did not even have to express it. They met those expectations because they did not want to let him down.

Why does influence depend on the relationship? Because when a child sees that his parents and teachers respect him and do everything in their power to help him succeed, he begins to trust and respect them in return. As the adults continue working for the child's benefit, affection grows, and so does the child's receptivity.[1]

Think about your own experiences. How cooperative are you with a manager whom you trust and respect? Are you willing to experiment with his ideas? You probably cooperate with him and are open to his suggestions. On the other hand, how cooperative are you with a manager whom you distrust or do not respect? You are probably less cooperative, and even if you follow his suggestions, you do so grudgingly. Children are no different.

When motivating, relations must be more than peaceful. The positive relationship we are referring to is more than an affiliation in which the child and adult are at peace with each other and have no distrust or disrespect for one another. Although there is nothing negative about this type of relationship, it may not be strong enough for real influence to occur.

The kind of relationship we are referring to is one in which both parties feel good about each other and show it. They trust and respect each other, and each tries to make the other feel important. In other words, positive things are happening between them. This is important, because when there is a lack of trust or respect, even if there is no *dis*trust or *dis*respect, the outcome of an adult's motivational attempts may be minimized.

The relationship and performance are both important. When bringing out the best in children, our goal is to work for the child's benefit, not ours. Our intent must be pure and unselfish. But this is not enough; even with a noble intention, we may still do things that harm the relationship. For example, suppose we moti-

---

1. Based on *Mishlei* 27:6, as explained in the beginning of this chapter.

vate children by screaming, punishing, criticizing, hitting and using harsh words. Although we have the child's welfare in mind and the child even responds to our pressure, the relationship may be weakened because the child resents our negative treatment. And once the relationship is weakened, our influence will be weakened, too.

Does this mean that we should go to the other extreme by avoiding any sort of pressure, so that the child will never resent us? Does it mean that we should provide a challenge-free environment, avoid calling the child to task for failure, and protect him from the penalty of poor performance?

While this approach may preserve the relationship for the meantime, it will cause another problem; the child will become spoiled and learn to dodge responsibilities.

If parents always shelter a child from the effects of poor performance, the child will never suffer any consequences and may never develop a sense of responsibility. As he grows older and continues to neglect his duties, his parents will not be around to protect him from the consequences, and he will be forced to suffer the penalty. Even worse, if he traces his problem to the way his parents treated him as a child, he may begin to resent his parents even after many years.[1]

Yes, the adult/child relationship is important; without it, adults will not be able to influence children. But performance is also important; without it, children grow up without a sense of responsibility. Our job, then, is to balance the two carefully. This notion is illustrated in the following parable.

There was once a farmer who owned a chicken that laid golden eggs. Day after day the chicken produced its eggs, providing the farmer with more and more gold. The farmer eventually became fabulously wealthy. But he was greedy. He wanted more gold, and he wanted it now. So he cut open the chicken, expecting to remove all its golden eggs. To his surprise, he found none.

Now the farmer had a bigger problem. With the death of his chicken, he had brought about the end of his financial growth.

The farmer was not forced to cut the chicken open. It was his choice to do so. In fact, he had had three options to choose from.

---

1. See *Make Me, Don't Break Me,* Ch. 5, on the topic of teaching children responsibility.

The first option was to focus solely on the chicken, which we will call the "producer." He would vigilantly watch its health and guard it from any harm by building a temperature-controlled coop and making strict rules about who could visit the chicken. In fact, his focus on the producer would be so intense that he would disregard the safety of the eggs, which we will call the "output."

The second option was to focus solely on the "output" — the eggs. He would build a special vault to store them and hire armed guards for round-the-clock protection. In fact, his focus on the output would be so intense that he would ignore the producer, leaving it vulnerable to sickness and other unforeseen harm.

The third option would be to focus on *both* the chicken and the eggs — the producer and the output. He would build the special coop so that the chicken could continue to lay eggs, and at the same time hire armed guards so that the produce would continue serving his financial needs. In other words, he would consider the balance between the producer and the output.

In this parable, the farmer chose the second option. He focused on the output with such intensity that he totally neglected the welfare of the producer. But he did more than that; he dealt the producer a fatal blow.

There is a moral for us in this parable. As parents and teachers, we are constantly formulating expectations for our children. No matter what the goals are, we have three options: We can focus on the producer (the child), the output (performance), or both.

In the first option, we would focus solely on the producer — that is, the child — by providing a challenge-free environment that would ensure his happiness, security and peace of mind. In fact, our focus on him would be so intense that we would ignore his "output" by overlooking low standards of performance and neglect of duties. With this leisurely setup, our hope is not only to keep the child happy, but also to enhance our relationship with him.

The problem is that our disregard for the output would leave the child vulnerable to another danger — he may learn that poor performance is acceptable and never develop a sense of responsibility. While he may not feel the penalty of such behavior as a child because we are protecting him from it, he will certainly feel it as an adult when he cannot hold onto a job and his friends and family lose respect for him.

What will be the status of our relationship then? If he realizes that his permissive upbringing planted the seeds of his problems as an adult, he may lose respect for *us*, leaving us with the kind of relationship we were trying to avoid in the first place.

In the second option, we would be like the farmer, focusing solely on the output — that is, the performance. We would make strict demands on the child to live up to high performance standards; and whenever he fell short of those standards, we would offer sharp criticism and unsympathetic punishment. In fact, our focus on the output would be so intense that we would ignore the child's welfare by coercing him into performing well, and we might even withhold praise if he *did* meet the expected standards. With this stringent setup, we would hope to help the child develop a strong sense of responsibility which would endure throughout his life.

The problem here is that our disregard for the child's feelings will leave him open to other dangers, such as reduced self-esteem, nervous habits and a weakened relationship with us. Not only will these symptoms interfere with his success as a child, they will sharply reduce the quality of his performances as an adult — exactly what we are trying to avoid in the first place.

And what will be the status of our relationship then? As the child matures and becomes increasingly independent, we still want him to trust and respect us, to share his new experiences with us, and to return to us for guidance. But he may never forgive us for the restrictive environment we created and the pain we inflicted on him as a child. His hurt may preclude the possibility of a warm relationship. Just as the farmer's single-minded focus on the output damaged the chicken and cut off its future output, our single-minded focus on performance would injure not only the child, but his future accomplishments, as well as the relationship we have with him.

In the third option, we would focus on both the child and his performances. We would demand high standards of performance, and whenever the child failed to meet those standards, we would let him suffer the full consequences. But we would also praise the child, provide rewards for good performances, and offer encouragement whenever he faltered. We would consider the delicate balance between the producer and the output, and create an environment conducive to the child's growth and development.

What will be the status of our relationship in this case? It will be exactly as it should be. Although the expectations are high and the child is left to suffer the consequences of poor performance, he will understand that we support him, respect him and care about his welfare. He will feel valued and will continue seeking our love and guidance, even as an adult.

Exercising the first option creates a permissive environment. Exercising the second option creates a restrictive environment. Exercising the third option creates a balanced environment in which the child's goals are achieved and his self-esteem flourishes. He is on his way to becoming a successful adult, and we will have accomplished our task.

So when a child forgets to clean his room, fails to hang his coat up, comes late to dinner, or neglects any other chore or rule, remember the fable of the chicken and the egg. Don't ignore the problem, and don't criticize the child in a way that will reduce his self-esteem and weaken your relationship with him. Respond in a way that will balance the child's emotions and performance. This will result in a healthy sense of responsibility and a strong relationship.

Take the lead in initiating a positive relationship. When a relationship with a child goes awry, some parents and teachers refuse to take the first step to repair it. "There are two people in this relationship," they say. "I am one, the child is the other. Let him come to me first. After all, I am the adult and I deserve respect."

If the child is particularly difficult, the adults may add, "This child is so difficult. He has no respect and his attitude is terrible. Sometimes I get the feeling that he acts out intentionally just to aggravate me. I cannot deal with him. Let him first signal to me that he wants a good relationship. Then I will reciprocate."

An adult who thinks like this is making a mistake. First of all, children do not have the maturity, experience or skill to initiate compromise and create mutual understanding. Adults do have these advantages. It follows, then, that they should take the first step in repairing or creating a relationship.

Furthermore, parents and teachers have the job of bringing out the best in children, and their influence is always severely diminished in the absence of a healthy relationship. Thus, if parents and teachers fail to create the proper relationship, they have not done their full job.

The pretext used for not taking the first step is that they, as adults, are in a position to demand respect. Rightfully so. Their *position* certainly deserves respect. But do *they* deserve respect? In most cases, true respect is earned; it is not the result of a demand. If the adults do not take steps to create a positive relationship now, they may never get the respect they think they deserve.

Parents and teachers ought to consider what the children in their care might be feeling. Maybe they have low self-esteem and are unsure if their authority figures respect them. Maybe they have never been given attention, and they have learned that the only way to get it is by being obnoxious. Maybe they have failed at other relationships, so they think that every relationship is doomed to failure.

If this is the case, can children be blamed for not taking the first step? Their conditioning is holding them back. But with enough attention, respect and sympathy from adults, they will very likely change their attitudes and reciprocate. And as they do so, the relationship will flourish.

Reciprocity is all we can expect. If adults respect and trust children, children will want to give it back. If adults show that they value children, the children will want to do the same in return. The dynamics of reciprocity are very powerful.

Be consistent. Parents and teachers sometimes threaten children with penalties for their misdeeds, but when it comes time to enforce the consequences, they do not follow through. Many times, the reason they avoid doing so is because they are afraid the child will become unhappy or hostile, jeopardizing the viability of the relationship.

This is a mistake. When adults carry out their commitments, the children see that they keep their word. From this, the children learn to trust and respect their authority figures. But when adults do not keep their commitments, the children learn to have little trust and respect for them.

To compound the problem, when parents and teachers do not enforce penalties, they eventually lose control of the children. The reason is simple: Without a penalty for misconduct, children have no deterrent. With no deterrent, they will continue doing the things they are not supposed to do. And as they continue doing those things, the authority figures lose control.

"But," inconsistent adults ask, "when children are unhappy about the penalty, our relationship with them unravels. Isn't it better to keep the relationship tight by keeping the children happy?"

True, children are happy when they avoid a penalty. However, they are not happy when their authority figures do not keep their word. Nor are they happy when structure is eliminated from their day-to-day activities. Even worse, when children learn that they can run circles around the adults, they begin to ridicule them, further reducing any sense of respect and weakening the viability of their relationship.[1]

Imagine a brick wall. On one side is a prize, on the other side are people who would like to break through to take it. These people chisel away at the wall, testing it for weak spots. Once they find a weak spot, they dig at it until it becomes larger and larger. Soon they are able to penetrate the wall. But what would they do if they could not find any weak spots? They would realize that the wall is impregnable and would lose their drive to penetrate it.

Children are the same. They want the prize on the other side of the wall — power and control. So they look for weak spots in their authority figures by violating rules and waiting to see if the penalties will be enforced. If the adults do enforce the penalties, the children realize that these adults mean business and would stop testing them. But if the adults do not enforce any consequences, the children will continue chiseling away at them until they have taken control of the home and classroom.

Does this mean that adults lose the control and respect of their children if they overlook penalties only occasionally? Yes, to some degree. The reason is that they send unclear messages to the child, and each time the child considers breaking a rule, he thinks, "When I broke the rule last week, nothing happened to me. Maybe this

---

1. See *Make Me, Don't Break Me*, pp. 147-163, on the topic of enforcing penalties.

time, too, nothing will happen to me." So he continues chiseling away at the adults' structure, trying to take control of his environment.

Let's go back to the original question: Will enforcing penalties weaken a relationship? We can now see that if adults are fair and consistent, enforcing penalties will not weaken relationships. In fact, when adults enforce a penalty with the understanding that the child himself chose to take it by behaving in an unacceptable manner, the child learns to take responsibility for his own actions and will voluntarily avoid unacceptable behavior in the future.

Relationship Bank Account

When you first enter a bank to open an account, you have a zero balance. You open the account with an initial deposit and continue to increase the balance by making subsequent deposits; the greater the deposits, the higher the balance. You decrease the balance by making withdrawals; the greater the withdrawals, the lower the balance. If your goal is to become wealthy, you make as many deposits and as few withdrawals as possible.

A relationship works the same way. Before you become acquainted with another person, whether he or she is an adult or a child, the balance in your relationship bank account is as good as empty. Once you have become acquainted, you either make a deposit or a withdrawal every time you say or do something. If the interaction is positive and leaves the other person with a good feeling, it counts as a deposit, and the balance in your relationship bank account increases. If the interaction is negative, however, it is a withdrawal, and the balance decreases. Obviously, if you want to become relationship-wealthy, you will maximize your positive interactions and minimize your negative ones.

A smile, a word of praise, a show of sympathy, a pat on the back, a half-hour of undivided attention, or any other value-giving gesture are all forms of deposits and serve to increase the balance in the account. Criticizing the other person, arguing with him, not giving him attention, making unreasonable demands, withholding praise when he deserves it, or any other value-detracting gesture are all forms of withdrawals and decrease the balance.

There are many behaviors that can go in either direction; the same behavior can be a deposit at one time and a withdrawal at another. Take listening as an example. Listening is generally a deposit because it shows value for the other person. In some instances, though, it can be a withdrawal; for example, you may listen carefully to another person to test him for honesty or to interrogate him for more information. This is a withdrawal because nobody appreciates being doubted or interrogated.

Setting limits on children is another example. Many parents and teachers, as we have discussed, believe that children do not appreciate limits; therefore, they consider prohibitions a withdrawal. This it true only when the limits are unreasonable or unnecessary. However, when there is mutual trust and the child sees that the limits are within reason, it is not so. In fact, setting limits may even be a deposit because children appreciate the structure that these rules provide.

To children, the world is chaotic. There are many decisions to make and directions in which to go, and they are not secure choosing these paths all on their own. They want structure. They want adults to give them direction by setting guidelines for them and creating a framework of rules with which they can live comfortably. Although their actions may indicate that they want full independence and control, deep down inside they do not want it. They want rules that will bring security to their lives.

Making withdrawals. When your cash balance in the bank is low, you are not in a position to make a large withdrawal; and if your account is overdrawn, you are not even in the position to make a small withdrawal. On the contrary, you are in debt to the bank and must pay it off.

For this reason, a wealthy person always keeps a cash reserve in his account; this way, he will be able to make periodic withdrawals. And since his goal is to remain wealthy, he only makes withdrawals when he has a justifiable need.

When it comes to relationships, we also want to maintain a high balance in our accounts. This means that we are cautious about making withdrawals. However, in our daily exchanges with other people, we invariably do make withdrawals by saying and doing things which have a negative effect, either because we slip or because we are required to do so. For example, the *mitzvah* of *tochachah* may require us to rebuke someone. He may prefer not to hear the criticism, but we are still obligated to offer it. Or perhaps the *mitzvah* of *tochachah* does not apply, but we slip and criticize him anyway; once we do the damage and make a withdrawal, we cannot rescind it.

In both cases, our input is a withdrawal from the relationship account. This is not a problem, as long as the account's balance remains high. However, if the critique is particularly biting, it is a significant withdrawal and may leave the account with a dangerously low balance.

In any relationship, both parties periodically act in value-detracting ways which threaten to weaken the bond. For example, friends, relatives and spouses may exchange insults and criticism. This leads to quarrels and hurt feelings. Will their relationships suffer as a result, never to rebound to proper health? If the relationship was strong enough before the action — that is, the balance in their account was high enough to withstand the withdrawal — it will tolerate an occasional bump.

However, if the relationship was not strong to begin with, it may not be able to tolerate the strain of an occasional insult or criticism. While the insult may be accidental and the criticism appropriate, the other person may resent it and become alienated. This is the reason that the same insult or criticism may cause two people to drift apart, while two others remain friends. The key is the balance in their relationship account *before* the incident. If the balance was high, it will tolerate the strain, but if it was low, it may not.

This notion is true in any relationship, but it is especially relevant for teachers, parents and managers. Suppose an employee or a child breaks rules, performs poorly, or shows up late to work or class. He or she has been warned many times about the problem, and a reprimand or other penalty is now in order. If the authority figure in question has been building the relationship account by making deposits of trust and good will, the two can afford to dip in now and withdraw a reprimand or another kind of penalty. True, the balance is now lower; however, the action will not seriously deplete the account. Sufficient funds remain in reserve for a continued effective relationship.

But if the account is already low, the authority figure has a problem. Suppose he has been light on praise and heavy on criticism, and he never made his employee or his child feel important. In this case, their relationship account has started out with a low balance. And now that a penalty is in order, it may not be carried off so effectively, because every negative action is another withdrawal and will only serve to decrease an already depleted balance. This will lead to resentment, resistance and an even weaker relationship.

And if the account is overdrawn to begin with, another negative action will only cause an already troubled relationship to deteriorate. Because there are no reserves, the parent or manager cannot enforce consequences without further damaging the relationship and bringing about more resistance and resentment.

These managers/teachers/parents have a problem. On one hand, they have to enforce a penalty; on the other hand, they cannot do so with real effectiveness. What should they do?

If possible, they should avoid delivering the consequence. They should try giving another chance or provide a lighter alternative. They can even ask the employee or the child what they think should be done, and if the suggestion is reasonable, consent to it.

They should then begin to improve their relationships by making daily deposits of good will and value-giving gestures. They should also begin to manage their people with positive motivational techniques instead of coercion and pressure, at the same time avoiding criticism, sarcasm and other devaluing gestures.

Consider the relationships you have with the people in your life. Each one has a different account. Are the balances high or low? Is there a need to increase the balance in any account? If there is, do so by making deposits of appreciation and good will. And before taking any action, consider how it will affect the relationship bank account.

YOU CAN DO IT

The ideas in this book can work for you if you are willing to make the effort. As your attitude improves and you become more productive, you will feel assured that you have done the right thing. You can do it, because Hashem planted the seeds of greatness within you. With your persistence and His help, you will truly see *SUCCESS!*

Glossary

Glossary

Aharon Hakohen	Aaron, the high priest, brother of Moses
Avos	Pirke Avos, Ethics of our Fathers, part of the Mishnaic code
Avraham	Abraham, our forefather
Bamidbar	Book of Numbers
Beis HaMidrash	study hall
Beracha/Berachos	blessing/s; Berachos is also the name of a Talmudic tractate
Bereishis	Book of Genesis
Ben Torah	A Yeshivah student, one who studies Torah
Bris Milah	circumcision
Chazal	Torah sages
Chessed	kindness
Chometz	leaven
Chumash	Five Books of Moses
Chutzpah	nerve, arrogance
Davening	praying
Devarim	Book of Deuteronomy
Emes	truth
Gemara	see Talmud
Halachah	normative Jewish law

Hashem	G-d
King Dovid	King David
King Shlomo	King Solomon
K'rias Shema	three paragraphs of the Torah recited twice daily, beginning with the words Shema Yisrael
Lashon Hara	disparaging remarks concerning another person
Maggid Shiur	Torah lecturer
Middah/Middos	character trait/s
Midrash	collection of interpretations on Scripture, usually containing a moral
Mishlei	Book of Proverbs
Mishkan	the Tabernacle
Mishnah	early codification of Jewish law
Mitzvah/Mitzvos	Torah commandment/s
Mon	Manna
Moshe Rabbeinu	Moses, our teacher
Parnassah	livelihood
Rashi	commentary on the Bible and the Talmud
Rosh Kollel	head of an institute of higher learning
Rosh Yeshivah	head of a yeshivah
Selichos	prayers pertaining to penitence
Shas	the complete Talmudic work
Shabbos	Sabbath, Saturday
Shemos	Book of Exodus
Shmuel	Samuel the prophet
Simcha/s	joyous occasion/s
Talmid Chochom	Torah scholar
Talmud	Compendium of discussions on the Mishnah. The basis for Jewish law, as practiced.
Teshuvah	repentance
Tochachah	rebuke

Torah	the entire body of Jewish literature. Sometimes it refers to the Five Books of Moses.
Tzadik	righteous person
Tzedakah	charity
Vayikra	Book of Leviticus
Yaakov	Jacob, our forefather
Yeshivah	institution of Torah learning
Yetzer Hara	evil inclination
Yosef	Joseph, son of Jacob

Biographical Notes

Biographical Notes

Baal Shem Tov — Rabbi Israel Baal Shem Tov (c. 1700-1760) founded the school of service of G-d known as Chassidus. By translating deep kabbalistic ideas into a practical approach to life and people, the movement and its philosophy motivated scholars and masses of ordinary Jews to strive for higher levels of learning and service.

Bleicher, Rabbi Dovid — (d. 1944). A prime student of Rabbi Yosef Yoizel Hurwitz, "The Alter of Novarodok," Rabbi Bleicher was a prominent expositor of the teachings of mussar. He was a renowned educator who attracted hundreds of students. He established and led the Yeshivah Bais Yosef in Mezritz, Poland, and was also responsible for the founding of numerous other yeshivos in Poland.

Chazon Ish — Title of the works of Rabbi Avraham Yeshaya Karelitz (1878-1953), a Lithuanian scholar who spent his last twenty years in Bnei Brak. He held no official position, but was acknowledged as a foremost leader of Jewry. His works cover all aspects of Talmud and *halachah*.

Chofetz Chaim — Rabbi Yisrael Meir Kagan (1839-1933). He was known by the title of his book, *Chofetz Chaim*, which details the laws of *lashon hara* (forbidden speech). Renowned for his piety, humility and scholarship, he authored many books covering the gamut of Torah and Jewish life. Recognized as a worldwide leader and *halachic* authority in his generation.

Dessler, Rabbi Eliyahu — (1891-1954). One of the outstanding personalities of the mussar movement. Held leadership positions in Russia and England before settling in Israel, where he served as the *menahel ruchani* (spiritual supervisor) of the Ponevezh Yeshivah. His teachings were published posthumously in the four-volume *Michtav M'Eliyahu*.

Feinstein, Rabbi Moshe — (1895-1986). Born in Russia, he settled in New York in 1937, where he became the *Rosh Yeshivah* of Mesivta Tifereth Jerusalem. Reverently known around the world as "Reb Moshe," he was respected as the greatest *halachic* authority of his time. His responsa, collected in *Igros Moshe*, deal with every facet of contemporary life.

Finkel, Rabbi Nosson Tzvi — (1849-1927). Known as "The Alter of Slobodka," he was among the most influential Torah personalities at the turn of the century. After serving as principal of the renowned yeshivah in Kelm and founding the yeshivah in Telshe and the Kollel in Kovno, he established the yeshivah in Slobodka which he later transplanted to Chevron. In Slobodka, he attracted many of the greatest minds in the Yeshivah world, and many of his students went on to serve as the leaders of the Torah world.

Grodzinsky, Rabbi Avraham — (1883-1944). *Menahel ruchani* of the Slobodka Yeshivah, where he was a leading influence. Author of *Toras Avraham,* a classic work of mussar thought.

Hirsch, Rabbi Shamshon Raphael — (1808-1888). Rabbinic leader of the Orthodox community of Germany; a fiery leader, brilliant writer and profound educator. Served as Rabbi in Frankfurt-am-Main for 37 years, where he vociferously opposed the growing Reform movement and virtually created the new German Orthodoxy.

Hutner, Rabbi Yitzchak — (1906-1980). Raised in Warsaw, Rabbi Hutner was a close disciple of "The Alter of Slobodka" both in Slobodka and later in Chevron. A noted educator and profound thinker, he headed Yeshivah Rabbi Chaim Berlin and authored the multi-volume *Pachad Yitzchak* and other scholarly works.

Katz, Rabbi Chaim Mordechai — (1894-1964). Born in Europe, he came to the United States in 1941, and with his brother-in-law Rabbi Eliyahu Meir Bloch, re-established the famous Telshe Yeshivah in Cleveland, Ohio. His lectures on mussar were published under the title, *Be'er Mechokek.*

Keller, Rabbi Chaim Dov — A contemporary Torah leader and thinker, Rosh HaYeshivah of the Telshe Yeshivah-Chicago.

Kotler, Rabbi Aharon — (1892-1962). Founder and *Rosh Yeshivah* of the Yeshivos of Kletzk, Poland and Beth Medrash Govoha of Lakewood, New Jersey. A pioneer in the American yeshivah movement, he was the foremost proponent of the *kollel* concept and revolutionized Torah life in America. He championed the cause of dedication to non-vocational Torah scholarship.

Levenstein, Rabbi Yechezkel — (1884-1974). A disciple of the Chofetz Chaim and Rabbi Yeruchom Levovitz, he went on to study in Kelm. After the passing of the latter, he assumed the position of *Mashgiach* in the yeshivah in Mir. He stayed with the Yeshivah during World War II, when it was uprooted to Shanghai and later to the United States. He later became *Mashgiach* of the Ponovezh Yeshivah in Bnei Brak. His works include *Ohr Yechezkel* and *Kovetz Inyanim.*

Levovitz, Rabbi Yeruchom — (1874-1936). A prominent mussar personality, best known as the *Mashgiach* (spiritual supervisor) of the Mirrer Yeshivah in Poland; he was famous for his profound insights into human character. A disciple of Rabbi Simcha Zissel Ziv of Kelm, he authored the *Daas Chochmah U'Mussar.*

Lipkin, Rabbi Yisrael — (1810-1883). Known as Reb Yisrael Salanter. As a young man, he was already recognized as one of the leading lights of his generation. He effectively established the mussar school of thought, which concentrated on spiritual achievement through self-analysis and improvement.

Lopian, Rabbi Eliyahu — (1876-1970). A prominent mussar personality in Kelm and London, he began a new career when he settled in Israel in his eighties. His lectures were published posthumously under the title *Lev Eliyahu.*

Luzzato, Rabbi Moshe Chaim — (1707-1746). Renowned for his works on ethics, philosophy and kabbalah. His most famous book was *Mesilas Yesharim,* which remains a basic mussar text to this day. In addition, he wrote many other seminal works.

Maharal — Acronym for Rabbi Yehudah Loewe ben Bezalel (1526-1609), one of the seminal figures in Jewish thought in the last five centuries. Chief Rabbi in Moravia, Posen and Prague. Author of numerous works in all fields of Torah, in most of which he presented the concepts of kabbalistic mysticism in terms comprehensible to most scholars.

Maharsha — Acronym for Moreinu HaRav Shlomo Eidel's, of Ostroah, Poland (1555-1632). *Rosh Yeshivah* and rabbi in a number of the leading communities of Poland. Author of monumental commentaries on the *halachic* and *aggadic* sections of the Babylonian Talmud. In the *aggadic* commentary he formulated many basic ideas of Torah and its philosophy of life.

Me'iri — Rabbi Menachem HaMe'iri (c. 1249-c.1306), one of the Rishonim (early commentators). He wrote commentary to Scripture and Talmud as well as other works, including *Chibur HaTeshuvah* on repentance.

Pliskin, Rabbi Zelig — Contemporary educator, author and lecturer. Currently a senior lecturer at Yeshivah Aish HaTorah in Jerusalem.

Rabbeinu Bachya — (1263-1340). Torah commentator and kabbalist who wrote an encyclopedic Torah commentary which considers the plain meaning, along with Midrashic, philosophical and kabbalistic exegesis. He also wrote on a broad range of topics.

Rabbeinu Yonah — (1180-1263). Rav and moralist of thirteenth century Gerona, Spain. Rabbeinu Yonah wrote commentaries on portions of Scripture, *Avos,* and several tractates of the Talmud. Among his mussar works, *Shaarei Teshuvah* has been a basic text for the last seven centuries.

Radak — Acronym of Rabbi Dovid Kimchi (1160-1235), a French Bible commentator whose classic and profound commentary on Prophets is included in most large editions of the Bible.

Ralbag — Rabbi Levi ben Gershon (1288-1344). Best known for his commentary on Bible, he was also a talmudist, philosopher and astronomer. Wrote a book on astronomy and invented an instrument for precise measurement of heavenly bodies.

Rambam — Acronym for Rabbi Moshe ben Maimon ["Maimonides"] (1135-1204), a pre-eminent Torah scholar of the Middle Ages. His three major works are: *Commentary to the Mishnah*; *Mishneh Torah,* a comprehensive code of Jewish law; and *Moreh Nevuchim* ("Guide for the Perplexed"), a major work of Jewish philosophy. He was also royal physician in Egypt, where he influenced thousands of people through his writings and teachings.

Rashi — Rabbi Shlomo ben Yitzchak (1040-1105). Known as the "father of commentators" because of his clarity, brevity and profundity of understanding. His commentaries on the Bible and Talmud have been the basic tools for all scholars, from his time until today. Lived in France, where by the age of twenty-five he was considered one of the leading talmudists of his day.

Rosh — Acronym of Rabbi Osher ben Yechiel (c. 1250-1327). One of the Rishonim (early commentators), he was considered the spiritual leader and *halachic* authority of German and Spanish Jewry. His *halachic* code is printed in all full editions of the Talmud. In addition, he wrote *halachic* responsa, commentaries on Torah and Talmud, and *Orchos Chaim,* an ethical work.

Salanter, Rabbi Yisrael — see Lipkin, Rabbi Yisrael.

Schwab, Rabbi Shimon — (1908-1995). Contemporary rabbi and thinker, who served for over sixty years in the rabbinate on two continents. He climaxed his distinguished career as spiritual leader of the Hirschian Kehal Adath Yeshurun community in Washington Heights, N.Y.

Schwartz, Rabbi Yoel — A contemporary Torah scholar and educator, living in Israel. He has written over twenty books, and is widely acclaimed for his vast knowledge of Torah thought.

Shapira, Rabbi Klonimus Kalmish — (1889-1943). Chassidic Rebbe of Piaseczna and martyr in the Warsaw ghetto. Author of *Chovas HaTalmidim* and *Hach'sharas Ha'Avreichim,* works that guide youngsters and adults into the realms of Torah life and kabbalah. As an educator he put his ideas into practice and left an indelible impression on his students and followers.

Sh'lah — Rabbi Yeshaya Horowitz (1560-1630). Known by the abbreviated title of his monumental work on Talmud, law, ethics and kabbalah, *Shnei Luchos HaBris.* Rabbi in Poland, Frankfurt, Prague, and Jerusalem; one of the leading Torah scholars of the early-seventeenth century.

Shmulevitz, Rabbi Chaim — (1902-1979). Born in Lithuania, he was considered a master educator at the age of only twenty-two. After the German onslaught of World War II, he traveled with the Mirrer Yeshivah to Shanghai, China, where he led the yeshivah during its five-year exile. Later became the head of the Mirrer Yeshivah in Jerusalem, where he was famous for his mussar talks.

Twerski, Rabbi Abraham, M.D. — A contemporary Torah scholar and psychiatrist, considered one of America's leading experts in the field of substance abuse rehabilitation. Famous for his lectures and books, which combine Torah knowledge with modern psychology.

Vilna Gaon — Rabbi Eliyahu ben Shlomo Zalman of Vilna (1720-1797), is referred to simply as "The Gaon," in recognition of his peerless genius. Considered the greatest Torah scholar in many centuries; acknowledged leader of non-Chassidic Jewry of Eastern Europe and spiritual father of the Yeshivah Movement.

Volozhin, Rabbi Chaim — (1749-1821). The prime disciple of the Gaon of Vilna. He is considered "The Father of the Yeshivah Movement." At the urging of the Gaon, he established the Volozhin Yeshivah — the first with an established curriculum and levels of study. The yeshivah became the prototype for yeshivos throughout the world. Among his works are *Nefesh HaChaim, Ruach Chaim,* and *Chut HaMeshulash.*

Wolbe, Rabbi Shlomo — A disciple of Rabbi Yeruchom Levovitz, he is a contemporary mussar personality and one of its most influential teachers. Author of *Alei Shur*, he established the Beis HaMussar in Jerusalem, where he has initiated a renaissance of mussar study and its application to daily life.

Ziv, Rabbi Simcha Zissel (of Kelm) — (1824-1898). One of the primary disciples of Rabbi Yisrael Salanter, he founded the Yeshivah of Kelm. A leader in the Mussar Movement, and mentor of its next generation of teachers, his thoughts on various topics of mussar were later collected in the book, *Chochmah U'Mussar*.

Index

Index

NOTES

NOTES

NOTES

NOTES

NOTES

NOTES

NOTES

NOTES

NOTES

NOTES

This volume is part of
THE ARTSCROLL SERIES®
an ongoing project of
translations, commentaries and expositions
on Scripture, Mishnah, Talmud, Halachah,
liturgy, history and the classic Rabbinic writings;
and biographies, and thought.

For a brochure of current publications
visit your local Hebrew bookseller
or contact the publisher:

Mesorah Publications, ltd

4401 Second Avenue
Brooklyn, New York 11232
(718) 921-9000